Intrepid Woman

Intrepid Woman

BETTY LUSSIER'S SECRET WAR
1942–1945

BETTY LUSSIER

NAVAL INSTITUTE PRESS
ANNAPOLIS, MARYLAND

Naval Institute Press
291 Wood Road
Annapolis, MD 21402

Library of Congress Cataloging-in-Publication Data

Lussier, Betty.
Intrepid woman : Betty Lussier's secret war, 1942-1945 / Betty Lussier.
    p. cm.
Includes bibliographical references and index.
ISBN 978-1-59114-449-6 (alk. paper)
1. Lussier, Betty. 2. World War, 1939–1945—Aerial operations, British. 3. World War, 1939–1945—Personal narratives, American. 4. Air pilots, Military—United States—Biography. 5. Air pilots, Military—Great Britain—Biography. 6. Women air pilots—United States—Biography. 7. Women air pilots—Great Britain—Biography. 8. Great Britain. Air Transport Auxiliary—Biography. 9. Great Britain. Air Transport Auxiliary—History. 10. World War, 1939–1945—Participation, Female. I. Title.
    D786.L87 2010
    940.54'4973092—dc22

                                        2010022131

Printed in the United States of America

14 13 12 11 10   9 8 7 6 5 4 3 2
First printing

All photos are from the author's collection.
Interior design and composition by Fineline Graphics LLC

Dedicated to Alejandro, his father,
and his Sicré uncles

Contents

Illustrations

Foreword

THE AIR TRANSPORT AUXILIARY (ATA) was a group of pilots who delivered aircraft between factories and frontline airfields for Britain during World War II. The ATA was composed of civilian men and women from twenty-eight countries who together made a major contribution to the Allied victory. They performed the vital function of delivering planes from factories to squadrons, and shuttling aircraft back for repairs, thus freeing pilots for combat duty.

Betty Lussier, the daughter of a decorated World War I pilot, learned to fly a Piper Cub as a teenager growing up in Maryland. Thus began a lifelong love affair with aeronautics. In 1942 the determined twenty-one-year-old responded to Britain's call to aid the war effort and was quickly assigned as an ATA pilot. Betty and her comrades hold the distinction of being the first women ever to officially ferry aircraft during wartime.

ATA women pilots eventually were cleared to fly aircraft to the continent. As Allied armies liberated European countries, recapturing airfields and building new ones, British Spitfires, Hurricanes, Typhoons, and Tempest fighters; Mosquito fighter-bombers; and Lancaster, Halifax, Barracuda, and Hudson bombers were flown to the aerodromes almost immediately by ATA men and women ferry pilots to support the invading ground forces.

After the war ended the ATA flag was lowered for the last time at White Waltham, Berkshire (ATA headquarters), in November 1945. One hundred seventeen British women served in the ATA, together with a number of women pilots from around the world. These included women from the United States (25) and from Argentina, Australia, Canada, New Zealand, Poland, Siam (Thailand), and South Africa. In all, ATA men and women pilots delivered 308,567 aircraft, including 57,286 Spitfires, 29,401 Hurricanes, 9,805 Lancasters, and 7,039 Barracudas.

One hundred seventy ATA ferry pilots were lost during the war.

On 15 March 2008 British Prime Minister Gordon Brown announced that all surviving ATA women pilots and ground crew would be awarded a special badge of honor for their courageous service and bravery during World War II.

When Betty resigned from the ATA she joined the Office of Strategic Services as a counterespionage agent. There she entered the elite division known as X-2, where she was one of the few Americans trained and authorized to analyze German messages and deliver them to combat headquarters. This is Betty's recounting of her wartime experiences.

—*Capt. James E. Wise Jr., USN (Ret.)*

Acknowledgments

I OWE SPECIAL GRATITUDE TO Ricardo Lussier Sicré, Ray Cole, Mona Houghton, Capt. James E. Wise Jr., and Wendy Lukasiewicz for their able assistance in the preparation of this manuscript.

Intrepid Woman

PART ONE

Flying with the
Air Transport Auxiliary

CHAPTER 1

Life in Maryland: The Early Years

WHEN MY SISTER, NITA, AND I first got the idea to go to England and help hold back the Nazis we were teenagers, students at the College Park campus of the University of Maryland. We had been in high school when the Nazis annexed Czechoslovakia, and then stunned the world by storming across Europe, forcing the British Expeditionary Force into the sea at Dunkirk, and occupying a defeated and surrendering France. The Germans then turned their mighty wrath on the British Isles. Nita and I watched and listened as the British, all alone and ill equipped, sought to defend themselves in the skies against the German Luftwaffe. We wondered why our government offered no help. We were too naïve to understand the politics involved, but we knew that the British needed help and we were ready to do what we could. In our youth we did not see the absurdity of two girls from a Maryland farm going to war against the formidable fighting force that was Germany.

For both of us 1940 was our first year at the University of Maryland. Nita was a freshman. I was a sophomore, having completed my freshman year at Washington College on the Eastern Shore of Maryland where we grew up. I had enrolled in Washington College because our oldest sister, Jane, had gone there before me and the campus was close enough to our farm to allow me to live at home. Our parents were dairy farmers. My sisters and I had been raised on a series of farms, starting with a ranch on the plains of Alberta, Canada, and ending on a flat patch bordering the Chesapeake Bay. There, we girls—no boys in this family—filled in as farm labor because the Great Depression was still on us, and our father could not afford to hire enough men to work the 350 acres that were his. It had been convenient for me to attend Washington College, live at home, and continue doing my share of the farm work.

Dad bought Huntingfield Farm at a bank foreclosure auction for $15,000. An ancient Indian tribal gathering ground, still rich in stone arrowheads, axe heads, and other artifacts, it would have been an idyllic place for us to grow up if the Depression had not been so severe. When we first moved to Huntingfield, the farmhouse had no electricity, no telephone, and no indoor plumbing. One of our daily chores was to trim the wicks on the oil lamps, wash their sooty globes, and fill them with kerosene. We pumped our water by hand from a crude well and hauled it indoors in pails, and we used a wooden outhouse. As we sold more milk and our financial situation improved, Dad had the house electrified, added an indoor bathroom, and installed a telephone. We hailed these improvements as great triumphs and gratefully enjoyed the convenience they added to our lives.

Outside, it never got any easier. Our father had opted for dairy farming because he loved cows. That translated into a barn full of cows that had to be milked by hand twice a day every day of the year. No days off. Our first encounter of the day would be at 4:30 in the morning and the second at 4:30 in the afternoon. At some point in between, one of us daughters, with a driver's license or without, had to drive the hundred-pound milk cans in our pickup truck to the milk collection station, more than ten miles away.

To keep the dairy herd going, we had to raise their food: corn for ensilage, soybeans, and clover or alfalfa for hay. We also had to raise wheat and tomatoes as cash crops to pay for other food for the cows. Like my sisters, from the time I was twelve years old I knew how to plow and plant, harrow and harvest, run all the heavy machinery, and drive the pickup truck when it was necessary. It kept us busy. About the time I was graduating from high school, we were able to afford electric milking machines. While the machines did speed up our work in the barn, we still had to wash the cows' udders, attach and detach the machines, "strip" the remaining milk from the udders, and drive the milk to the station.

Although we never had any extra money, things were reasonably priced in those days. We bought our first-ever car for $500. It was a brand new four-door Ford sedan, painted dark blue. I spent many Sundays lovingly waxing its surface while listening on its radio to the Yankee ballgames—Lou Gehrig, Joe DiMaggio, Yogi Berra, all in their prime, all out there playing ball. Cigarettes were five cents a pack and everybody smoked. Gasoline was going for fifteen cents a gallon. We could get into a first-run movie for a nickel in the nearby town of Rock Hall. Jeans could be bought for $1 a pair and only farmers like us would be caught dead wearing them.

After we moved to Huntingfield we never again had time or money for vacations. Somewhat replacing vacations, our mother set up a summer camp for girls on the farm, which bordered the Chesapeake Bay. My sisters and I served as counselors, although we were not any older than the campers themselves. Playing with those girls in our free time was easier than milking cows or picking tomatoes in the 90° heat of an Eastern Shore summer. We learned some useful skills, too, at Mother's camp: I helped our father build the modest cabins that housed the campers. From the glamorous redheaded swimming coach, Reds, we learned to swim faster than any other girls in the region. And we did all the stuff that campers do: campfire building, archery, beading, volleyball, storytelling. Whatever the camp needed, we learned it, and then we taught it. When Mother's camp closed down at the end of each summer, we returned to our academics, having made many new friends.

Although we did not have any other choice, we were fortunate in our schools, both elementary and high school. We drew a series of intelligent, dedicated teachers who taught curriculum every bit as edifying as that taught at the private schools on the Western Shore of Maryland, schools that were attended by those children whose parents had the money to pay the steep fees. In our rural classrooms, even before we got to high school, we had learned to conjugate Latin verbs—amo, amas, amat—enabling us to identify word origins for the rest of our lives. In other classes, we built impressive models of medieval forts to help us understand our connection with our ancestors.

While we were still in high school, our parents astonished us by bearing three more babies, all girls. The first child, Roberta, died within three days of her birth from the same lung condition that had killed one of the Kennedy babies. The other two were twins, born prematurely and named Suzanne and Joanne. Only Suzanne survived. We older girls decided our parents were trying for a baby boy, since our father was the last male in his line. Growing up among so many adults, Suzanne soon became the pet and plaything of the family.

Both of my grown sisters were naturally good looking. Jane resembled Elizabeth Taylor without the lavender eyes; Nita was a dark beauty. I was plain and so perversely accented my plainness in all the ways I could, by chopping short my blond hair and wearing distinctly unflattering clothes. When the other girl graduates dressed up for our class prom, I wore an inappropriately short skirt and refused to learn how to dance. I substituted my lack of grace and good looks with belligerence. I was always getting kicked off the athletic teams (field ball, basketball) for rough play. But I did combine my aggressiveness with a high sense of justice for all. I was forever on the lookout for bullies. On my first day in class after we moved to Huntingfield Farm, our teacher had to leave the room for a short time. As soon as she closed the door behind her, a big, stocky boy jumped up from his seat in the back of the class and started picking on a smaller, skinny boy, kicking him in the shins, tweaking his ears until the tears came, and punching him in the body where it would leave no mark. I waited for someone to speak up. Surely someone in our class would intervene and stop this unfair harassment. Nobody did. I weighed the pros and cons of interfering. On the one hand, I wanted so much to blend in, to make a demure good impression on my new classmates. On the other hand, how could I let this big bully's behavior go unattended? My sense of justice won out. I got up from my new desk, walked back to the scene of the crime, and politely asked the bully to stop what he was doing, and to leave the kid alone. The bully laughed condescendingly and continued what he was doing. I doubled up my hand, drew back my arm and clocked the bully right square on his jaw with my fist, hard enough to cause him to sprawl out in the aisle on his back. I returned to my desk. The bully scrambled to his feet and resumed his seat, while the victim wiped up a bit of blood. There was dead silence in the room, when the teacher reentered it. Nobody said a word and she took up our lesson where she had left off. Neither the victim, aghast at being saved by a mere girl, nor the bully, aghast at being dethroned by a mere girl, spoke to me for the remainder of that semester, but the axis of power had shifted. It had been established that no more bullying would take place, at least not if I was anywhere in the neighborhood.

The year I enrolled at Washington College, I was only on the campus a few weeks before I realized that Washington's strongest feature was its role as an informal marriage mart. For the most part, the girl students were there to show themselves off in the most favorable light and make the best possible marriage. Their future was a choice of marriage or the prospect of teaching or nursing and being tagged "an old maid." The boys, to be fair, were intent on getting their degrees and starting careers, but they also were shopping for the most suitable life partner. This meant a young woman who, after the honeymoon, would cook for them, clean house, raise a number of children, and entertain the boss on cue, all without spending much money. After the graduations in June, there was always a flurry of weddings. I did not fit in at Washington College because, hard as it was to get it across to my suitors, marriage was not my priority. I was still intent on saving the British nation.

I did acquire TC, an endearing, enduring new boyfriend. TC was what we rural people called a city boy. He was born and raised in Catonsville, a suburb of Baltimore, by a doting mother and father. His father had been one of the innovators of the skin-cream product Noxzema. I think they stirred up the first batches of the stuff in TC's basement. TC had the most remarkable vocabulary, and he diligently added a few new words every single day of his life. He was never separated from his dictionary. He remembered the words, too. He had a great memory. When he visited me at Huntingfield, he always got up at 4:30 in the morning with Nita and me. In the barn, he would rush around and try to lift all the milk cans for us. The cans weighed one hundred pounds apiece and, with our country physiques, we were much stronger than he was with his city muscles. He had a marvelous sense of humor and did see the ridiculous situation he had put himself in by falling in love with a farmer. Dad sneered and shook his head: "TC will never last." But he did. In spite of all the obstacles, he hung in there and defended his self-appointed position as number one in my affections.

When I finished out my freshman year at Washington College and transferred to the University of Maryland, over on the Western Shore, TC came along, intent on keeping hold of his prize farmer-student girlfriend. My sister Nita, who had just graduated from high school, also went to that university. Going to the University of Maryland presented a whole new set of problems. In order for us to attend, our parents sacrificed to pay the modest tuition fees and Nita and I worked at two jobs each to pay for the rest of our expenses—room and board, books, clothes, travel to the farm on weekends, and ice cream. One of my jobs was conducting lab tests to detect tuberculosis in dairy herds. I was paid from $15 to $18 a month for this work, depending on how many hours I put in. This became my base living money. My other job was to clean house and cook for a pair of university professors, husband and wife, in exchange for my room and board. Nita had a similar job with a different university family. After working at our jobs for a time, we commented to each other that love must have an awesome power to make any intelligent woman cook and scrub floors like that for the rest of her life. As a third job and for a little extra cash, we both babysat at nights for whichever university professors had a dollar, wanted to go out, and called us. We could study after our little charges went to sleep.

At the same time as I was accepting TC as my basic boyfriend, Nita had caught the eye of one of the most popular athletes on campus. His name was Kenny Reecher, and he was gorgeous to look at, with black wavy hair, dark eyes, and such an engaging manner.

When we began discussing going to England, the Battle of Britain was still raging over the English Channel, and, to our dismay, the English seemed to be losing. Nita was doing well in her class work, but I was earning a series of Cs and Ds in mine, and the academic route seemed endless to me. Along with my jobs and my course load, I was enrolled in the newly created Civilian Pilot Training (CPT) program. This was a program our government had dreamed up in order to build a reliable supply of civilian pilots. All the universities with adjacent airstrips were participating, including the University of Maryland. It was looking more and more like the British Isles were going to fall to a Nazi invasion and that our Atlantic coastline would be the next Nazi target. In the event that the United States would be drawn into a war, these CPT pilots could be called upon to patrol the coastlines, be on the lookout, and report by radio any invading Nazi U-boats they spotted.

It had been hard for me to get into the CPT course at Maryland, although I was as well qualified as any of the male applicants. I had learned to fly already back on the Eastern Shore in a small plane, a Piper Cub J5, that belonged to a friend of my parents. The designers of the CPT course had in mind a tidy pool of young men as their finished product, not to be disrupted by any of the messy details that women pilots would entail—separate toilets and all that. But I was insistent. To my advantage, their qualifying rules did not specifically exclude women would-be pilots.

"Show me where it says women cannot apply."

They could not show me and so I crept in under the wire.

Nita was not so fortunate. The CPT was happy to turn down her application. At seventeen, she was too young, they told her. We did not stop trying to get her accepted, but it was never to happen and it would cause our wartime objectives, hers and mine, to diverge.

Taking part in the CPT course overloaded my already supercharged schedule. The course required me being on the airfield at dawn for the flight exercises. That part was easy because of the many years I had been rising at 4:00 in the morning to milk the cows. For a preferred activity, piloting a plane at sunrise instead of milking cows was no contest. At the other end of the day I had to complete 150 hours of class work during the academic semester in such subjects as power plants, navigation, theory of flight, and meteorology. On the one hand, the actual flight work was not troublesome because of my previous flight time on the little, fabric-winged Piper J5 on the Eastern Shore. I just had to upgrade to a more powerful engine. On the other hand, the class work covered new ground for me and took hours of intense concentration. In between I had to fit the lab job, the household duties job, the babysitting, the miserable academics, and some stab at a social life with patient TC. To me, attending a war with Nita sounded like taking a paid vacation compared to carrying out our exhausting and hectic schedules.

Nita and I continued to talk constantly about going to England. We chafed at the fact that the United States was not assisting Britain in a more active role. In June 1940 President Roosevelt had persuaded Congress to approve the Lend-Lease Act, allowing the United States to supply some old war-useable materials to the British, Liberty ships among them. We all knew that President Roosevelt was sympathetic to the British plight, but he had to placate the influential isolationist voices in Congress and act on the advice of such notables as Charles Lindbergh. Lindbergh had visited Nazi Germany and was impressed with its power, certain of its ultimate victory. He came back to this country espousing his view Americans should stay home and sit out the European war. Congress, too, was advocating a hands-off policy in the conflict. There were men who thought Hitler could be appeased with more "small" concessions, like Czechoslovakia and Poland.

"Peace for our time," Neville Chamberlain declared, waving his useless nonaggression pact with Hitler over his head.[1]

The lend-lease assistance that Congress did approve in March 1941 may have been the major reason the British were able to hold out in the face of the fierce Nazi aggression. In 1940 alone some 3 million tons of ships and materials had been lost at sea to the marauding Nazi U-boats. By the following year, the losses had increased to more than 4 million tons, including 1,300 lost ships. That was only on the seas, while in the air the British had fought through what became known as the Battle of Britain and, wonder of wonders, were still unconquered.

You could say the Battle of Britain began in June 1940. The French had already surrendered without putting up much resistance. The British Expeditionary Force, which had gone hastily to their rescue, was pushed into the sea at Dunkirk. To illustrate how one-sided the coming sky battle would be, in June 1940 the German Luftwaffe had around 3,600 aircraft, including bombers, 2,700 of them crewed and serviceable. At the same time, the British had only 871 single-engine fighters—of which only 644 were useable. It was 644 against 2,700.[2] It did not look like too much of

---

1. Neville Chamberlain, "Peace for Our Time," September 30, 1938. Available at http://www.britannia.com/history/docs/peacetime.html.
2. Christopher Chant, Brig. Shelford Bidwell OBE, Anthony Preston, and Jenny Shaw, *World War II: Land, Sea and Air Battles, 1939–1945*, London: Octopus Press/Treasure Press (1986).

a contest would ensue. Hitler did not think so either. He had convinced himself, after Chamberlain had weakly backed down, that the British would not resist his invasion. France fell to Hitler's army in June 1940. During that same month he demanded what he called "terms" from the British government. "Terms" meant, How did the British government want to surrender? To nobody's surprise but Hitler's, the British responded with a resounding, "No deal."

At that unexpected news, an enraged Hitler unloaded on Britain the worst attack in the history of air war beginning in July 1940. Against England's forward air bases, against all identified radar stations, against the airfields, against the coastal defenses, he sent waves of one hundred or more bombers to clear the skies over Great Britain before he invaded by land or by sea. In two days of August alone, 1,485 planes were counted droning over England with their deadly bomb loads. Of the 644 British planes available for defense in those months, 450 of them were destroyed or seriously damaged by the German attackers during the several weeks of the onslaught, and 230 pilots were killed or wounded.[3] The Royal Air Force (RAF) pilots attacked the German bombers around the clock, some of them not sleeping for twenty-four hours at a stretch. They would stay in the air until they had reached the limit of their fuel supply, land briefly for refueling, grab a bite to eat, jump back into their planes clad only in shorts because of the heat, and take to the air again. RAF's Fighter Command was on the verge of collapse. For the British civilians watching helplessly, it was a heart-wrenching experience, and for the engaged pilots it was a life-or-death experience.

Without the opposition of the Fighter Command, Hitler's boats could have motored across the English Channel handily and his troops could have come ashore in England. It was looking grim indeed.

Fortunately for England and the rest of the world, Hitler then made his first big strategic blunder: Fighter Command had bombed Berlin, acting on the well-known principle that the best defense is a swift offensive, however insane it seemed. Hitler, angry at this unexpected defiance, reacted emotionally instead of keeping his cool. He ordered hasty revenge. For that he had to call off temporarily his attacks on the Fighter Command positions. This slight respite was just what Fighter Command needed to regroup. Regroup they did, and so successfully that when the Luftwaffe resumed its attacks on the Fighter Command positions they were no longer able to subdue the British pilots. Hitler sustained such losses that his air war had to be cancelled in July of 1940.

3. Ibid.

The British had lost 915 of their all-types planes. The Germans had lost 1,733 of theirs.[4] By October 1940 the British could declare themselves the winners of the Battle of Britain. The threat of invasion, although not entirely put to rest, was greatly diminished.

⁂

In December 1941, after the Japanese struck at Pearl Harbor, everything changed. I was sitting with TC, my ever-present boyfriend, in his little blue Nash on the university campus when we heard the announcement. It was early morning in Hawaii, mid-afternoon in College Park, and TC and I had finally found some time to be together. We had been listening to a program of quiet music—Artie Shaw, Benny Goodman, Glenn Miller, the Dorsey Brothers—when an agitated voice cut in abruptly with news of the sneak Japanese attack on our naval facilities and ships at Pearl Harbor. We stared at each other in disbelief. After all, Japanese diplomats were still in Washington, DC, discussing our differences with President Roosevelt. We were stunned into silence there in the car, in the winter afternoon's semidarkness. The implications of being attacked by surprise overwhelmed us. Surely this would lead our nation into war. While the gruesome details poured out over TC's car radio, we slowly recovered our calm and began to talk about what this would mean to us. What would happen to us?

"It's scary," one of us said as we held each other's hand.

Then we talked about what service TC could be inducted into. I still insisted I would keep trying for service flying in England, one way or another. Our lives would change and we would need courage, for it is one thing to talk bravely from the safety of a motherly nation about going to the aid of a struggling ally, but it is something much more real when your own country becomes the victim of sneaky aggression and you must take a position.

And our lives did change. Within a few short weeks from that December night, TC dropped out of the University of Maryland and joined the Army Air Force. His explanation was that he did not want to serve on the ground in the Army and, if he waited to be drafted, that would be his fate. This is what he said, but I believe he wanted to stay near me in the sky and joining the Air Force might make that possible. TC began an intense training program that took him all over the United States—Maryland, Texas, Colorado, and Arizona, among many postings—as he began his climb to fighter pilot status. How I envied him, struggling as I was to gain

---

4. Ibid.

an hour or so of flying time each day. I envied the ease with which he, a man, was accepted into "the club" of learning to fly; everything was made easy for him. He did not have to find the money to pay for his room and board, he did not have to scrape together newly required equipment. Somebody else woke him up in the morning and started him on his way. They even paid him a little money for this privilege.

I kept my whiney complaints about the lopsided system to myself. As long as TC was doing his basic training in Maryland—the only trainee to wear pajamas at night and to use two washcloths, one for his face and one for his body—I would make the bus trip from College Park once a week to see him. The bus fare to Fort Meade was thirty-five cents; many times it was hard for me to gather together that amount of money. Once Nita had to borrow it from an admirer of hers, who was willing to invest thirty-five cents on the off chance of a future date with her.

After TC was posted away from Maryland, he kept writing to me from his various airfields: "I'm not mad at anyone. I just want to come home and marry you." Aside from his marriage aspirations, which I did not share, I would have changed places with him in a flash. I was still putt-putting up and down the Eastern coast, adding slow minutes to my flying time and enduring long hours of academic study and flight indoctrination. How willingly I would have changed places with TC. He could come home and "not be mad at anyone" and I would take his place up there in the wild blue yonder, fighting the ferocious Luftwaffe. But women were still an untapped resource in the U.S. preparations for full-out war. That was soon to change and we—women as well as men—would be swept along with the changes.

Nita and I made a new plan to get into the war. We decided to remain in college for one more semester. That would see us into 1942 when we both would be a year older. I could complete the CPT course and qualify for my private pilot's license. Nita would start private flying lessons that we would pay for with all our spare money. Spare money? Were we joking? When we both had a respectable number of flying hours we would get ourselves to England and try to join a flying service there.

Meanwhile we started looking into job possibilities in the Baltimore area so we would be ready for the day our college semester ended in June. It was always understood with our parents and TC's parents that we would all go back to college when the war ended. One way or another, we needed more money to make our plan work. The job hunt turned out to be the easiest part of our plan. With the wholesale departure of men to the military, there was a breathtaking array of jobs to be had everywhere, including jobs that had never before been open to women.

It was a job hunter's market for women. Suddenly, we women had become indispensable in cranking up the war machine and keeping the economy going. We found we could work almost any place we chose. In one day alone Nita and I presented ourselves at the Glenn Martin plant, makers of the B-26 bomber; at Bendix, manufacturers of radios; at Black and Decker, makers of small parts; at Montgomery Ward; and at the telephone company. We were received eagerly everywhere, immediately given application forms to fill out, and asked if we could "start Monday." The wages offered to us sounded downright luxurious compared to the meager amounts we collected from our campus jobs and the babysitting. The telephone company paid $16 a week, Montgomery Ward said $20 a week, and Glenn Martin dangled sixty cents an hour in front of our eyes. For an eight-hour day, six days a week, that would be an unheard of $28.80. We swooned in anticipation of how many flying hours all that cash would buy. Tempting as it was, since we were still attending classes at the university and could not "start Monday," we decided to hang back from making job choices until our semester ended, but we knew money-paying jobs were out there in abundance.

At one of the airports I used for my flights I picked up the most astonishing news: Jacqueline Cochran, America's fastest woman flyer, was recruiting women pilots to fly with the RAF in England. We could not believe it, Nita and I. It was our "dream come true." Someone else had our same idea to go over to England and help the British. I immediately made contact and was granted an interview, to take place when the recruiting team swept through Baltimore. During the few days before my interview I was walking on air, already seeing myself in the skies over England, saving a grateful nation from the Luftwaffe attacks. When I walked into the hotel where the interviews were being conducted, my hopes hit the floor again. There was Jaqueline Cochran and one or two other women whom I assumed were pilots. They were what I would call older women. For all my interest in aviation I had never met a seasoned woman pilot nor did I know that there existed groups of women banded together to promote women in aviation. Later I learned that most of these pilots owned their own planes and had hundreds of hours in the air. Some of them even owned or managed airports.

Jacqueline Cochran was the center of this scene. Being a foundling child, she had never known the exact date of her own birth. At that time she looked to me to be in her mid-thirties, a tall, strikingly attractive blonde.

There in the hotel room, accompanied by those self-assured women pilots, she must have been surprised to be confronted by a Maryland farm girl, a would-be war pilot. Maybe she was remembering back when she was a barefoot, hungry waif, foraging for food in a northern Florida sawmill town. Whatever her thoughts, she was extremely gentle with me and began our interview by reminding me that U.S. law forbade American women from leaving the country alone in time of war if they were under twenty-one years of age. My face must have reflected disappointment because she then remarked that the war could go on for some years and she expected to continue recruiting pilots. She suggested that I add my name to her waiting list. Without hesitation, I did.

After this turndown, when Nita and I realized that we would never become one of Jacqueline Cochran's pilots, I still plugged away at building up my flying time with whatever money I could scrape together. At the same time Nita and I both started looking for other ways to get into the war.

Our father's new activity, service in the Royal Canadian Air Force (RCAF), was a help to us. During World War I Dad had served in the RAF. There was no Canadian air force then and Dad, an American citizen by way of his birth in Chicago where his father was constructing a church, had volunteered before the United States had declared war. In his Sopwith Camel, just like Snoopy's, he had become a decorated war ace with a handful of downed German planes to his credit. Perhaps that is where my original interest in flying came from, although Dad and I never talked about aviation, only about crops and cows. Now our father had put Huntingfield Farm into our mother's hands and gone off to join the RCAF. In World War I he had been a teen-aged pilot; in World War II he aimed to be a forty-five-year-old pilot. At first the RCAF turned him down flat. "Too old to fly," they said emphatically. But after Dad staged a dramatic three-day sit-down strike on the steps of the Air Ministry in Canada's capital city, Ottawa, they were embarrassed, snatched him inside, and said he could join up if he passed all the tests that the younger men had to take. He passed all the tests; after all, he had the body of a fourteen-hour-a-day farmer. The RCAF probably intended to park him behind some desk, as an "old war hero," but he earned a promotion to the rank of squadron leader quite soon and was given command of the wireless wing of a Service Flying Training School, a unit that gave air time to future aerial radio operators. Although, as commanding officer (CO), his place was in the office and not in the air, Dad made at least one flight every day as the pilot for a student in his Service Flying Training School. Pity the poor, quaking wireless student who got the commander as his pilot.

Dad did have one occasion to save the life of a student. He was on a routine flight in a Gypsy Moth with a trainee when the little stud that joins the bell crank and the aileron arm snapped, causing complete loss of aileron control. Dad immediately climbed to some 4,000 feet and ordered his trainee to jump. They both were wearing parachutes. The kid froze and would not budge. Dad decided he could not very well jump himself and leave his passenger behind, so he gingerly descended in wide, awkward, flat turns and landed in that manner, without injury or further damage to the plane.

For relaxation, Dad knitted sweaters and socks. At night in the officers' lounge Dad would relax with his clicking knitting needles while unbelieving noncommissioned officers would line up outside to peek in the window and see their CO knitting. Being the father of many girls, Dad was accustomed to cross-gender activities.

Fortunately for Nita and me, Dad's aerodromes were just over the United States–Canada border—first in sophisticated Montreal, later in rural country near Buffalo. When our hopes of going to England with Cochran dimmed, Nita, always more practical than I was, turned her efforts toward volunteering for service in Canada. On our free weekends we started driving up to Canada and spending time with Dad. Nita got in contact with the Canadian women's services. They were less strict about age limits for service, and Nita was considered a Canadian because of her birth in Alberta. We took advantage of Dad's VIP status to fly all the hours we could on his supply of Gypsy Moths and Ansons. After dark we attended the service dances, under Dad's watchful eye, and when he was not looking we flirted with his best-looking pilots.

One time, on our nine-hour drive back to college from Dad's field, we detoured through the Allegheny Mountains and stopped in Lock Haven, Pennsylvania, where the Piper Aircraft plant was located. The plant was tucked down into a valley with its long, narrow airstrip hugging the mountain on one side and bordered by the state road on the other side. There must have been two or three hundred planes neatly lined up on the length of the runway, awaiting delivery, rows and rows and rows of them. Inside the plant dozens of industrious men and women were putting together more Piper Cubs. This light model was desperately needed for the Army and Air Force communications units and for civilian air patrol use. We asked about jobs. I could imagine myself ferrying all those Cubs to their destinations. Out came the application forms and we were told our wage would be thirty cents an hour. We were spoiled already and compared this offer unfavorably with the sixty cents an hour that the Glenn Martin plant was dangling before our noses. But we did leave our résumés.

The war was going badly in the Pacific. Bataan had fallen to the Japanese and the Philippines were crumbling. As a nation, we were unprepared to fight a war that far from our shores. I do not suppose even those in charge in the Pentagon had imagined such an eventuality. By the end of December 1942, the Japanese were well in control of the Malay Peninsula.

That same year many things happened at once in my life: Mother, weary from the struggle of farming without adequate help, sold Hunting-field Farm, loaded some stuff and little Suzanne into a trailer and moved up to Canada to be with Dad. What thoughts must have gone through her mind as she gave up the struggle with the land and tried to decide which of her lifelong accumulated possessions were going with her to Canada and which she would leave in Maryland. That June Nita and I dropped out of the University of Maryland, although it was always understood with our parents that we would finish college after the war. Nita committed to service with the Canadian Women's Auxiliary Air Force in a ground capacity. She had grown tired of chasing elusive service in the air over England. I sighed and once more sorted through the job possibilities around Baltimore, eventually taking work at the Glenn Martin plant. At least they were building an interesting product, the medium-sized B-26 bomber, and the sixty cents an hour they paid influenced my decision even more. I volunteered for the night shift from 4:00 in the afternoon to midnight so I could continue flying during the daylight hours, further building up my flying time to impress Cochran. When did I sleep? I didn't sleep much, for sure.

Nita, not one to be idle while she waited for her marching orders from the RCAF, took a job with Montgomery Ward, working normal daytime hours. We both moved in with our sister Jane and her husband who lived in an apartment in downtown Baltimore. Jane had become an inspector for the U.S. Navy. They assigned her to inspect munitions assemblies at a small plant in Elkton, Maryland, which is halfway between Baltimore and the Eastern Shore. Jane's husband, Albert, was working at the shipyard in Baltimore, building Liberty ships and waiting, like Nita, for his call-up to the Army. Those two, Jane and Albert, spent all their off-work time over on the Eastern Shore. Huntingfield Farm had been sold, but Albert's family lived in Rock Hall and it was to their house that Jane and Albert returned on the weekends. The presence of Nita and me in their apartment was a crowding inconvenience to them, but they graciously put up with us. With my night work schedule and their many Shore visits, we managed to keep out of each other's way.

America's entry into the war had changed the tempo of life in Baltimore. Everyone was caught up in what we called "the war effort." If you were not in one of the fighting services, you had better be employed in the supporting services, building ships or airplanes, assembling machine guns, or tamping ammunition into shells.

In his State of the Union speech that year, President Roosevelt announced that in 1942 we would produce 60,000 military aircraft, 45,000 of which would be combat planes—bombers, dive-bombers, and pursuit planes. If that did not shock us, he added that the production would jump further to 125,000 units, including 100,000 combat planes, in 1943. Tanks, too, would roll off the assembly line to the tune of 45,000 in the current year and 75,000 the next year. He expected us to produce 20,000 antiaircraft guns in the current year and 35,000 the next year. On the seas we would be launching 6 million tons of merchant shipping in the current year compared to the 1,100 tons we had produced in 1941. In 1943 launchings alone would escalate to 10 million tons. To quote our president in his State of the Union speech, "These figures and similar figures for a multitude of other implements of war will give the Japanese and the Nazis a little idea of just what they accomplished in the attack on Pearl Harbor."[5] I was surprised that President Roosevelt would reveal so much delicate information in his State of the Union speech. I suppose he decided that the scare factor was more advantageous than concealing facts.

When the British read these figures, they must have been blown clear away, as I was. Yet for all our preparations and blusterings, between January and May 1942 the Japanese steadily took over the Philippine Islands; our troops under Gen. Douglas MacArthur were forced to abandon the Philippines and flee to Australia. Those troops left behind under Gen. Jonathan Wainwright were soon forced to surrender to the Japanese invaders.

Baltimore, being a serious seaport, was crowded with sailors on their last leave. Soldiers, too, were present everywhere, en route to the next base. To be in uniform gave the wearer a special status and we civilians vied with each other to accommodate and pamper those service persons who crossed our paths. Nita initiated a conversation with a young sailor on her bus one day and ended by giving him all of Mother's Toll House cookies that she was supposed to be bringing to me. After work late one night Nita and I walked past a uniformed boy passed out on the sidewalk in the rain. When we noticed his RAF shoulder patch as we passed, we

5. State of the Union Address, Franklin Delano Roosevelt, January 6, 1942. Available at http://www.presidency.ucsb.edu/ws/index.php?pid=16253.

returned, hoisted him up between us, and dragged him home to Jane's apartment. We stripped off his wet clothes, put them on a radiator to dry, and stretched him out under a blanket on the couch, still unconscious. In the morning "RAF" was still sound asleep. Nita and I had to go out so we wrote him an innocent little note excusing ourselves, telling him there was food in the refrigerator if he woke up hungry, and asking him to engage the lock on the door when he left. It did not occur to us that this British airman would do us any harm or take any of our belongings. In our cars, too, we always picked up uniformed hitchhikers and thought ourselves lucky to be able to help them on their way to war.

For a couple of months in early 1942, Nita and I fell into a fairly regular routine. She went off to work at Montgomery Ward's in the morning. I would sleep for an hour or two, then rise and meet Reds, the swimming coach from Mother's summer camp, at a nearby pool for a training session. Nita and I were the strongest swimmers on Reds' team—she in backstroke and myself in butterfly breaststroke. He entered us in as many swimming meets as we could schedule, but our training was haphazard. Reds was only one generation removed from Germany so the war presented him with a moral dilemma: he did not like what the Nazis were doing, but he did not want to kill any relatives. He solved his problem by joining the U.S. Merchant Marines. In the weeks before he departed Baltimore for training in New England, he carried around with him the Merchant Marine manual and read chapters when he was not busy. One of the chapters he was mastering was emergency procedure in case his ship was torpedoed. He felt he had it pretty much memorized until my sister Jane looked over his shoulder one day and scoffed, "Don't you know that ships are bombed from the air just as frequently as they are torpedoed?" Reds looked quite alarmed. "I'll need to get another manual," he said.

I took him flying with me once, his first flight ever in an airplane. In those days, very few people had ever been up in an airplane. I strapped him into the rear seat, and off we zoomed. I had been flying my pattern for about half an hour, waiting to hear from Reds how impressed he was. No sound came from him. I looked over my shoulder to see if at least he was enjoying the ride. There he was, slumped back in the corner with his nose buried in the Merchant Marine manual. I could not believe it. I didn't say a word, but I yanked the stick over and put the plane into a vertical bank, first in one direction, then, sharply, in the other. Reds was too stubborn to say a word, but when I looked again he had closed his manual and was looking somewhat green.

After my swim workout with Reds, I would go out to one or another of the several private airfields on the outskirts of Baltimore to fly up some time and add to my total hours. I had my choice of Rutherford where I had made a deal with the manager, a woman, to exchange cleaning and sweep-up duties and work on the student logbooks for time in the sky, or at Logan airfield (since abandoned) where Carl held sway. Carl was chief pilot and instructor at Logan and owned a 225-horsepower Waco and a Piper Cruiser. For $6 an hour I could fly his planes. On weekends when I was not working overtime at the plant I would go out to Rutherford. On working nights I would fly out at Logan.

The war was closing in on all our airfields. One day when I arrived at Logan field, I came across about twenty little Piper Cruisers in Army garb. They were preparing to take off en masse so I paused to watch them get into the air. They rustled down the taxi strip, one behind the other, and wheeled around in threes at the end of the runway. Then into the air they went, one after the other, a 180° (half circle) over the runway, and off into the sky to some Army destination.

Another time I dozed off working my pattern at three thousand feet. If I had crashed, I wonder what would have upset Carl the most—losing his precious Cruiser or losing me. Fortunately, when I fell asleep I had my hand resting on the throttle and as I relaxed into sleep, I shoved the throttle wide open. The sudden burst of power jolted me awake. I emphatically stayed alert for the rest of my hour in the air and I didn't tell a soul about my indiscretion.

Many times if Carl did not have a student he came along with me and gave me a free lesson. He was a first-class instructor and I learned a lot of technique from him. On the rare days when the sky was clear (there was generally some industrial smog over Baltimore to contend with) we would spiral up to five thousand feet. From there we could see all the way across the Chesapeake Bay to where Huntingfield Farm curved along the Bay Shore. One day the wind was up to thirty-five miles an hour. This is too windy for a light aircraft, but Carl and I were there at the airfield and Carl had canceled his student lessons so we ventured upstairs. We positioned ourselves at three thousand feet directly above the airstrip. There were no other planes in the sky so we faced into the wind and opened the throttle, full throat. Nothing happened. We sat there in the same position for ten minutes, laughing out loud. It was a strange feeling to be sitting in the air with our throttle wide open going nowhere. Carl finally signaled me—I was the pilot—to dive down to one thousand feet where there was less of a gale and we were able to make some progress. With our landing, the field was closed to any further flying that day.

And soon it would be closed officially and indefinitely to civilian traffic, along with all the other airfields along the Eastern coast. The war was getting closer to our lives and more personal. Carl's beloved Waco was requisitioned by the military. In one last, nostalgic flight, I followed Carl in the Piper Cub to deliver her to her new handlers at a nearby military base, and "ferried" Carl back to Logan field. After our Waco delivery, Carl dropped me off at Jane's apartment. Later that night he telephoned me and formally asked me for a date. His request caught me by surprise. There was a big age difference between us and I thought of him more as a father type. While I was thinking up an excuse that would not hurt his feelings, it did cross my mind how great it would be to have a boyfriend who owned not one, but two airplanes. It only crossed my mind fleetingly. It probably crossed Carl's mind, also. He would be thinking, "This woman is crazy about flying and I've got two planes. . . . " In my refusal, TC took the rap. "No, Carl," I answered, "My boyfriend would not like it if I dated you or anyone else. We said we wouldn't."

From then on, because the field was closed to civilian traffic, we saw little of each other. Carl did come to some of our swimming meets, but I felt embarrassed talking to him anymore.

By coincidence, Carl also worked on the night shift at the Glenn Martin plant for the same reason I did: to free up the days for flying. Before Logan field was closed to civilian flying, after our flight time, Carl would give me a ride in his car to the plant. Driving was twice as fast as taking the streetcar. At first it was strange for me, working in the dark, but I soon became adjusted to the new tempo. The job I had been assigned was called "runner," a person who procured by whatever means the little nut, bolt, or subassembly that was holding up the general assembly line. The job took me all over the plant. On my travels into the various departments, I detected so much inefficiency and waste that I trained someone else for my runner duties, declared myself the efficiency person, and began to work out better procedures for the lagging departments. I must have been doing a good job because before too many weeks went by I had a desk in the plant supervisor's outer office and the walls were full of my charts showing how to move all the parts faster.

To get home after my eight hours of labor at the plant, I hitched a ride with a wild bunch of kids from the rough part of town. We tore through the midnight sleeping city at about eighty miles an hour in their dilapidated coupe, top down, rain or shine, the kids scruffy and dirty from their assembly line, longhaired and smelling of tobacco and sweat. We always had to make one or two pit stops for beer, but every morning they delivered me safely to Jane's apartment and waited until

I was safely inside before roaring off with their perforated muffler. Eventually, everyone in my gang was inducted into the services and I had to find another ride. The replacement was a sedate older man who wore a necktie, rode with all the windows of his clean sedan rolled up and the radio playing softly, which was boring after those raucous kids. I missed them.

Most of the time I was able to avoid thinking about the temptation of a social life and keep my eyes steadfastly on my long-term objective of getting to England and helping to hold off the Nazis. But one stifling hot night, just as my coworker dropped me at Jane's apartment (he did not wait until I was inside), I heard a melodious peal of light-hearted laughter. I looked across the street to see where the laughter was coming from and saw two couples making their way along the sidewalk. They were about my age, all four of them, and dressed in their finest clothes: the boys were in formal tuxedoes, the girls in lovely, long dresses. One dress was of fire-red taffeta, the other of ethereal baby-blue chiffon. They continued to laugh and chatter among themselves as I watched them out of sight. For a quick moment I felt a stab of jealousy. Why was one of those couples not TC and me? Why was I hot and exhausted and fed up instead of dressed in a lovely red robe and telling funny jokes? I went into the apartment, dropped on the bed, and closed my eyes. Before I fell asleep, the joys of a carefree social life had faded into the background and my true objective was back in the forefront.

To achieve my goal—getting to England—I had one remaining untapped resource. During World War I my father had had a favorite squadron mate, a Canadian named William Stephenson. They had flown together daily in their Sopwith Camels on missions over the lines in France; on more than one occasion, they had saved each other's life. Now this intimate friend of Dad's had been named by Churchill as the head of British intelligence efforts in the States, a unit discreetly known as British Security Coordination (BSC), housed in New York City at Rockefeller Center. Before Cochran swept onto the scene with her promise of flying jobs in England, I had been badgering William Stephenson for a job with his BSC outfit. At one time he had been recruiting couriers to carry sensitive documents between Washington, DC, and New York City—no Internet in those days. Reluctantly, he let me interview for that job, an interview that I failed miserably. Too naïve, too open, too young. I guess they concluded that I could not keep a secret. Another time Stephenson presented my credentials to a former squadron mate who had remained in the RAF and risen mightily. The answer came back loud and clear: "If Betty were a boy, I could use her today, but. . . ."

Well, I was not a boy and never would be so frustration reigned.

Quite unexpectedly, in July of 1942 I received a letter from Stephenson informing me that the British government was launching a new program in which they would pay the passage of any British citizen living in the United States who agreed to return to England and engage in war service. Stephenson reminded me that because I had been born in Canada the British considered me one of their citizens. He instructed me to contact the British consulate in Baltimore and learn the details. It turned out to be true. England was desperate for war workers. Deaths in combat, deaths in the many bombings, aging workers, expanding labor needs in the war plants—all these factors were creating a shortage of workers and the British had started scouring the world for loyal citizens. Although it made me feel guilty and unpatriotic to the United States, I immediately declared myself a British citizen. After all, I had been born in Alberta, Canada, and Canada was a loyal member of the British Commonwealth. There in the British consulate in Baltimore they issued me a British passport before I finished asking for one and passed me along to a transportation officer to arrange my trip to England. The transportation officer was up in New York City so I took a day—rather, a night—off from work and caught an early-morning train north. At this point I did not expect to get to England; I was just following this latest lead to see how far it would take me before someone told me, "Too bad you are not a boy." At the time of the morning when I caught my train, Baltimore had a dreary air, noiseless, damp, still too early for workers to be afoot, but with a smattering of sailors and soldiers on their way to the next post.

Once in Manhattan I hurried to the British consulate where I filled out another sheaf of documents, was photographed, thumb-printed, given the title "British Volunteer 00623," and handed over to a British Army major who promised he would have me on a ship to England within two weeks. Two weeks. I was stunned. After months of interviewing, conniving, scheming, here I was on the threshold of departure for the war. Was I frightened? After my hazardous childhood on the farm, dealing with runaway mule teams, overturned wagons, raging bulls, and machinery that collapsed on top of my body, no, I was not frightened, but, yes, I was curious, elated, and open to a new adventure. And, of course, I would be fulfilling my self-assigned mission of saving the British. Now I needed to hurry back to Baltimore and tell everyone—my family, my employers,

Carl of the planes, Reds of the swimming, and, most of all, my patient boyfriend, TC.

TC was the one who took my news in the worst possible manner. Somehow, maybe because he was already in uniform, he thought he would be the first of us to go into active service. In a perverse way, he was offended because I was going off to war before he did. Most of all, being twenty-one, he was embarrassed to have to admit to his buddies that his girlfriend had chosen war service over marrying him and settling in to keeping the home fires burning. We had to say our last goodbye over the telephone because TC was in a fighter pilot course out in Texas and I was in Baltimore. There were lots of tears and fervent vows of faithfulness. We promised to write every day. I said I would await his arrival in England with impatience; surely his posting would be to a fighter unit somewhere in the British Isles.

When I told Reds, he immediately lost interest in me and my life since I would no longer be a body collecting swimming medals for his team. Besides, he had to worry about those torpedoes.

Carl was happy for me; he knew what flying meant to me. My coworkers at the plant signed up to receive postcards as if I were going on vacation.

My family—Mother, Dad, and sisters—just sighed and said, "Come home when you get tired."

After all the goodbyes were over, I was standing in front of my open trunk, trying to decide what I might need in this England where I had never been. Would it be hot like Maryland or cold like Canada? I had heard it would be foggy for sure. What should I give away or store for my return? By any standards I was leaving behind a hard life—the farm days that started at 4:00 in the morning and endured until the sun went down, with every type of tough physical work in between. I was leaving behind a university life where I held down two or three jobs to pay my way, studied my courses, and learned to fly, all at the same time. And I was leaving behind a loving family—father, mother, sisters. We disagreed on many of each other's attitudes, but we were respectful of each other and I knew I would miss them as I would miss all the fast friends I had gathered around me in my years of growing to twenty. Reds, Carl, TC. TC, my grown-up boyfriend would be at the head of my list. We had envisioned several carefree years together in college, getting to know each other better. If we continued to love each other, later on we might put our lives together and become our own family. All of this familiar, comfortable life was fading into the past—some of it, without doubt, never to be possible again. The friends and family—would they be there for me when I returned?

Would I return?

Before me awaited that little, besieged island called Great Britain. It was a total unknown to me, yet I was launching myself to give service in a time of British distress. Would there be a place for me? Would I fit in? Was I taking on unnecessary risks and maybe going to lose my life before it got started?

I put that last thought out of my mind because I knew in my heart I had made the right decision. I knew I was doing the right thing. I quit philosophizing and got back to the packing. Should I take this sweater or leave it for my sisters to fight over? What about books? Could I live without Salinger? Books weigh so much; I had heard that the British love books and read all the time. I would leave my books behind and acquire new ones in England.

It was my last full day and night on American soil. Stephenson had pressed a good supply of dollars on me so I treated myself to a matinee performance of *Porgy and Bess*, starring Todd Duncan and Etta Maten. It thrilled me beyond description. In the evening I took in a musical, *Let's Face It*, which did not thrill me. And then I was sitting on the bed in my YWCA room with the strains of Glen Gray's Casa Loma band drifting up from the street as I reviewed the life I was leaving behind and tried to imagine the new life about to open up before me.

CHAPTER 2

Betty's Favorite Day: Crossing the Ocean to England

THE FOLLOWING MORNING, October 1, 1942, I dragged my big trunk and suitcase out of the YWCA, put them into the back of a taxi, and headed for Pier 56. There I joined my fellow British travelers, six women and two men, in Customs where serious officials combed meticulously through our luggage before waving us onto our ship. I had been expecting a serious-sized ship. Instead, for the next three weeks my home would be a tiny Norwegian vessel—only two or three tons compared to the usual six or seven. Her name was M/S *Scebeli*. With some tactful maneuvering, I garnered a single cabin containing a nailed-down bed, a wardrobe, a sturdy desk, and a basin right in the cabin. There was even a light over the bed for late-night reading and space for my big trunk and suitcase.

After assigning us to our cabins, the captain shooed us off *Scebeli* until early evening. Most of us went looking for the last stateside supper. We had been told the grim facts about food in England: there was very little of it. Our egg ration would be one a month, if we could find an egg, and there would be no meat, except for the occasional tired old horse. Forget about bananas and oranges. My own last supper ended with ice cream. I knew I was saying farewell to my favorite food.

At 9:00 that evening we were all back on board, ready for an early morning departure when the tide would be most favorable. I stood on deck watching the crew stow last-minute cargo away in the hold. It was an eerie sight. On the dock, shadowy figures dumped huge crates marked "Wisconsin ham and bacon," the great winch creaking down to lift up the crates, swing them over the hold, and slowly lower them to the hands of more dark figures who grabbed them and steered them to rest. We passengers, exhausted from our last American day, retired to our bunks. Hours later— it must have been 4:00 in the morning—I rolled into the guardrail of my bunk with a thud and woke to the loud creaking and groaning of the hull and to the dismal boooop–boooop of the ship's horn. I guessed we had cast off. I dressed quickly and scrambled out to the blackness of the deck. As two stubby tugs towed *Scebeli* clear of the dock area, I hung over the rail. The tugs left us very soon and we moved down the Hudson River under our own power. I turned to watch the awe-inspiring skyscrapers of New York City fade out of sight, and silently saluted the proud, majestic woman with the torch, Miss Liberty, who watches over the harbor. A lump rose in my throat and I wondered if I would ever see her again.

The next morning when the breakfast gong summoned us to the table we were short one of the men. The Immigration and Naturalization Service authority had taken him ashore late the night before because he lacked his proper exit permit. Thus, the final passenger count was six women, one man. All the other women were British citizens who had been in the United States for only a short time. They spoke of this voyage as "going home" and looked on me as an oddity. The sole man, Bill Haines, was a clothing representative, and had been working in New York for a London firm. The captain indicated that all seven of us would be seated at one long table for our meals. He and his officers were seated at a separate, smaller table. They were all Norwegian: blond and mostly beautiful.

Our ship was well escorted until mid-afternoon of that first day. A destroyer trailed us for some hours and several patrol seaplanes circled above. Later we were joined by two fat dirigibles. The dirigibles stayed with us until dark, patrolling slowly ahead and out to either side, looking for suspicious dark spots in the ocean. We had passed a large convoy going in our direction as we left the harbor and the river behind. There must have been sixteen ships of various sizes, but we soon outstripped them. We had been speculating whether we would make our crossing in the convoy or lone wolf it. The company of all those other ships would have been cozy, but it seemed we were going to make a run for it without an escort. The crew reacted in two ways. Some were quite nervous, saying that alone we had less chance of surviving and being picked up if *Scebeli* was torpedoed and that we could run into submarines more readily. Others maintained that we would be a smaller target all alone and we could move faster, reducing our dangerous days at sea considerably. The crew's opinions seemed to depend on what their experiences had been on previous voyages across the Atlantic.

That first evening the sea became quite rough and our little ship rolled heavily. We landlubbers braced ourselves against the sudden jars and were glad to weave off to our cabins soon after dinner. It was a miserable night for all of us. Sitting on the edge of my bunk, I watched my room roll down to a 40-degree slope and then roll slowly back in the other direction. It reminded me of a movie scene of someone with a hangover. There was no way of writing the promised daily letter to TC. He would have to understand.

Our doors were all braced open. The captain had explained cheerfully that doors often jammed shut when a torpedo struck. Our choice seemed to be to close our doors and go down with the ship to a swift death or leave our doors open, get out, and deal with a slower death in the icy ocean. The captain said it was our choice. He said he slept with his door open. We all announced we would leave our doors open. We were cautioned to sleep in our clothing from that first night at sea until the end of the passage and to keep our life jackets on at night. I went along with the clothing advice, but there was no way I could get a night's sleep wearing that life jacket.

The next morning, only the lone Englishman, Bill Haines, and I made it to the breakfast table. All the others were prone in their bunks. Haines and I made the rounds with wet towels, water, and comfort. Over the next four days, the women returned to life one by one. Florence Searle was the one who intrigued me the most. She had worked in Hollywood as a script continuation person—the person who in each scene of a movie takes note of what time it says on the clock and assures that it is properly adjusted in the next scene. She notes all the costume details and the furniture locations. During our voyage she entertained us with many Hollywood stories.

The weather acted up again, but by now all of our inner mechanisms were attuned to the wild sea. Our ship pitched and tossed in mountainous waves. The sea changed from a peaceful blue to an angry black with waves swirling up into startling lashes of greenish-blue. Florence and I ventured out to our favorite perch, one we had discovered in a lifeboat. After only a few minutes, we were drenched with salt spray and we scurried back to our cabins to change clothes. Then we tried to go to the bow of the ship, but the sailors yanked us back because the waves were washing over the deck and there was the danger that we could go with them. The sailors finally stowed us in a small, sheltered corner on the second deck. From there we could get fresh air and be safe from the waves. We watched our ship dipping her nose right into the sea and saw waves pounding over the bridge. This was not the Chesapeake Bay, my only other deep-water experience. This was a frightening sight, but I liked the invigorating salt air. Florence and I endured there until teatime.

The next day, when the sea had settled down, I asked the chief mate if there was some work I could do. It would make the time pass faster and I was not used to being idle. Looking rather dubiously at my clean trousers and neat shirt, he offered me a brush and a can of battle gray paint and led me to the dizzy height of the bridge gun turret.

"This will keep you busy," he remarked, "Ships always need more paint." I set to work. Several hours later, one trouser leg rolled up, the other drooping around my ankle, shirt tails hanging around my hips, sleeves rolled up and hair caught in a ribbon, with dabs of paint on my face, I must have presented quite a picture.

The dinner gong sent me scurrying from the bridge, my paint can swinging from one hand. I had become accustomed to Norwegian meals, but they did differ in many ways from our farm fare. Breakfast was the same—fruit, toast, eggs, bacon, and coffee. Lunch was more elaborate: we always started with soup. Without exception, the next course was fish—fish with potatoes, fish with onions, fish with vinegar, or fish cakes. This course was followed by meat and potatoes, or chicken stew, or baked ham. Fruit ended the meal, if any of us had room left.

The Norwegian version of supper was peculiar to me. When we arrived at our table, it would be spread with a smorgasbord array of shrimp, ham, tongue, sardines, deviled ham, relish and pickles, and several different kinds of cheese. We were not expected to tackle this spread until we had been served a hot course, usually a stew. After the hot course, we fell on the smorgasbord and tried out all sorts of food combinations. It did occur to us that this luxurious meal before us was in great contrast to what we could expect in England. We even joked about possibly going to our watery deaths with full stomachs.

Darkness had enveloped the ship when we left the table one evening, but I sidled cautiously out on deck anyway. I was amazed once again at the inky blackness surrounding our ship. Peeking at the ocean, I caught my breath at the beauty of the ship slicing into the dark and throwing off phosphorescence. The unreal whiteness seemed like piles of angel robes whirling in a storm. I could not face the harsh light of the lounge again that night so I felt my way step by step along the deck to an iron ladder, then up onto the rear gun mount. I scrambled over a pile of rope and clutched at the gun barrel for support. A shadow moved on the opposite side of the gun base and a gruff mumble answered my greeting.

"Getting a bit of fresh air?" I asked.

"No, on guard duty," the shape replied in English and turned his back on me to peer off into the thick blackness. I realized suddenly that, of course, there would be a twenty-four-hour guard maintained during a perilous passage like ours.

The next morning I was awakened abruptly by the scurrying of feet on the upper deck and the sound of excited voices. I threw back the blanket and pulled on my shoes. I was fully dressed, as our captain had advised. Snatching my life jacket with one hand and running the fingers of the other hand through my tousled hair, I went out on deck. I stopped still in astonishment. Every gun was fully manned, the gunners looking grim. The chief mate was directing the aim of the big gun to starboard. I looked in that direction. It could not be, but it was: only six hundred yards away was a thin broomstick cutting through the sea before a white tail of spray. It was a periscope. My heart went into my throat. I wanted to move. Instead, I stood in the center of the deck and waited for it to rise up under me, waited for the silent torpedo that seemed sure to come. The gun crews also waited. Silence. Thirty seconds passed. A minute passed. Our ship lurched forward at full speed, zigzagging crazily from side to side in an evasive maneuver. The periscope disappeared. The moment had passed. The danger was over for the time being at least; my companions sleeping peacefully down below had missed the excitement. Surely that U-boat had spotted us, so why did they not send off a torpedo? We were never to know the answer. Perhaps they were empty and on their way to rearm. Whatever the reason, it was lucky for us on board *Scebeli*.

Sleep would have been impossible for me after that experience so I joined the gun crew stripping a machine gun on the rear mount. They accepted my offer of aid without comment and my hands were soon covered with grease as I carefully cleaned breeches and barrels. Those on guard were keeping a close watch for the reappearance of the U-boat and we began to load up more cartridge belts just in case.

After this scene, we carried our life jackets with us always and the steward gave us a drill on how to get into some new rubber suits. These suits were designed by the Norwegians; as yet they had not been produced in great enough quantities to permit distribution to all the Allied seamen. The suit was similar to a pair of child's sleepers. A string is drawn tight under the chin to secure the hood, which is attached to the suit, and the wristbands are elastic to make them watertight. Boots are attached to the suit and weighted on the soles with lead so that on leaping into the water the wearer automatically assumes a standing position. The suit enables a person to keep afloat and warm as long as the body can endure. The use of the suit is said to have saved thousands of lives, but I do not see how any sailor, spotting a U-boat, would have time to get himself into this suit before the torpedo arrives.

That afternoon I made my way back to the gun mount and helped the gunner dismantle and clean the machine guns. The gunner's name was Olaf, but he said to call him Ole. He spoke excellent English that he had learned at school, and he told me the story of his war years. Although he was only twenty-two years old, he had been at sea a number of years in the Norwegian merchant navy. In that capacity, he had pretty much covered the world: Africa, South America, the East Coast and West Coast in the United States, and Canada, besides every country in Scandinavia. When France capitulated to the Germans, Ole's ship was caught in the French Moroccan port of Casablanca. The German invaders offered him and the other crewmembers tempting bribes to continue sailing their ship under the German flag. When the crew spurned this offer, they were thrown into a prison camp near Tangiers. In a breathtaking escapade, Ole and some companions sneaked past the guard on a moonless night, stole a small lifeboat, and put out on the Mediterranean Sea. It took them three days to cross the Strait of Gibraltar to Spain safely. The day after their escape another small boat attempting to escape from Oran, Algeria, was detected and those crewmembers returned to the prison camp.

Next in his life was a trip to England for a gunnery training course and to sea again as a gunner in the British Navy. His first treacherous voyage through the Caribbean guarding an oil tanker ended in the Bahamas when a U-boat torpedo found its target. He told me how the first torpedo struck the paraffin, which does not explode, instead of the benzene, which does explode, giving the crew enough time to evacuate the tanker, and how the captain stayed on board with Ole and four other sailors to try and get the tanker to shore. Ole received the Norwegian War Cross for that action. They were only eighty-five miles from the Florida coast when the torpedo struck, but no aircraft or destroyer or even launch was able to go to their rescue. Moments after the captain had given up on his efforts to get the wounded ship to port and ordered the rest of the crew to abandon ship, the flames got to the benzene and the tanker blew sky high.

There followed for Ole and his fellow crewmembers a fairy-tale two weeks in Nassau, with the Duke of Windsor as their host, and then up to Canada for more gunnery training. Since all his perilous adventures were caused by the Nazis, I asked Ole how he felt about the invaders of his homeland. He raised his blond head, looked out to the horizon with his blue eyes narrowed and murmured, "We will have our vengeance one day."

There were more hair-raising tales from the gunners and from the Norwegian crew. There were hours of serious instruction for all the passengers on the guns, and lazy hours of dozing on the upper deck in the sun. I found a perfect place that was conducive to writing. It was up on the third and top deck, jammed right into the bow of the ship. I had only to rise up a bit and I could see our nose plowing through the water. When the sun was full overhead, it turned the ocean a beautiful deep blue; when the spray leaped up against the sun the white foam melted away into a bright green. We even had schools of dolphins join us on calm days, racing with our ship and playing in the water.

At other times I would stand upright in the bow and let my eyes slowly follow the horizon around in a full circle. It was awesome to see nothing but water on all sides into what seemed to be infinity. There were wispy white clouds overhead in a robin's egg blue sky; the sun made a silvery, blinding pathway from the horizon to the ship. In those magic moments, with no periscopes in view, I was glad to be making this voyage on a small ship.

One night we sighted some lights on the horizon. I happened to be on deck at the time. There was much rushing about until a radio communication identified the lights as belonging to some Swedish ships running food to Greece. The ships of neutral countries (including Sweden) always ran fully lighted and the rules of war protected them.

My father's birthday was October 10 and two things happened that day. The captain proposed a toast to him with all the passengers joining in. It was a warm, sincere tribute to someone they knew only by reputation, and it pleased me very much. The other event was the reception of a communiqué over *Scebeli*'s wireless: a BBC résumé of the military situation in most of the world (see Figure 2.1).

```
REUTER NEWS M/S "SCEBELI" SATURDAY OCTOBER 3rd 1942.
                    Occupied Europe and Germany have been given hell last
   twentyfour hours as British, American and alied 'planes carried out
   a none stop raid.British bombers covered Rhineland with high explosive
   and thousands of incendiary bombs.Many fires were started.British heavy
   bombers also attacked Liege in Belgium.Famous American flying fortresses
   went to France attacking several coastal towns towns including Bologne
   and Le Havre.Yesterday Americans lost 17 bombers.Many squadrons of
   American, British and alied fighters escorted bombers on their none stop
   raid. Six of the escoting 'planes were lost.Shipping were attacked off
   French coast by new American built torpedoplanes.
                    Stalingrad is still stubbornly resisting the Germans.
   The Re Army keep up their offensive North-west of the city and have
   pushed germans back at several point. Here the Russians captured 130
   crippled German tanks being used as trnch defense.Holding firm other fr
                    Airactivity is keeping up in Egypt.In the Tobruk harbour
   one ship set aflame.There is no change on land front.
                    In New Guinea alied forces are pursuing rapidly retreating
   Japs.Our bombers attacked supply ships off New Guinea coast setting two
   On fire.Canadian and American bombers attacked Japanese instalations on
   Aleutians Islands destroying six Zerofighters, one submarine believed
   sunk and several transports damaged. We lost on bomber.
                    .In Poland 500 Italians have been arrested because they've
   gone on strike telling Germans 14 hours a day is too much working on
   railways.
                    ---------------------------

        Kindly Switch off electric fans after seven o'clock tonight

   helping to facilitate the wireless correspondense.

                                            Thank You...Radioo
```

FIGURE 2.1 *Reuter's News Release*

R.A.F. D.O.
U.K. Port of Landing,

       Miss Betty Ann Lussier has been accepted as a British Volunteer for War Service in Great Britain.

       She comes from a family with a fine record of public service, and is strongly recommended.

       She would like to be placed as a Ferry Pilot.

       If this is not possible, her appointment to the Women's Auxiliary Air Force might he considered.

       Otherwise she is well qualified for the Women's Auxiliary Territorial Service as a Motor Transport Driver.

John W. Taylor

His Majesty's Consul

British Consulate,
   Baltimore, Maryland.

   18th September, 1942.

FIGURE 2.2 *British Consulate Letter*

As the morning of October 13, 1942, dawned a shout came down from the bridge, "Land in sight." I felt a strange exhilaration at the sound of that wind-carried announcement. It meant that *Scebeli* had once again defied the odds and almost made it into port, carrying me along. At the time I was standing on the aft gun mount, peering into the mist when very slowly a few dim peaks emerged in the distance: Northern Ireland.

The captain mounted a double guard to bring us unscathed through those last dangerous hours. He opened a bottle of champagne and toasted the good fortune with all his passengers. He admitted that we had brought him good luck in spite of the sea myth that women are bad luck on board a working ship.

Late in the morning, after we sighted land, the bell buoys began to appear and a harbor loomed ahead, with its contingent of queer, fat barrage balloons tethered and floating overhead. Other ships began to pass us, each with a balloon anchored to the rigging and floating ridiculously overhead, looking for all the world like fat children towing toy balloons on a string. In spite of their frivolous appearance, those barrage balloons had a serious purpose. They were there to discourage dive-bomb attacks from the German Luftwaffe fighter planes patrolling the coastal regions, on the lookout for potentially vulnerable targets.

After a brief stop at Mersey River, my fellow passengers recognized our entry port as Liverpool. The end of our journey came with a bang. We docked. We were inspected by the Immigration officials. We were inspected by the Customs officials and presented with our letters of identification. We were scrutinized by the Censor officers. My precious journal was confiscated for a closer reading. Seeing how upset I was at losing my journal, the officer assured me I would get it back in due time. The Customs officials admonished us not to use Xs and Os in signing off our letters in the future. Why? According to them, these symbols made it too easy for us to send coded messages. And we were told politely not to ask for anything from our overseas families and friends—not stockings, not chocolate. In other words, the British were too proud to ask for any handouts. "Do not send your size numbers, either," they told us. The British may have had their backs to the wall, they may have been clothed in old clothes and hungry, but they still had their pride and they were emphatically not letting us ask for any silk stockings.

Finally, we were questioned, one after another, by a representative of the UK Ministry of Labour. No potential spies were going to get into Britain through Liverpool. More important than whether we were warm bodies ready to work for England seemed to be that we were of good family and impeccable character, as witness the letter that accompanied me from the British Consulate in Baltimore (see Figure 2.2).

Our baggage was tossed onto the dock. Quite suddenly we were free to leave *Scebeli*, free in England. The officers and the crew lined up formally on their deck to bid us an affectionate farewell. I took a long last look at the staunch little ship, thought of the bravery of its men, ready to head out on the treacherous sea again, and turned to meet my unknown future.

CHAPTER 3

Welcome to London and Maidenhead

WE TRAVELERS WERE NOT entirely on our own, at least not yet. An official from the UK Ministry of Labour was waiting on the dock. He gathered us all together and checked us off on his list, herded us into a van with our luggage, and drove us to the railway station, where he bought us all tickets to London. Apparently, everything starts in London and we needed to be there to begin our new lives. Through a long, dark night the train hurtled over the English countryside, but we were unable to see anything because of the strict blackout restrictions. We dozed off and on but were too excited to sleep. Everyone except me was coming home, and they were eager to meet up with their families. Early the next morning we stepped off our train and into the hands of another cheery Ministry of Labour representative who led us through the streets of London on foot at high speed for a first breakfast at what one of our women dubbed a "hostile," instead of a hostel. It was that—cold and forbidding—but the food was warm and welcome. By then we all had realized that our main means of transportation was going to be our feet. Private cars were absolutely unheard of in those days in gas-starved England, so we would get accustomed to trotting around behind sturdy-legged English men and women.

After that initial meal we were walked back to the Ministry of Labour and whisked around from department to department, collecting all the identification and ration cards that we needed in order to call England our home. We presented those letters we had brought from the British Consulate in the United States, and explained in what ways we were qualified to contribute to the war effort.

Bill Haines, our lone male from *Scebeli*, was offering to be a steward on a transatlantic plane or ship. Even our hazardous voyage across the Atlantic had not changed his mind. My five women companions signed

```
:58x.
ADC.
                    MINISTRY OF LABOUR & NATIONAL SERVICE.

                           Barnsbury Road.N.1.

.o Chief Recruiting Officer.
........ WAAF                              14 OCT'42
.................
...............

                       Overseas Volunteers.

        This is to introduce Miss B.A. Lussier  who has come to this
country under the Overseas Manpower Scheme and has volunteered for
service in the WAAF (Ferry Command Service)

        No further reference relating to his/her freedom to join the
service need be made to the Ministry of Labour but should any difficulty
arise with regard to his/her application would you please communicate
with the Ministry's Overseas Manpower Committee, Hanway House, Red Lion
Square.W.C.1. (telephone number Holborn 8454).
                                   Yours faithfully,


                           DEPUTY MANAGER.
```

FIGURE 3.1 *UK Ministry of Labour Letter*

up right away with the Women's Auxiliary Air Force, although Florence still hoped to find work in an Army film unit. My letter stated firmly that I wanted to be placed as a ferry pilot.

We were all given letters that named our skills so that we could more easily be placed in a job that suited us. The new letter I was given from the Ministry of Labour seemed to buy into the plan I had for myself (see Figure 3.1).

The other women and Haines, all bona fide citizens born in England, had places they could call home; at the end of our grueling day with the Ministry of Labour, off they went to their friends and relatives, leaving their addresses with me and vowing to keep in touch. Haines said he was headed to his home in Maidenhead, a small town about thirty miles west of London. Maidenhead! That was where I was headed, too. William Stephenson's English secretary, Alice Green, lived there and I had been told to stay with her until I sorted out my future. I was tempted to ask Haines if I could tag along with him to Maidenhead, but found myself too shy to make the suggestion. Off he went to Maidenhead without me. I had been given a letter to present to the "Ferry Command," now identified as the Air Transport Auxiliary (ATA), and a rail ticket to get myself and my luggage there. On closer inspection I read that the ATA headquarters was also in Maidenhead. Bill Haines, Alice Green, and the ATA could all be found in the small town of Maidenhead, a remarkable coincidence.

Although I had been instructed to let Alice Green know when I landed in England, I had not done so. I would be landing on her doorstep as a surprise, if she were even at home when I finally called. With my rail chit from the ever-helpful Ministry of Labour, I set out for Maidenhead on my own. Before departing London, I asked a teashop server for a glass of water, please. She looked at me as though I had demanded champagne and in a harried voice replied, "I only have four glasses and there are thirty-five people in front of you waiting for water, so you will just have to wait your turn." I boarded the next train for Maidenhead waterless, while she served customer number thirty-three.

In my short, sheltered life I had never felt such utter desolation as when I stepped off that train in the dark with my cumbersome trunk and bedraggled suitcase, and stood in one of those quaint red English telephone booths for twenty minutes while a kindly "inquiry directory" tried to locate a Miss Green. I had not been to bed since rising Monday morning on *Scebeli*, and now it was Tuesday morning. Nor had I changed clothing or eaten a real meal since our debarkation breakfast in the "hostile" in Liverpool. I felt quite forlorn being alone in a foreign country for the first time. Suddenly a friendly, warm hello echoed through the receiver. It was "Miss Green" who soon became "Alice," but she was listed in the telephone directory under her married name of "Alice Dott." A wizard telephone operator had found her. As soon as I heard her voice, the whole picture changed for me. No longer was I a deserted stranger there on the railway platform, but a welcome visitor with a place to call home. It struck me forcefully that an important element of being able to cope with any situation is to have a stationary person or a stationary location to call home. For the years I had known TC, he had been my solid person and Huntingfield had been my solid location. Now I could see my center shifting to Alice Green.

She was eager to see me, rushing down to the station in the dark with her husband, David Dott, in tow to deal with the trunk. Her welcome might have been embarrassing except she was English and more restrained than demonstrative. Stephenson had never bothered to describe Alice to me, but in my mind I had pictured a staid, elderly old maid, administering devotedly to Stephenson's secret secretarial needs. Instead, Alice was absolutely beautiful. She was tiny, with perfect features and the lovely English complexion—peaches and cream—that comes from living in the English climate. I would hazard she was between thirty-five and thirty-eight years old when I met her. She had been married for fifteen years to David and they owned a house within walking distance of the station. Together, David and Alice moved me right in as one of the family.

Alice might have added me generously to her family, but she showed no mercy about pushing me on to my fate. As soon as I awakened on my first morning in her house, she fed me a sparse English breakfast—no eggs, no sausage or bacon, no butter or jam. I had already turned over my ration cards to her. After breakfast she asked me, "Do you like to walk?" When I answered with enthusiasm, she trotted me downtown to the station and put me on a bus going to White Waltham aerodrome, where the ATA was located. On the bus I met a youth in an ATA uniform with a "USA" shoulder patch. He directed me to the ATA commandant's office. Another one-mile walk put me in front of a closed door. I rapped timidly and a booming voice bellowed, "C'mon in."

The commandant, a gray-haired, heavyset woman in the navy blue uniform of the ATA, grabbed my hand and almost pumped it off. Then, with her forty-year-old eyes, she scrutinized me and the Ministry of Labour letter I held in my hand.

She inquired suspiciously about my age. I called myself twenty-one, giving myself a couple of extra months. Twenty-one sounds more serious than twenty and I would be twenty-one in December. I could see her mentally noting, "Too young." While the commandant was giving me the once-over, various women pilots stuck their heads in her office door; to my dismay, they all had gray hair and were in their forties at least. Nevertheless, I was thrilled to see them, actual women pilots on duty, and I wished they had come on in the office and talked.

The commandant asked me many more questions: the origin of my murky citizenship, how I had managed to get across the ocean alone, who paid for my passage. I told her about the U-boat sighting, hoping she would sympathize with me more. Throughout this part of the interview she remained quite reserved and only relaxed when I told her about my father—how he was a decorated ace fighter pilot in World War I and how he was flying again in this war. After that bit of news, she asked for my logbook so she could check my flying hours. When I said I did not have it with me, she asked me to bring it back the next day. She stood up, gave me another one of her bone-crushing handshakes, and sent me out the door. A mile back to the bus stop, a mile down to the Ministry of Labour, and another mile to Alice's cottage. With all that walking I had time to reflect on my first interview with the ATA and I decided that while I had not made a great impression, as I am sure Jackie Cochran had on whoever interviewed her, I was still in the running. Why else would the commandant ask me to bring back my logbook for inspection?

Once back inside Alice's house, I was looking forward to putting my feet up for the evening. Alice had other plans. "Why don't we walk your

AIR TRANSPORT AUXILIARY

HEADQUARTERS — WHITE WALTHAM AERODROME, Nr. MAIDENHEAD, Berks.

TELEPHONE — LITTLEWICK GREEN 251

PAE

17th October 194?

Miss B.A.Lussier,
58 St. Marks Crescent,
Maidenhead, Berks.

Dear Madam,

Referring to your application for a position as ferry pilot in this
organisation, will you please report to the undersigned for a flight test,
medical examination and interview on any weekday, except Monday, convenient
to yourself, arriving here not later than 9.30 a.m.   It is essential that
you let us know beforehand the date of your visit.

Will you please bring with you your passport and five photographs to the
following specification exactly:-

1½" x 1½". Photographs to be clear and distinct, of head and shoulders only
and printed on thin matt paper.

The cost, up to 3/-, will be reimbursed on your arrival, but travelling
expenses must be borne by the candidate.

Presentation of this letter will be necessary for admittance to the aerodrome.

Your log book is returned herewith under registered cover.

Yours faithfully,

Y. A. R. Ohchinson
Chief Instructor.

Enc:

FIGURE 3.2 *ATA Medical and Flight Test Letter*

logbook back to White Waltham tonight? I need some exercise." Off we
went, another five miles to the aerodrome and five miles back. On that, my
second night at Alice and David's house, I slept like the dead.

A week later I was summoned by formal letter for my final encounter
with the ATA recruiters, my flight test, a physical examination, and yet
another interview (see Figure 3.2). After wringing my hands all week and
feeling I was going to be turned down, I was quite encouraged by the tone
of the letter. Surely they would not ask for five photographs if they were
going to send me away. With mixed feelings I boarded the now-familiar bus
in Maidenhead to take me to the ATA headquarters in White Waltham. On
the ride over I worked myself up into a good state of nerves. I was terrified I
would fail something: the medical, the flying part, the final interview. After
coming so many thousands of miles, would I fail my last interview?

All my life I had been careful never to let myself be put into a position where the events of a single day or of a single action would turn my entire life in one specific direction or in the opposite direction, or in a position where I would not be the one making the choice. I believed in always keeping options open and being the one who made the choice. Yet here I was at such a point: my future was going to be chosen for me, and I would not make the choice. My future course depended one way or another on the outcome of this next encounter. If I passed, I could go on in the field of aviation, perhaps for the rest of my life. If I failed, I would be shoehorned into some profession not of my choosing and not nearly as exciting as flying.

While waiting for that letter, I had taken time to think about why I was making such a painful effort to get into the sky over Britain. Of course the main attraction was that incomparable feeling of freedom and control when I was up in the sky, far above the earth. Another part of the appeal was that flying was an out-of-the-ordinary profession; women are scarce up there and it is a challenge to break those barriers. I was thinking, too, of those young women, yearning to be pilots, who would come after me. If I could endure, their pathway might be smoother, their acceptance by male pilots more ready. In addition, I dreaded monotony and being surrounded by walls as I worked. Hard as the labor was, working on the farm had given me a preference for being outside. Up in the sky, no flight is ever the same and there are no walls to keep me confined. And, of course I was still intent on wanting to help to save the British nation, whether they wanted my help or not.

From the waiting room, where I had put in an idle hour, I was hustled into the medical examination room. Here not one but two doctors gave me a thorough going over. There was some whispered exchange between them, loud enough for me to overhear, "Is she too short?" They actually measured my legs again, from my crotch to my heel, and seemed to decide that the leg parts were long enough. We filled in some more forms, identifying all the diseases and conditions I did not have and had not had. They then returned me to the recruiting officer. The recruiting officer was annoyed to see me appear so near lunch time and sent me off to the pilots' canteen for a bit of nourishment. In the canteen I observed more female ATA pilots and confirmed to myself that they were all older and surely well entrenched in the field of aviation. When I went back after having a sandwich, I was presented with a helmet and a parachute, introduced to the chief instructor, and shoved into a truck. We motored around the airport apron, the driver and I, to a sad-looking Tudor—a basic, tandem aircraft used by many flight schools in England. I was bundled into the front cockpit with the chief instructor swinging gracefully into the rear. I felt awkward trying to get comfortable sitting on top of the strange parachute. In Carl's planes we never wore 'chutes. After all my nervous worry, the test was a letdown. It consisted merely of a takeoff, a left-hand circuit of the field, and a landing. My instructor did not seem to pay much attention during our flight. After we landed he told me I would hear from what he called "the section board." More waiting seemed to be in my future, but on the bright side they had not eliminated me yet.

I discovered something weird that day. Sitting on top of my dresser at Alice's house I had a photograph of my father in his uniform. When I stood directly in front of the photograph, with the light reflecting a certain way, I seemed to be inside Dad's uniform myself, with his service cap on my head and his wings over my heart. Was it an omen?

Alice must have noticed how on edge I was not knowing my flying fate, because she insisted on taking me to London for a day of serious sightseeing and some not-so-serious theater. She did not invite me: she just said we were going and off to the train we went. We spent quite some time in St. Paul's Cathedral. It was a most impressive structure, so massive and spacious. Nothing I had ever seen in the States compared to it. The rear of the building had suffered quite a lot of damage from two or three direct hits during the German bombing. It was amazing to me that the rest of the structure had escaped damage because all the buildings for two blocks on three sides had been razed—with just bare ground left and no buildings. The Germans obviously had been intent on bringing down the entire cathedral. They had been determined to be the force that destroyed this symbol of British history. For safety's sake, the cathedral should have been closed to all foot traffic, but the British would never have allowed the Nazis to do that to their dignity. So she stood in all her solemn majesty—wounded, but receiving as many of her subjects as wished to come in and pray.

Alice walked me up several of the famous streets in central London: Cheapside, Fleet Street, the Strand, and Bond Street. I liked the streets where all the shops would be devoted to the same product, like the street with printers, or the street with books stalls. With Alice standing by patiently, I peeked into many of the fascinating little courtyards, called mews, off the main street. They truly represented the old, old London. They still bore the names originally given to them to describe what was sold there, like Poultry Street and Wood Street. The streets wound narrowly in and out, ending in the minute, circular courtyards surrounded by buildings with quaint small-paned windows and latticed walls, the second story jutting out over the street and almost touching the building jutting from the opposite side of the street.

In the afternoon we took in an English musical. It was called *The Dancing Years* and starred the famous Ivor Novello, the British equivalent to our Rudolph Valentino. Besides starring in the show, Novello had written the book and composed the music; Christopher Hassall had written the lyrics. "Dearest Dear, if I could say to you—in words as clear—as when I play to you—you'd understand how slight the shadow that is holding us apart." Very schmaltzy, but that show already had survived one thousand performances and the English audience was still enthralled. Maybe, for a space of time, the show took them out of their grim reality and into a perfect world.

I had only been in England a week, but I knew with a firm conviction that the Nazis were never going to conquer the English. Oh, the Nazis might get to the beaches in their boats, they might land inland with their gliders, but every inch of the way they were going to be opposed by every English person standing. The Germans would have to kill every man, woman, and child before they could take possession of this tiny island. Already every directional sign on the entire island had been removed in preparation for the invasion. No English person was going to help the Nazis find their way around when they got here. Every last English person was devoted 100 percent to preventing a conquest. Their own private ambitions and goals had been set aside, and they concentrated completely on their personal contribution to winning the war, be it dying by the hundreds in the air as hastily trained fighter pilots or by working twelve hours a night assembling Bristol bombers as David did, or by serving thirty-five people water with the four glasses remaining from the latest bombing, or waiting in line two hours for that one egg a month.

Winston Churchill spoke for all of England when he defied the Nazis with his brave words: "We shall not flag nor fail. We shall go on to the end. We shall fight in France and on the seas and oceans; we shall fight with growing confidence and growing strength in the air. We shall defend our island whatever the cost may be; we shall fight on beaches, landing grounds, in fields, in streets and on the hills. We shall never surrender."[1]

My heart went out to the English and I knew with renewed conviction why I had come over here from my sheltered America and why the English

---

1. Winston Churchill, Speech Before Commons, June 4, 1940. Available at http://history. hanover.edu/courses/excerpts/111chur.html.

were going to triumph, this year, or next year, or at the end of however many years it took.

That week of waiting to know my fate yielded three notable milestones. First, I witnessed my first Nazi air raid. Alice was in London and David had gone off to see a movie before going to work (he worked a night shift), so I was alone when the mournful wailing of the air-raid warning signal sounded. It was so calm and quiet that I thought at first it was just a fire alarm. There were lots of those as a result of constant damage to the electric systems. It lasted about half an hour during which time no bombers appeared in the sky and I did nothing because I knew Maidenhead was well west of London and contained no targets valuable enough to merit a dropped bomb. Then the shrill, cheery "all clear" sounded and it was over—my first, but not my last, air raid.

The second milestone was a shock: to hear for the first time an Englishman, turned traitor, reading the German news from Berlin. In a calm, convincing, beautifully modulated voice, he read out a distorted, lying version of the days' events. My first reaction was one of sadness to hear this lovely English voice betraying his country. Then I had an overwhelming surge of anger and I wanted to be sitting opposite this traitor and just stare into his lying eyes and make him answer me—why, why, why?

The third milestone happened at White Waltham aerodrome. I was there on one of my many forays to the ATA offices and my visit coincided with an improbable visiting group. There was King George VI and Queen Elizabeth, our Mrs. Eleanor Roosevelt, Winston Churchill, Lloyd George, and Gen. Jan Smuts, the South African prime minister. They all had motored out together from London to open and dedicate the new ATA canteen. I suppose they also were curious to see firsthand the unusual mix of pilots from many countries and of both sexes. They democratically greeted all the ATA pilots who happened to be on duty that day. As I was not in uniform yet, if I ever was to be, I was not invited to meet the visitors, but I could look on from the sidelines. After this event, Mrs. Roosevelt stayed on in England for some weeks. I think she felt comfortable and at home in that country where she was accepted with love and respect and not criticized for "meddling" as she was so many times at home.

❧ ☙

As the week wore on with no word one way or the other from the ATA, I made my required weekly visit to the Ministry of Labour. I went to collect the equivalent of $2 per day they were giving me for my maintenance until

I had a paying job. I also went to report my daily doings. England did not want strangers wandering about the countryside without purpose. After chiding me for not reporting to her on Monday as she had requested (by now it was Thursday) the woman in charge gave me my money. Almost as an afterthought, she picked up a letter from the pile on her desk and began to read aloud to me. It was a letter notifying the Ministry of Labour that one B. Lussier had been accepted for service in the ATA. I was without words. If she had been an American, I would have thrown my arms around that woman's neck and given her a bear hug. I had convinced myself the ATA was going to turn me away and here it was, the official notice that I was in.

I walked out of the shabby hut about three feet off the ground and strolled along the street cheerily chatting to myself and smiling on all the citizens I passed who were not aware that they were looking on the new savior of the RAF. I even gave the bit of Alice's cake I had been hoarding to a hungry stray dog and stopped to chat with a group of disinterested five-year-old boys on their way home from school for lunch.

Still no official letter came to me from the ATA. I wondered if the Ministry of Labour was mistaken. But, no, I had seen their letter with my own eyes. Bureaucracy was at work. I was meant to suffer and wait with patience. Subconsciously, for all my expressed doubts, I must have expected to be accepted because only the week before I had taken my brown shoes to the shoemaker and asked him to dye them black. Black was the required color for ATA foot attire.

More days of waiting for the mail and more nights of sitting by the fire with Alice clickity-clicking on her knitting needles after David went off to work. I had been in England for only two weeks, but being idle was making me irritable about the little things: No milk, my favorite beverage. No fruit. Very little heat. No exuberant Americans with whom to carry on nightly conversations. I missed that. I was not exactly homesick, but I longed for more news from the States, from my family, and from TC, my boyfriend. And this climate was hard to accept. There was heavy fog all night and early morning, burning off about noon, then a drizzly rain in the afternoon, and back to the fog when the sun went down. I understood why English women had such lovely complexions—creamy, spotless, and without wrinkles: they had no sun damaging their skin.

Alice felt compelled to keep me busy during the tedious wait for my marching orders from ATA. On Armistice Day she took me to Westminster

AIR TRANSPORT AUXILIARY

HEADQUARTERS — WHITE WALTHAM AERODROME, Nr. MAIDENHEAD, Berks.

TELEPHONE — LITTLEWICK GREEN 251

TRG.

Miss B. Lussier,   4th November, 1942.
58 St. Mark's Crescent,
Maidenhead.

Dear Madam,

    It is now possible to commence your training and you are requested to
report at 9 a.m. punctually on Wednesday 11th inst., to the School Adjutant,
Luton Aerodrome, where the initial part of this training will take place.

    Please bring with you:-

1.   Ration cards.
2.   Unemployment insurance card.
3.   National health card.
4.   Form N.S.2. if you have registered for the armed forces.
5.   Notebook, pen and lead and red pencils.
6.   Civilian gas mask.

-2-

We shall also want to know the name and address of your bankers.

Kindly acknowledge receipt of this letter.

Yours faithfully,

Chief Instructor.

FIGURE 3.3 *ATA Assignment Letter*

Abbey to plant a cross in the ground they called Remembrance Field. Each
year the grass plots all around the Abbey were opened for the people to
put up their little crosses. It was heartbreaking to see the large crosses with
"Canada," "India," "Australia," printed on them and see all the small
crosses so sadly surrounding them. Each cross represented a person's life.
Many of the crosses bore the names of the loved lost one: "To Bill," "For
Tom." These were the souls sacrificed from World War I and here we were,
doing it all over again. We seem never to learn the futility of war.

    On our way home that day we passed a shop with an epitaph from
World War I, emblazoned in big, black letters all the way across the
window. The occasion was the release of a new movie, carrying the poem's
title, "Went the Day Well?" This short, simple verse stirred my heart,
especially seeing it on that special day:

Went the day well?
We died and never knew,
But well or ill,
Freedom, we died that day for you.[2]

Although we still felt besieged in England, the war was going better for the Allies in Africa. It was November 1942. Operation Torch, the recapture of North Africa from the German Army by the Allied Forces, had been mounted, with a three-pronged thrust. American troops were landing in Casablanca from the United States. More American troops were landing in Oran, carried there in British ships from England, and a contingent of all-British troops was going ashore in Algiers. French naval forces were opposing the landings in support of the German military and many unnecessary casualties occurred. But the Germans would have to adopt a new strategy if they wanted to stay in Africa.

The letter I'd been waiting for so impatiently finally arrived, assigning me to the ATA flight school and ordering me to report one week hence in Luton (see Figure 3.3). Luton was the site of the main training unit, ground and flight, for the ATA; nearby Barton-in-the-Clay seemed to be a sort of elementary school where the first flight work was undertaken.

---

2. John Maxwell Edmonds, "Four Epitaphs," *The* (London) *Times*, February 6, 1918.

CHAPTER 4

It's Official: I'm an ATA Student Pilot!

ON RECEIVING THE LETTER from the ATA, I was immediately in seventh heaven. Until that exact moment, in spite of the advance notice from the commandant at the Ministry of Labour, I did not believe it was ever going to happen. I believed that somehow at the last moment the ATA would reject me, my legs too short, and I would be sent to drive ambulances. Now all my petty complaints about the English climate and the English authorities melted away. I loved everybody. I even found room in my heart to love the fog. By more good luck, Luton was not far from Maidenhead. That town and the adjacent White Waltham, the ATA headquarters, are about thirty miles west of London, while Luton and Barton-in-the-Clay are thirty-three miles to the north of London. I could take the train into London both ways to make the connection. Like all roads leading to Rome in the Roman Empire, all roads lead to London in England. It appeared I could sleep at the Guys' house during the week when I was flying, while leaving my stuff at Alice's and spending my off time at her house. That is, if Alice was willing to have me. And she said she was.

On my last weekend before I reported to flight school, David and Alice entertained several friends and relatives. We were nine bodies in all. Alice was the perfect hostess. She prepared lovely meals—breakfast, dinner, tea, and supper every day. This was no small feat in food-scarce England. The women guests drove me insane with their chatter about everyone in general and their personal acquaintances in particular, all accompanied by the patriotic clack, clack of their knitting needles. Perhaps if I had known some of the people they were gossiping about I would have been more interested. As it was, when the women gathered around the radio for a BBC broadcast about the war I sneaked outside. It was just dusk and I took a mile-long fast walk. On the way home, I crossed with two male figures. We peered curiously at each other through the blackout, and as we got closer, recognized each other: one was David and the other was Stan, one of the guests. They suggested I join them at the pub. It was another new experience for me, waiting in front of a shuttered pub for it to open. Pubs did not open until 7:00 at night and closed again at 10:00, which was not very much drinking time. There was a quaint old swinging sign out front, and a low ceiling and uncovered rafters inside. The traditional dartboard was nailed to a wall, with a newspaper photograph of Hitler tacked over the bull's eye. There was also a billiard table and card tables and the exhausted workers who went with it all. The women were having their drinks in a separate section of the pub. When I asked David why this was so, he shrugged his shoulders and said, "It's always been like that." I never had an opportunity to ask Alice what had led to this custom. Did the women prefer to be only with each other, or did the men prefer they drink separately? For the moment, I moved in among the women and enjoyed my lemonade.

After the drink, on our way home, David, Stan, and I had an animated conversation. David talked about the service members who came to speak at his plant from the British Navy, the RAF, the British Army, and the Merchant Marines. Stan worked as an air-raid police officer and had seen some horrible sights. He explained to me many of the freak things that he had seen bomb blasts do: they blew a one-ton slab of clay about two hundred yards to land right on top of a prostrate man and force his body right through the cement sidewalk, blew a cornice off the top of a tall building and on top of three men lying in the protection of the building, and ripped people right down the middle, from head to feet. Oh, war is not a glorious experience for the civilian, and he has no brass buttons to pull together over his torn chest.

❧ ☙

There was a pea soup fog in progress the next morning when I left for the flight school. Alice insisted on wading through it up to London with me. She claimed she had work to do for Stephenson, but I could tell she did not trust me to find my way to Luton without her. Secretly, I was glad to have her along to guide me. The dense fog, a mixture of the smoke from the burning of soft coal and the usual fog, was disorienting. Alice led me through it and accompanied me right up to my train.

"Now don't forget to get off at Luton station," she reminded me, as if I would make that mistake.

I was certainly taking this big day calmly, considering all the weeping and wailing I had been doing the previous week. Arriving at

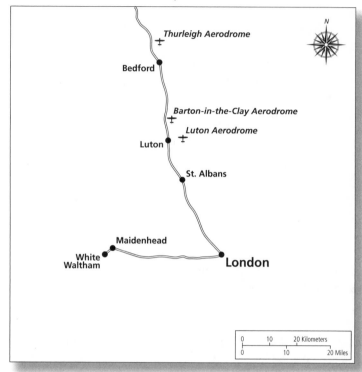

MAP 4.1 *The Local Geography*

dismal Luton in the dense fog was certainly the happiest day of all my twenty years. I was overjoyed and wanted everyone at the aerodrome to share my youthful enthusiasm for being there. After the many months of grueling night work at Glenn Martin's and the exhausting days spent flying in squares to add flight hours to my log book, here I was, where I had dreamed of being, about to become England's ace pilot. Well, maybe not the ace pilot of all pilots, but at least a good, competent ferry pilot, familiar with the local geography (see Map 4.1), one able to contribute to Britain's defense.

That first day in Luton brought me down from my cloud-nine perch and onto the level of everyone else who was just getting through the day's grim war work. I was handed another fistful of forms to fill out and present at the right desk. I was issued with my flying kit: an oversized, zip-up, warmly lined khaki flying suit with a silk inner flying suit; a helmet with goggles; silk gloves for warmth with leather gauntlets to go over them; sheepskin-lined boots; and a couple of coverall-type flying suits made of a denim-like cotton material for when it got warm. There was also a parachute, our lifeline in the sky if we found ourselves in deep trouble.

We were ordered to find ourselves a gas mask, an item hard to come by in Britain, and never to be separated from it.

After morning tea, noon lunch, and afternoon tea, while collecting my kit and manuals—so many manuals that I should have been forewarned the path in front of me was going to be rocky—I was given a distracted motor pool driver who did not bother to introduce himself. The end-of-the-day syndrome. In his camouflaged car, through the waning light and with the headlights off, he drove me lickety-split to the far side of Luton, to the small aerodrome called Barton-in-the-Clay. It was at Barton, they had informed me, that I would receive my primary training as required. "You will be there about a month," they prophesied. Barton did not seem to be much more than a grassy meadow with one dirt runway. I deposited my flying kit in the locker that was assigned to me. I was instructed to check my parachute into a special storage room where it would be well guarded and inspected periodically and reissued to me every time I had a flight to make. Our instructors must have foreseen parachutes tossed in the corners of pubs if they let us take them home, and did not trust us with them away from the aerodrome.

As soon as he could scoop me up, the driver whisked me back to my new home in Luton. "This is it," he announced and dumped me, my suitcase, and my trunk out in front of my assigned billet, then skedaddled away. I looked up at the house. It was similar to the Dotts' and the English equivalent of Baltimore's row houses—a cozy, two-story brick dwelling, with a carefully tended lawn in front. When I rang the bell, Mr. and Mrs. Guy, my new billeteers, both nervously came to the door of their house. There ensued one of those embarrassing moments when none of the participants knew what to say to each other. We knew we had to live together for the next month because their government had ordered it thus, but would we tolerate each other, the staid English couple and the brash American volunteer? Would we even like each other? And what were the Guys thinking? They must have been expecting an English male pilot of a certain age. Whatever their thoughts, they opened the door wide to me, took my suitcase, wrestled my trunk aboard, and welcomed me over their doorstep. They showed me upstairs to what surely was their best bedroom. I was humbled by the gesture and hoped I could live up to whatever expectations they had. I determined right then and there to be a model tenant. After my scant possessions were unpacked (I had left all my treasures at my room in Alice's house), I joined the Guys for a modest supper in their dining nook off the kitchen. We talked shyly, getting to know each other. After our meal, I offered to help with the washing up, but Mrs. Guy was adamant about doing it herself. Maybe later on she would relent. I retired to my new room early to write some letters home and prepare myself mentally for my first day as a student pilot in England.

The next morning, without any ceremony, I was drawn into my new Barton-in-the-Clay life. Our classes took place in a couple of makeshift wooden huts, similar to the one at the White Waltham headquarters. I arrived on time with my notebook and pencil and shuffled into our first class with my fellow students. We were divided into two groups of about ten students for each class. Our class had two women besides me and seven men. I was the youngest in the class and they all had many more flight hours. Right away I realized I was wearing the wrong wardrobe: a skirt and silk stockings. It was freezing in the hut. After all, it was November and cold. The wiser, more-sensible students were wearing the fleeced-lined flying boots that had been issued to us and were occupying all the chairs around the cast-iron stove stoked with lumps of coal. The blackboard across one end of the classroom was full of complicated diagrams purporting to explain to us what happens when we press button A. Actually, there was only one diagram and two intelligent-looking instructors in RAF uniform. One soon revealed himself by his lecture as a mastermind on engines and other mechanical subjects; we nicknamed him "Boost." The other was a navigation expert whom I dubbed "Egbert" because he seemed like an Egbert. That first day, not one word was said about flying. It was as though flying was a minor detail and only the navigation and the mechanics had importance. Some of the students seemed to know each other and they sat together, ate lunch in the canteen together, and, at the end of our long day, left together on the bus for town. The outsiders, myself among them, huddled over our notebooks on the fringes, taking copious notes and trying to keep warm. I ended the first day of my new life in a decidedly dejected mood.

Every once in awhile—now was one of those "awhiles"—the situation in which I had put myself flooded over me and I felt like I was going to drown. I had spent so many months struggling and conniving and pleading to get to England. When I was well on my way on board *Scebeli*, I thought the big battle was behind me, a thing of the past. Now I was discovering that the fight had only begun. My troubles with the Ministry of Labour, then the duel with the ATA, turned out to be minor blips on the screen. The real battle was still ahead, the battle to master all the navigation in tricky, treacherous British skies, and the mechanics, not to mention flying the aircraft itself. Airplanes? I dared not raise my head from my notebook long enough to even think of the planes yet. And all the time I thought those 150 hours of ground school in the CPT program at the University of Maryland were going to serve me for air navigation in Britain. Here it all was again, all of it, only applied to the British conditions, the endless fogs, the camouflaged and unidentifiable aerodromes, the barrage balloons popping up all over the sky, the engines—all of it foreign to me. I pulled Mrs. Guy's best sheet up over my ears, shut my eyes, and tried to get enough sleep to help me face the next day at flight school.

The second day went better for me and I got along pretty well out at the field. I was wiser than yesterday and pulled on my flying boots like everyone else. In the morning I listened intently to Boost delivering a long lecture on airfoils and sat through an enlightening session on the mechanics of instruments. In the afternoon there was a lecture by Egbert on finding the distance covered using the computer. Last, we tried to convert statute miles to nautical miles to kilometers. We were told that the French insisted on using kilometers in their planes, while the Fleet Air Arm (the branch of the British Royal Navy responsible for the operation of aircraft) insisted on knots because of their sea connection, and the RAF stuck to the statute mile. This was going to complicate the lives of us ATA pilots to no end, but I understood already that, unlike the pampered military pilots, we were expected to cope with whatever was thrown at us.

Toward late afternoon of that second day, the perpetual fog unexpectedly cleared just enough to allow a few ships off the ground with the pilots of the class ahead of us. I went out on the tarmac to watch the takeoffs and landings—or "circuits and bumps" as the British dubbed them. The trainer they were using was a Magister of about 125 horsepower with a cruising speed of 135 miles per hour and tandem cockpits to accommodate an instructor and a student pilot. It was similar to one of our Fairchild models and oh so noisy.

In the evening I went for my first drive in the blackout. The Guys had to collect their fortnightly groceries from a co-op station and they invited me to accompany them. It was amazing to me how they managed to follow the narrow country roads with their headlights on dim. Bicycles, pedestrians, buses, dogs, even an occasional cat, all popped up in front of the Guy's car, which was driving on the wrong side of the road, by my standards. It was distracting, but to me it was a wonderful feeling to be tearing about in a real, live, full-sized car again after so many weeks of foot travel. I realized how spoiled Americans are with cars to take us everywhere and I told the Guys about it. They only smiled and kept their attention on the busy road before them.

⚓ ⚓

I was waiting anxiously for some letters from home—not exactly homesick, but longing for something familiar in this foreign world around me. How was TC doing with his fighter pilot training? Did little Suzanne notice that her sisters had all deserted her? I looked and looked at the different houses around me and all the different people I was associating with now and tried to decide what it is that makes our own particular home seem positively the only place like it in the entire world. It might all hinge on one word: familiarity. These strange places and new people were a trial for me to adjust to and I longed to be back on the farm for a few hours where everything was familiar. (Of course, I knew full well that within hours I would be chafing to be out of there again.) With the arrival of some letters, my mood soon lifted and I read with joy about TC's latest checkout in a P-47, bringing him that much closer to me; about Nita's quest for enemy submarines on the west coast of Canada; about Dad's daily patrols with his wireless students; and about Mother's trials with my impish baby sister, Suzanne.

Word came to me of several Marylanders in the service who were wending their secret ways to Great Britain and who might be calling to give me company. Even if they were not particular friends of mine, I eagerly looked forward to seeing and talking to someone from home. I was feeling lonely and longing for support in the letters from home, but at least the war was going better than expected. Under General Montgomery's command, the British Eighth Army, intent on carrying out Operation Torch, was advancing with amazing rapidity in North Africa. It was a thrill to hear about their victories as German general Erwin Rommel retreated before them. Maybe the most notable accomplishment of the British Eighth Army was that they had broken the myth of the invincible German forces.

By the third day at the field, I was leaving all my doubts and loneliness behind and fitting right in.

One day I was absorbed in solving wind drift angles and ground speeds when CO Woods put his head in the door of our classroom and called, "Lussier, get your gear on, weather test." We had learned already that CO Woods never wasted many words. I was startled to be chosen. He must have been feeling sorry for me, sorry that I had not been in the air since my arrival. I quickly clambered into all the cumbersome equipment and trotted out after him to the plane. The gear weighed me down so much that I had trouble breathing. By the time I got my parachute on, I was gasping. It was such a contrast to the free and easy outfits we wore to pilot Carl's Cub through the air over Baltimore.

Once settled in the plane, a Magister, the CO signaled for me to do the flying. I got us into the air with self-conscious maneuvers; after our weather check (bad weather as always, but what else in the British skies?) he shouted for me to take us to Luton aerodrome. Fortunately, I had looked up the heading to get to Luton that morning and off I went, exuding confidence. While in the air, I got my first topside view of English countryside. During my entrance test I had been so engrossed in making a good impression that I had not taken in the surroundings. Now my spirits soared. After landing in Luton, we handed over our Magister for servicing and picked up another one, in better shape, to get us back to Barton. Once on the ground again in Barton, I realized I had just completed my first unofficial ferry job for my new boss, the ATA. I had delivered an ailing aircraft to the shop for repairs and ferried a healthy plane back to the work site.

The iffy October weather continued into the afternoon and, following a couple of classes with Boost and Egbert and a tea session, we were dismissed early. The rush up to London was universal, but I was not ready to face London yet. I needed a touch of home. I took the first train going in Alice's direction, to Maidenhead. I sat in a corner of the compartment and practiced my Morse code, using my flashlight. A British paratrooper left his seat and moved closer to talk to me. He had harrowing tales to tell of his jump training. He commented that at first he had thought I must be a spy, Morse code and all. While waiting for my connection in Paddington Station, I talked to a Welsh schoolteacher. She was teaching in a village called Didcot, near Oxford, and she invited me to visit the famous university town in the future. I promised I would look her up. During my walk up the hill to Alice's from the railroad station, I pondered how strange it was that I should be walking in a total blackout three thousand miles from my home and feeling quite natural about it.

The next morning when Alice brought a cup of tea to my bedside (she was letting me sleep in because I had begun my training and she figured I must be tired), there was a huge smile on her face.

"Letter from Texas," she announced crisply.

I could tell it gave her pleasure to bring me my first letter from TC. I ripped open the envelope and for a few minutes I was holding hands back there in Baltimore and impatient for the time in the future—soon, I hoped—when he might be joining me in England as a fighter pilot.

On my way back to my billet in Luton, I stopped in London at the old, established clothier, Austin Reed, to be measured for my ATA uniforms. I was quietly dismayed at how unappealing they had managed to make the uniform, navy blue and shapeless. While I was in one of the fitting rooms, I looked out to see Mrs. Winston Churchill come bustling into the shop with her youngest daughter in tow. The Churchills believed firmly in everyone pitching in. Their daughter was being fitted for an Auxiliary Territorial Service uniform and mother was doing the critique. I silently wished her well with the uniform. Mrs. Churchill looked striking, tall and regal and handsome. I had not realized how tall she was. Her hair was white and she had flawless pale skin—that British fog again. I noticed, too, that she was wearing mended silk stockings like the rest of Britain's womanhood and somehow, to me, that made her more human. Her daughter seemed to be about my age and she was voicing some quiet complaints about the styling of her uniform. I realized that, English or American, all young women want to look their best.

Before I caught my train back to Luton, Alice treated me to my first "hotel tea." She took me to the Ritz Hotel. English hotel tea is almost like a fourth meal, elaborately set up on little round tables for two or four, with carts wheeled among the tables, carts filled with thin, bite-sized cucumber sandwiches, cakes, and pastries. There was a choice of many exotic teas. I wondered how the Ritz did it all on their sugar ration. That evening Mrs. Guy must have been disappointed at the way I just picked at the contents of my supper plate.

The next day I was scheduled for my first formal instruction in the Magister trainer. All those weather rides with our CO did not count as learning. The satellite aerodrome, Barton, from which the primary flying course was conducted, was located about five miles from the main aerodrome, Luton. We were taken there in a British Army transport. The ride was over country roads; I was astonished when we suddenly pulled into a farm lane, rumbled right up to a tumbledown barn, turned sharply between two haystacks, and came into sudden view of a small grass aerodrome. This was it. This was our first training facility.

My flying kit seemed to weigh a ton that first day as I pulled on layer after layer and shoved my feet into the clumsy boots. But there was no heat in the Magisters and I knew I would be glad for the boots once I was in the air. Thus clad, I staggered over and collapsed onto a bench to await my instructor who was taxiing the low-winged Magister over from the dispersal area. I was being turned over to the only woman instructor at Barton. I had been hoping for one of the men, my childhood conditioning kicking in and telling me that men make better instructors, but some of my fellow students insisted this woman was the best pilot. She introduced herself to me, we shook hands, and then we took to the sky. Up we went into the bit of space assigned for our exclusive use. We had only been in the air for half an hour before I was captivated by that old-fashioned, noisy plane and was referring to her quite spontaneously as "Maggie," like all the other students did.

I piloted around our plot of the sky fairly well, although the flaps system and the very sensitive elevator trim took some getting accustomed to after flying Carl's easygoing, forgiving Piper Cub. The instructor had me shoot a few takeoffs and landings and then said we would continue in the afternoon. But after lunch the fog rolled in, washing out all flying, and I spent the time until closing with my maps. I learned that Britain has seven hundred aerodromes and, once in the air, we pilots would never be more than fifteen minutes from at least one of them. That piece of information was supposed to give us comfort, but the cunning manner in which these landing strips were camouflaged was bound to make them hard to find. Besides, when your engine stops up there in the sky you are going to be too busy to remember soothing details like how many aerodromes there are.

The following day, without any further instruction, I soloed the Magister. It was not intended that I solo so soon. It came about through a chain of misunderstandings. My assigned instructor, the lone woman, called in sick so I was handed over to one of the men. He seemed to be hazy about how much instruction I had been given previously and evidently thought I had a lot more hours than my introductory session yesterday. He took me up and had me carry out a few lackadaisical circuits. Once back on the ground, he climbed out of the front cockpit. As he slid down the Maggie's wing, he looked over his shoulder and inquired, "Do you feel happy?" Rather puzzled, I assured him that I "felt happy."

He smiled, satisfied, shoved his pipe stem between his teeth and, as he turned his back and strolled off across the field, assured me over his shoulder, "You'll be all right." He had set me loose. I could not believe it. It was so soon. Should I tell him I was not ready? Of course not. This is the intrepid pilot here.

For a moment, sitting there behind all that horsepower—actually only 150—she seemed like a monster, but I could not admit that I was not ready for this. My first circuit was one of adhering strictly to "the rules." As soon as I circled back and touched down all in one piece, I opened my mouth and let out a terrific yell, so thrilled was I. I scampered through a few more takeoffs and landings, but none of them compared with the feeling I got from that first time. So haphazard was our paperwork that my two instructors never did compare notes and realize they had sent their American up into the sky alone without proper checking out.

Dad had a similar experience in World War I. He volunteered for the Royal Flying Corps (part of the RAF). He was sent to Texas for basic training. There was an acute shortage of aircraft for training purposes so the pilots-to-be had to juggle for time in the air. My dad's instructor had one particular pet student and gave that student a noticeable amount more airtime than he gave my dad and the other students. To the instructor's acute embarrassment, his pet kept refusing to solo, saying he was not ready, even when he had an unheard of eight or nine hours of dual instruction.

One day all the students were lined up on the tarmac and the instructor called out his pet's name to solo. The pet refused once more. "Why, any one of these students would solo if I told him he is ready," the instructor bellowed. He glanced down the line of students at attention. "You, Lussier, you'd solo if I told you to, wouldn't you?" "Yes sir," said Dad, stepping forward with only two hours of experience under his belt, unbeknownst to the instructor. Into the sky went Dad on the joy ride of his life. When he returned to earth with a passable landing, he became the instructor's new pet, with free access to the trainer planes.

The rest of that day I was designated duty pilot. It surprised me that the ATA and the RAF would put an operational airfield, albeit a training field, into the hands of a twenty-year-old foreigner, but the ATA was impartial to age or sex. If you were accepted, you would share all the responsibilities. It was one of the features I liked most about the ATA.

CHAPTER 5

Duty Pilot Adventures

BEING DUTY PILOT KEPT ME FROM getting carried away with the joys of flying. Everything happened on my watch: A herd of horses broke loose from their nearby corral and stampeded across my field. A plane landed crosswind under the nose of a plane correctly landing upwind. As if to reward me for all this stress, I looked up in the sky to see a huge, graceful glider passing silently over my head. That sight helped remind me of our wider purpose in being here. Gliders like the one I was watching overhead would someday land our combatants in France for a final struggle with the Nazis.

Normal duty pilot days allowed us time to exchange flying stories with idle pilots and staff, when we were not dealing with galloping horses. One idle pilot told this tale: A pilot was hopelessly lost after dark and searching about in the blackness for his aerodrome. He suddenly spotted a flare path and decided to sit down on it, although he did not recognize it as his home field. He made a perfect circuit and was coming in on his final approach, right in the center of the flare path. His plane sank lower and lower. Just seconds before he was to touch down, he leaned forward and, looking over the nose of his aircraft, shouted in amazement to his copilot, "Lord Almighty, there's a train coming right down the middle of my flare path!" One more could-not-possibly-be-wrong pilot.

One day I received a welcome cablegram from Ole, the Norwegian gunner, informing me that *Scebeli* had once again made it across the Atlantic unscathed, into the port of Cardiff. Shortly thereafter I burst into my billet late one evening to see on the hall table a pair of fur gloves and a familiar navy cap with "Kgl Norsk Marine" (Kongelig Norsk Marine, or Royal Norwegian Navy) printed across the front. There in the living room was Ole himself. We spent a long evening going over the details of his journey to North America and back. I had thought their destination had been New York City, but I had been wrong: *Scebeli* had put in at dreary little Saint John up in Canada. They had suffered an uncomfortable trip coming back to England, with rough weather all the way and even a snowstorm. They had taken the northerly route this time. A short way from Newfoundland they passed right by two U-boats, both on the surface. According to Ole, the weather was too choppy to support a sea fight from either side. That seemed incredible. Maybe the U-boats were out of torpedoes, but two unarmed U-boats together? And why would they make themselves so visible by cruising on the surface?

Ole told me that one huge French submarine had been refueling regularly at a Halifax facility for months before someone discovered she was in the hands of a Nazi crew, that she was refueling and going back out on the ocean to sink Allied ships and not Axis ones. When the British discovered the true activity of the French submarine, they sank her.

Ole claimed that the German espionage system was so efficient in the southern waters that the U-boat commanders received the Allied route courses at the same time as the Allied ship's captains. There must have been a spy among them. They could lie in wait along the way because the Allied captains were subject to court martial if they varied their assigned routes.

The Guys graciously let Ole sleep on their living room couch and he stayed with us for a few days of his short shore leave. That gave me time to tell me more Norwegian horror stories.

A doctor, now in London, had been working inside occupied Norway. Doctors were the only Norwegians allowed to use cars and this particular doctor was transporting patriots clandestinely to the Swedish border where they were spirited down the coast and over the North Sea to England. The Gestapo eventually captured two young resisters who knew about these activities and began to torture them for the doctor's name, a torture that consisted of breaking each bone in each finger one at a time. Think of the pain. The boys could not stand it. One of them broke loose from his bonds and leaped out a window, falling ten stories to his quick death. The remaining lad crumbled under the torture and revealed the doctor's name, but the doctor was warned in time to get over to England. This brave patriot had to make the hard choice of leaving his children at the mercy of the invaders, a hard choice for anyone.

Ole assured me that many bridges and railroads in Norway had been mined secretly with explosives and that the organized underground was waiting and ready for the Allied support, whenever it was to come. They were a nation of courageous fighters.

Then it was time for Ole to go back to his war and me to mine, out at the aerodrome. The morning Ole was to leave, I sneaked over to Luton in my assigned Maggie trainer to show off a little for him, but apparently he had departed already for the railway station and only Mr. Guy was there to give me a feeble wave.

~~@ @~~

By now I had become familiar with all the pilots in my group. One of the most notable was the world-famous John Cobb, who had become the fastest man in the world behind the wheel of a racing car in 1939 when he had been clocked at more than 369 miles per hour, a record he surpassed in 1947 when he achieved the astonishing speed of just over 394 miles per hour on the Utah salt flats. When he came to ATA I do not know if he was holding a pilot's license already, but he went about his training assignments just like the rest of us.

Our top world-famous flying colleague was Jim Mollison. He was not technically in our group, but he mingled with us each day because he was assigned to the Luton Number Five Ferry Pool. Being years older than me, he was not a friend and I hardly knew him beyond a nodding acquaintance. Mollison was a good friend of Bill Haines who I had traveled with on *Scebeli*, though. When Bill found out that Mollison and I were flying from the same dispatch office, he took the occasion to issue a strong warning to me: "Beware of socializing with charismatic Mollison," was the message.

It was unnecessary advice; there were no sparks between us. Instead, Mollison was a huge pilot idol of mine. He was the British equivalent of Charles Lindbergh, adored and idolized throughout the aviation world. Jim was the first pilot to fly solo both the north and south routes across the Atlantic Ocean, feats he accomplished in 1932 and 1933. In 1931 he had set Australia–Britain record at seven days, five hours. In addition, he was the first pilot to fly solo from Great Britain to the Cape of Good Hope, crossing the dangerous Sahara Desert and the continent of Africa in four days, seventeen hours. He must have possessed a body of iron and a mind of steel to endure the trials he put himself through. In the 1930s and early 1940s he built a reputation for being absolutely fearless in the air and resolutely determined to reach whatever goals he set for himself. In 1932 he married Amy Johnson, a pilot herself, who had already achieved a few honors of her own in her short life; they divorced in 1938. Amy had joined the ATA in 1940, but was killed in a flying accident in January 1941. Her accident was described as a tricky delivery flight, but some insist it was an unauthorized flight to London for a personal evening. In any case her plane dove into the Thames Estuary, near London, in a thick fog, with no chance of rescue.

Besides the celebrities, there were many competent pilots who had been judged unfit for combat but were able to do ferry work. Regardless of our level of competence, all of us had to endure the months of review at Barton-in-the-Clay. One of the other women pilots was Tanya, a glamorous, young, blond beauty. We had one Polish pilot, Maurice, a refugee from Warsaw, and one New Zealander, Scotty. Then there were the English pilots: training at the same time as the pilots in our group were thirty pilots no longer able to serve with the RAF. They were considered healthy enough and skilled enough for ferry service, though. One or two of them would join our ground school classes.

I began to sit daily with Scotty, Peter, and Tony. Scotty was the New Zealander. He had been refused an RAF commission because his slight stutter might pose a problem giving orders in a crisis. Scotty was the playboy of the Western world, equipped with a motorcycle, a roadster coupe, and connections that kept him supplied with fuel for his machines. He also had a fat wallet to pay for the upkeep on his toys. After Scotty related some of his schoolboy exploits to me, I could understand why he was not at all popular with the authorities. On a whim one night, he and his school buddies telephoned the police and told them that the dean of a rival college had been murdered. When the police raced to the scene of the reported crime, the dean himself opened the door. The howl that the press raised reached out of New Zealand as far as England, according to Scotty. Equally rude and insensitive, they rented a rowboat from a renter they disliked, rowed it into the middle of the lake, punched a hole in the bottom, and let it sink. They swam back to the shore and raised a ruckus with the renter because his boat was rotten. They even had the nerve to threaten a lawsuit. Although time had passed since those childish episodes, Scotty did not seem to have changed much. He was always the first to rebel. Now he was shopping for a baby rabbit to turn loose in our navigation class. I do not know why Scotty and I became fast friends, since he spent his free time cruising the pubs, chugging down ale, and I always drank water or lemonade. Maybe it was because he came to depend on me to locate him at the last pub of the evening and steer him to his billet for enough sleep to keep him awake in class the next day.

Peter, one of the English pilots with whom I became close friends, was an aspiring lawyer, a graduate of Cambridge University, and a thrilling conversationalist. He could discuss philosophy, religion, or world affairs with equal authority.

Tony Hay was one of the RAF pilots. From an aristocratic London family, he was so handsome that my TC would have fainted with jealousy if ever he saw me with Tony.

Peter, Scotty, Tony, and I were each other's best friends. We arranged ourselves in a row at our classes, wrote jokes to each other, and defied Boost and Egbert to teach us something we did not know already. I think we were hoping they would pass us out of there more quickly just to get rid of us, since we knew how to fly the planes. But the ATA teachers took seriously the groundwork they thought we should master and held us tenaciously to our desks until they were satisfied we had learned what we needed to stay alive up there in the sky.

Soon we had graduated from solo circuits around the Barton-in-the-Clay aerodrome area to longish cross-country flights that took us all over England, Scotland, and Wales in our Magister trainers. Our flights tested our navigational ability and taught us to deal with the fickle English weather, never to trust those beautiful blue skies that greeted us in the morning because there was a 50 percent chance that they would turn to dismal fog by mid-afternoon. There were two dozen cross-country routes, and each of us had our favorite: passing over someone's house we wanted to impress with our skills, or getting back to base early so we could keep a date in London. We would be trying to trade off our assigned cross-country trip, if we did not like it, for one we preferred. We had quickly figured out that our instructors never checked to see which pilots had completed which cross-country routes. As long as all the cross-country chits were turned in and marked completed at the end of the flying day, they were content.

We were being pushed along in our training and mistakes were being made. Our instructors explained that ferry pilots were needed desperately out there in the real world. Inevitably we suffered accidents. Our first aircraft write-off occurred shortly after I joined ATA. It slapped all of us sober for a time, and cured us of writing silly jokes to each other in class or trading cross-country routes. It was one of the recently arrived RAF pilots on his first solo flight. He was practicing forced landings and misjudged his distance. He caught one wheel of his plane in a high-tension wire, tripped off and dropped onto the ground, nose first. Luckily an alert farmer, spreading manure nearby, witnessed the accident and was able to drag the pilot out before the aircraft blew up. The plane was a complete burnout. The pilot was taken to a local hospital, condition critical. He would recover, but he would not fly again for the ATA.

Next, one of our cadets, flying a Magister, was making an emergency landing in the meadow of a nearby farm. He failed to notice a tractor that happened to be working in the same field, landed right on top of it, and killed the farmer driving the tractor. Our pilot was seriously unnerved for weeks afterward.

Just when we were relaxing and convincing each other that accidents come in pairs, a third crash occurred. It was indeed horrifying. A Wellington bomber smashed through a watchtower and a hangar when an engine failed on takeoff. The resulting mess fired the buildings and, besides killing all the bomber crew, killed twelve of the hangar personnel. We were left speechless.

While we were still obsessed with death in the air, two of the new RAF cadets, no more than twenty-one years old, interrupted to tell us that it had been no picnic on the ground during the Battle of Britain. For six consecutive months London had been blitzed every night, and these two were among those assigned to get the clearing up done as best they could. One cadet said he had worked at his daytime job for seven days and on each of those seven nights had reported for voluntary air-raid duty. He said he did not know how he stayed awake for a week, but he knows he did and it seemed to him like a distant and horrible nightmare.

"I expected to wake up any moment and find it was all a dream."

Then when they saw our worried faces, the boys laughed and joked about going home one morning, pulling open their front door, and having it fall off its hinges into their hands. They could laugh, but it could not have been so witty when it happened.

As we were lamenting the Wellington accident, a young RAF Scot told us about being asleep in a Wimpy (the Wellington bomber's nickname) when it spun into the ground from two hundred feet of altitude. It broke its back right through the center. Fortunately for this young man, he was in the rear half while the rest of the crew, unfortunately, was in the front half. Emergency workers managed to fish him out of the wreckage, but the others burned to ashes in the ensuing explosion. The Scot told us that he saw this accident repeatedly in a frequent nightmare and always hoped his companions died on impact.

We began to take our cross-country practice missions seriously now because our whole class wanted to get out of backwater Barton-in-the-Clay and into the next phase of our training at Luton aerodrome. We reported on time each morning to our wooden hut, grabbed our cross-country chits from the operations officer, mapped out our routes as quickly as possible, taking into consideration the present wind conditions and cloud cover. We had strict orders to fly "visual" at all times, so detours around identified cloud banks had to be factored in.

Not wanting to make it too easy for us, our instructors had never pointed out that Barton-in-the-Clay, our home aerodrome for the moment, had a lovely, high hill jutting up over the south approach. We discovered on our own that the hill could be spotted from more than twenty miles away, serving us as a comforting landmark.

One morning on a cross-country that took me to Cardington I witnessed a bizarre scene. It was early in the day and I had taken off before the ground haze had burned away. It hung over the terrain like an opaque blanket, and there was a sharp line delineating where the clear sky began. I was flying on that line, with blue sky above, cloudbank below. The haze had enveloped the little town of Cardington completely—or at least where Cardington was supposed to be because I certainly could not see it. Just then, a barrage balloon poked through the clouds in grotesque fashion. I had never seen anything like that, but I had been told to get accustomed to looking for and avoiding the barrage balloons that each possible target of a Luftwaffe attack threw into the sky.

FIGURE 5.1 *Sketch of Balloon Barrage over Cardington*

Another day that December I was flying alone in the open cockpit of a Magister, cold as an iceberg, with snow slicing past, obscuring my goggles.

I heard a loud humming and looked up to see nine or ten Flying Fortresses passing about one thousand feet over me, all in perfect formation. They seemed so warm and companionable to each other, filled as they were with young American men. I wanted to be up there with them, and not in my cold, lonely, snowy cockpit. I felt left out.

Before we finished the basic phase of our training program in Barton and were sent over to Luton for the second, more intense, phase, we cadet pilots allowed ourselves some fun times in the sky—fun but dangerous. Maybe it was our way of injecting a bit of drama into the ho-hum routine of practicing maneuvers and flying our cross-countries accurately. Maybe it was the suspense of it: Will we be caught by Egbert or Boost? And if they spot us playing around, what will they do to us?

One day one of the RAF cadets and I crossed paths in the operations room. He was clutching a chit for one of the routes and I was holding a maneuvers-to-do list. Our eyes met at the door. We did not know each other very well, but I knew his name was Johnny.

"What are you up to this morning, Johnny?"

"Oh, just a repeat of the same route for the third time."

"I've got air space off the south end of the runway," I informed him, waving my chit under his nose.

"Why don't we meet at 'the chimney' and do some formation flying? I've got one thousand feet."

We agreed to meet at one thousand feet over the chimney, a derelict factory, in fifteen minutes. I arrived first and circled around at one thousand feet for five minutes. No Johnny joined me. I flew another circuit and still no Johnny. Looking up, I noticed another Maggie circling at two thousand feet and decided that Johnny had misunderstood my altitude. I climbed to two thousand and wing-waggled the other Maggie. The pilot responded by whooping down on my tail in a classical dogfight challenge. I zoomed all over the sky, as much as you can zoom in a slow-moving Magister, trying to shake him off my tail. Why was Johnny drawing me into a dogfight when we had agreed on formation flying? He suddenly formatted competently on my right wing, too close, and off we went, following the railway track. He broke away after a few miles, with me following, and together we spiraled down to four hundred feet over a town. There we formatted again, followed the railway tracks back to Barton, and neatly landed, one after the other. I trundled my plane over to the dispersal area and headed back to the operations room to turn in my "maneuvers" chit.

Passing through the ready room to drop off my parachute, I saw Johnny stretched out in an armchair, reading a magazine. I dropped my 'chute on the floor and remarked that he certainly got down in a hurry.

"Not really," he answered, "I never went up. My plane went U/S [unserviceable]."

I almost passed quietly through the floor. When I explained to Johnny my illegal encounter, the two of us dashed into the operations room to read the daily assignments. We discovered to my immense relief that the mystery plane was piloted not by an instructor, but by another RAF cadet. We sought him out and frightened him in reverse, telling him we thought he had formatted on one of our instructors, maybe Egbert. He started protesting that the other pilot in the sky had challenged him first and led him on. Before he caught his bus to town, we confessed the truth, much to his great relief.

Almost without our noticing it, the cross-countries became routine—smoothly executed and right on the mark. We knew where we were from one end of England, Scotland, and Wales to the other. Now we pilots were able to understand why our instructors put us through these seemingly infantile exercises. The day we would be called on to step into an unfamiliar airplane and deliver it to Prestwick, Scotland, the navigation required to get us there would not be a problem. We would be able to set our course competently, secure in the knowledge that our calculations would help us to arrive over our destinations and we could concentrate on handling the machines.

One of my near-perfect cross-countries occurred on an unlikely day. The visibility at Barton was way down, and Egbert, always looking over my shoulder, advised me to forget about my assigned cross-country and stick to circuits and bumps.

"Maybe the haze will lift this afternoon and you will still have time to complete a cross-country. And, by the way, I don't see your gas mask. Did you find one?"

"Sure, sure," I said.

Some inner madness urged me beyond safety that day. I had been instructed by Egbert to stick to take offs and landings, but when we got in the air, if we encountered milder weather conditions, we were allowed to take advantage of them. I assumed Egbert would approve of my reverting to my original flight plan, and I set out quite blithely toward the east coast. Flying in that direction, east, was always an added hazard because rogue

Nazi planes were known to cruise the English Channel and dart in on any hapless, unarmed planes they might spot. I do not know why the Nazi pilots did that. Surely they knew their target would not be a British fighter pilot ace, but only an over-aged civilian pilot in an unarmed transport plane. Maybe that was what attracted them, knowing they would not meet with any defensive fire, knowing they had a sure kill and could return to their home aerodrome and boast about bringing down one more of the hated British foe.

My course, this day, took me to Honington, past Cambridge and its university, over the town of Caxton, and back to Barton. I navigated neatly through my marginal visibility, trusting my compass and my wind-drift calculations. As we had learned to say, "It was downhill all the way." At the end of my flight, I arrived precisely over the Barton hill, landed, and hurried to find Egbert. Flying a perfect, predesigned cross-country is exactly like playing a perfect game of golf (without the Nazi raiders, of course): you want to explain it immediately to someone, anyone—blow by blow.

The Americans from Maryland began to trickle into England. They all had strict orders from their mothers to contact me when they were allowed to leave their bases. The first one I heard from was Corp. Bill Kelly. Kelly was a sidekick of Reds and had worked as a counselor at Mother's summer camp for several seasons, during which time he became an honorary member of our family. At the advanced age of twenty-five, we Lussier girls, still in our teens, considered Bill over the hill and thought it hilarious when he tried to date us. We told our boyfriends about him and giggled together. Teenagers can be cruel. I knew he had joined the U.S. Army and was in training somewhere. His arrival announcement came in the form of a letter. What surprised me was that it bore an English stamp; when I opened it, I read that he was stationed near Salisbury, which is not far from Maidenhead. Bill was forbidden to tell anyone exactly where he was. It was a treat to know that at least one of my old friends was so close; it made me feel less isolated. We quickly arranged for Corporal Kelly to spend the coming weekend in Maidenhead with his "cousin." It was always easier to get leave in order to see your relatives, thus I would be a cousin for the duration of the war. Bill arrived for his first visit on a December evening. I bounced into the Guys' house after a day at the airport and Mrs. Guy said, "I have a cup of tea ready for you," and coyly indicated the parlor door. I groaned inwardly, thinking to myself, "Not another cup of tea," steeled myself, opened the parlor door, and there was Corporal Kelly. (I learned later that he had made it up to the rank of sergeant at least twice, but his distinctly exuberant behavior kept earning him demotions.) The sight of him was such a pleasant surprise and I was as pleased as punch. Bill came burdened with two enormous boxes of long-forgotten American delicacies: peanut butter, chocolate bars, and Kleenex, all purchased at his unit's military post exchange (PX).

"I brought my lunch," he announced, much to the Guys' amusement.

Mrs. Guy had cooked dinner already so we stayed to share it with her and Mr. Guy. After the meal, Scotty called around because he and I had arranged to attend an ATA party together at one of the local pubs. We dragged Bill along with us. While the partygoers were eating their supper, Bill and I had a heart-to-heart discussion about "Everything." We recalled the fun of our Huntingfield summer camp days.

"You have grown up since then," Bill observed.

We agreed that pleasure is intangible. We evaluated the English. We firmly agreed that the United States was the most wonderful country in the world and that American men rate above English men. I thought guiltily about liking British Tony so much, but I did not mention him to Corporal Bill.

The ATA party dispersed right after the food disappeared; everyone had to report for work in the morning. Scotty and Bill had already become drinking partners. They, along with Peter, insisted we make a night of it.

"We have to show our new friend some ATA hospitality," explained Scotty and I could see I was headed into an evening at the end of which I would be putting everyone to bed. So we drank round after round of whatever the bartender shoved across the bar until closing time at 10:00 at night. By then I was a bit weary of English lemonade, which is all I ever drank on those outings. Just before the final bell, Peter put three shots of whiskey in one glass and gulped it straight down. In a few moments his usual shy, conservative manner disappeared like a Dr. Jekyll/Mr. Hyde transformation, and he started bouncing up and down like a yo-yo, quite out of control. After the bartender herded us out the door, we went in search of any other place that might be open. We skipped along the middle of the blacked-out street, singing loudly. I had to yank Peter down from a lamppost he was climbing and extricate Scotty from where he had slid under a parked truck. As we arrived in front of the George Hotel, we discovered a private party in session. I fixed all the ties on straight, thinking maybe if we joined this party I could find a sober dancing partner.

Scotty loudly claimed, "I can get us tickets to go in."

He disappeared for half an hour and returned without any tickets.

Peter said, "Let me try."

He, too, came back with no entrance tickets. All this time, Bill was standing demurely to one side, humming happily to himself.

Now he burst forth with, "Let me give it a try."

Off he went and returned almost immediately with a fistful of tickets. The glamour of a Yank uniform must be irresistible. We crashed the party and in one of their spotlight dances, surprisingly, Bill and I were spotlighted and awarded the equivalent of $3 worth of defense stamps. At 1:00 in the morning I dragged all three of my companions out of the party and poured them, one by one, into their billet beds around town. I put Bill in my bed at the Guys' house and curled up on the parlor couch under Corporal Bill's big Army coat. As the sun dawned I thought what a lovely day it had been.

CHAPTER 6

Old Loves, New Friends

I WAS THINKING A LOT ABOUT TC these days because it was just about one year ago that we had said our tearful goodbyes over the telephone, TC out in Texas at one of his training airfields and me at the YWCA in Manhattan. I had been trying to sort out my feelings for him, trying to remember, wondering if he had forgotten me over this long, lonely year. In my mind I kept evading the subject of our future together. Rather, I was waiting to see what TC would do first. Whenever I received one of his letters it brought him back to me vividly—all the slang he used seemed to make him so real. He wrote as many letters as he found time for and he professed one-woman-ness, but he was an impulsive lad and very, very personable. Surely during this year of separation he had met women to whom he was attracted, just as I had met and been attracted to other men. I thought that in my prolonged absence and his loneliness some woman could sneak into his heart and I could find myself dethroned. If that happened, I felt I would be able to tell from his letters that he had met someone else to be serious about. There was also his old high school sweetheart still about. She had never given up on the project of reclaiming him in my absence, although, for the moment, he still insisted on his fidelity and continued to ask for my hand in old-fashioned marriage. If he did find someone he loved more than me, it would be quite a blow to my ego, of course, but I prided myself on being unselfish enough to wish for what was best for TC. Our vision of our futures did not coincide or mesh. TC wanted to finish this war as quickly as possible, rope me into marriage, and return to live for the rest of our lives in the Baltimore ambience where he grew up. I wanted to roam the world, exploring what made it tick, helping to make it tick better, and never get married. If TC did not find another love, he might be following me from continent to continent, not really wanting that life, but wanting to be with me, just as he did when he followed me around my dad's cow barn.

He was quite as adventurous as I am, but he preferred to be adventurous in the quarry near Baltimore where we swam and dove from huge heights. He was smarter than I am, although I did not acknowledge his superior intelligence in public. He had the widest vocabulary of anyone I had ever met. Maybe the greatest difference between us was that he was gregarious and loved to be with people all the time, especially his close, childhood buddies. I was more retiring and tended to stand off from groups of people and observe. That could develop into our most serious problem in a future together. If TC were forced to conform to my pattern—and he would claim to enjoy it just as he claimed to love flying—I would always have the uncomfortable feeling that he would be happier "back home" in the middle of the local scene. I was prepared to one day receive a message from him announcing that he had found a new love, someone who would stay home, marry him, and lead a "normal" life. I told myself that I was prepared for such a rejection, but I still awaited with happy anticipation his pending arrival in England.

I was turning twenty-one and I wanted to celebrate the momentous occasion and the fact that I was finally old enough to travel legally outside my country without resorting to a British passport. Tony had turned twenty-one two months before me and he wanted to celebrate, too. On the actual day of his birth he stood guard all night at an air-raid shelter with the bombs dropping all around his post and the sirens wailing to keep people off the streets. None of our companions seemed interested in our momentous occasion so we agreed to join forces, just the two of us, and paint the town together. I donned one of the dresses I had filched from my sister Jane, Tony put on a tie, and off we went to London on the train. We saw an early show, were disappointed, and hardly remembered it afterward. We found a quiet restaurant and ate a sumptuous—for war-torn England—dinner. After eating, we had only half an hour to chat leisurely before the servers shooed us out the door and closed the place. That was the worst feature of embattled England's nightlife: they closed their doors at 10:00 and we were obliged to go home or transfer our festivities to the sidewalks.

Getting acquainted with Tony Hay took me into a whole new world. As far as I knew, none of my stateside acquaintances came from aristocratic ancestors. Tony's lineage was long and distinguished. He told me that his grandfather had been a well-known public figure in the Victorian era. He performed many benevolent deeds, so Tony told me. For his dedication to public welfare, he was rewarded by the queen with a knighthood and then offered a baronage. "Baron" is the lowest English title and cannot be carried on from generation to generation. Tony's family lost the title when his grandfather died. I could tell from the way Tony described it that he regretted not being able to keep a title in the family. The English are like that: independent and proud of their independence, but pleased to have their class distinctions and to pay reverence to a king or queen. Americans, on the other hand, feel strongly that all human beings are equal and therefore should not take titles that indicate some of us are on a higher plane than others.

Tony's father was like his grandfather. He had been given the best possible education, at Oxford University. He also did a lot of public work, but misfortune dogged him: through various twists of fate he lost a series of what should have been lifetime positions. The Hay family finances declined accordingly. Somehow, even with their limited means, the parents managed to give Tony the same excellent education that his grandfather and father had enjoyed. Tony was born early enough to have experienced both extremes of the family financial situation. He remembered being luxuriously wealthy but was living on a very restricted budget when I knew him.

Reluctantly, we caught the last train to Luton. It had been an ideal way to observe a monumental event, our coming of age. Two youngsters from two different countries, two different backgrounds, together engaged in the serious business of war, yet pausing for a few precious hours to honor the occasion of reaching the age of majority.

The next day a hideous crash brought us back to reality. Two Spitfires met in a head-on collision above Bedford town. The two craft spun in immediately, with no chance for the pilots to eject. One plane fell on a factory and the other plowed into a house. One of our student classmates saw it happen. All the sky in the world and these two specks meet in the same patch. It makes the point Egbert was always stressing: "When you are in the sky, never get careless about the watch for other craft."

"And by the way," he added, "I don't see many gas masks. Get them."

With his fierce will to get ahead fast, Tony passed the tests and was transferred to Luton aerodrome for the second phase of the training. He was an accomplished pilot. I did not know why he had been dropped from the RAF and he never chose to tell me. Peter, too, checked out, even while nursing a hellish hangover.

"Don't be long," he said to me as he departed for Luton, "I need someone to keep me in line.

Of our gang, only Scotty and Cadet Lussier were left in Barton. We were agitated to be left behind, but it was not to be for long. We buckled down and worked hard on our endless cross-countries, sometimes flying as many as three in one day. Sometimes I thought Egbert had decided to keep me there as the team mascot. At the end of most days, when I would be preparing to sneak off the field, Egbert would appear in the ready room and announce, "Roll out number twenty-six (which was a Maggie). I am going to take you on a tour of all the outstanding churches in the area." And he did and we returned to Barton aerodrome as the last rays of the winter sun were fading. Or he would beckon me out of our classroom, saying, "Come. I want you to see the landscape covered with this new snowfall." He never showed any signs of exploring his chances of getting a date with me so I decided he felt protective of me, knowing that I was one of the youngest pilots in the ATA and not wanting to be the instructor responsible for any mishap that could occur to me.

The remaining days of 1942 were reeling away. If the world were sane, I would have been on Huntingfield Farm in Maryland. Although already sold, my mother had yet to completely move off the farm. Besides milking the cows, I would have been reviewing the past year, as was my habit, and making plans for the coming year. I would have been on the telephone with TC—he spending Christmas with his family, me with mine—and we would have been planning a great New Year's celebration together. But that could only be a dream for now. I was thousands of miles away from the farm, engaged in what war service I was allowed, with no clear vision of what the future would bring me or even if there would be a future for me. The past year had been the most complex in my twenty years. TC had to be going through the same emotions. Pressed into a war for which he had no enthusiasm, flying fighter planes that guaranteed the pilots a short life span, his chosen girlfriend somewhere out there . . . what could he be thinking?

In England, New Year's day passed us from 1942 into 1943 with no change in our routine. It was just another day of duty. We reported to our operations room to be told, "No flying as yet, but stick around." The weather was completely closed all day, but we were not released. Aside from two feeble lectures, there was no attempt to educate us all day long. Consequently we collapsed before our little iron stove and got into earnest discussions about creation and existence, subjects that always perplex kids in their twenties. I longed to be up at the Luton aerodrome with my pals, Tony, Peter, and Scotty. Strange how fond you can become of utter strangers in a few short weeks. My mind kept drifting back to the previous New Year's day with Dad and the rest of my family in Montreal, a couple of flying hours in one of Dad's Tiger Moths, and time on the telephone with TC, somewhere in Texas.

David, Alice's husband, had two unmarried sisters who always visited over the end-of-year holidays. They sat quietly in the background and silently observed the festivities. I talked to them earnestly about women in aviation, extolling the joys of taking a flight. They had never been up in a plane. I was convinced that if they stayed long enough on their visit, I could coax them out of their long, black dresses and button shoes and into a flying frame of mind. But they departed after the holiday, still not won over to women in aviation.

The beginning of the new year combined with a grim downturn in the weather. Late that month I was walking toward my aircraft burdened with all my equipment. The sky was completely overcast with a 1,500-foot ceiling. There was a light, icy rain pelting down, yet everyone on the field was proceeding with the business of delivering planes, quite forbearing of all the inconvenience. It occurred to me what an uproar there would be if we could transfer our unit complete to Logan airfield in Baltimore where any light haze would have been the excuse to keep us out of the air and pack up business for the day.

I paid for that day of bravado in the open cockpit by catching a miserable cold. At first I tried to ignore it and went through the intense torture of flying with a cold. No more-exquisite punishment could be devised so innocently. The doctors know what they are doing when they forbade us to stay on duty with a cold. Since I hated to miss any days of possible flying, I did not report my condition. Egbert cheerily dug me out of the book *Guilty Men* in which I was buried and ordered me to "run out number twenty-six," which was tucked away in the back of a hangar. I stood there in the rain, supporting my 'chute for fifteen minutes while the mechanic fished the plane out for me. That was followed by another ten minutes of being stuck in the mud with all of us lending our weight to heaving it onto the tarmac. Another five minutes passed while Egbert ambled out of the hut onto the tarmac and got himself arranged in the front cockpit. Then he had me climb directly up to five thousand feet where the air was practically dripping with live icicles. My ears were screaming with pain as Egbert had me do a couple of ho-hum spins and a few half-hearted stalls. By that time I was quite deaf and his voice came through the intercom as though he were miles away. He had me execute a difficult forced landing on our way back to our field. That was it. I was ready to throw in the towel. I went to see the doctor, who sent me to bed early that evening and ordered me not to report for flying duties until two days hence.

This forced idleness led to a reflective afternoon walk with equally idle and reflective Scotty. We were sloshing down the street with the rain dripping into our collars and water soaking our ankles. It was dusk and a greater chill was creeping into the air. I turned to Scotty and confessed, "At times like this exact moment, I could give up everything and beat it back to the States without a single regret." I started to continue, but Scotty interrupted, "Yes, I know. When I first came over here I had spells of the same sort, times when all I wanted was to chuck England and get back to my home and things familiar. But then the sun would come out and things would look different. After you have been here awhile you sort of forget about going home."

I could see how right Scotty was. I knew when spring came and I was as busy as a bee and warm, too, why, then I would not dream of giving up. We ended our damp walk by going to see a new movie everybody was talking about: *Casablanca*, starring Humphrey Bogart and Ingrid Bergman.

Alice announced in great secrecy that William Stephenson, my father's World War I buddy, would be making an official visit to England in January. In his capacity as head of the BSC in the States he had been working to convince Churchill to accept some Americans for training in intelligence collecting and spy catching. The British, with their worldwide colonies, were masters at espionage and looked on us as naïve for never having created a spy service, nor seeing the need for one. Now that we had been drawn into the war, Stephenson was hoping to help the Americans get started.

My hope was more modest. I *wanted* to fly around with Stephenson while he was in England. He had told me that on his official trips he was assigned ATA planes and pilots.

"I will ask for you as my pilot," he had told me playfully, the last time we had met in New York. A cadet entrusted with the life in the air of a man as important to the war effort as Stephenson? I knew it would never happen, but I did yearn to tag along on at least one of his flights.

Most of the time when I returned to work, Alice rode on the train with me as far as London. She always said she had work to do in London, work she invented if she did not have any. She never liked to see me go back to work alone. In London we often went to the theater. One time we saw a musical called *Waltz Without End*. It was about the life of Chopin when he was dying of tuberculosis.

Then it was back to that cold, open Magister cockpit, snow slicing past and clogging my goggles. Back to flying our course estimations and hints from Egbert that my time with him was coming to an end. And more Flying Fortresses thundering overhead, telling me, "The Yanks are coming, the Yanks are coming!"

I knew it was time to move on when, on yet another nonflying day, Egbert rounded us up and gave us the lecture on observing correct engine temperatures. I knew it was time to leave because I had listened to that lecture four times. From engine temperatures, he eased into a discussion of not getting lost up there. He started out by asking tactlessly, "Who has been lost lately?" As if any of us were going to admit we had ever been lost in our lives. Before he dismissed us, he said, "I don't see any gas masks in your kits. Be sure to acquire them." Oh, yes, we would.

Tony called from Luton. He said it was to wish me a happy New Year, but I could tell he really wanted to report that he had checked out on the Hart with its impressive 500-horsepower engine and was moving onto the Fairchild. I felt a twinge of jealousy and gave Egbert a glare the next time our paths crossed.

Operation Torch, the recapture of North Africa from the German army by the Allied Forces that began in November 1942, had gone smoothly. Months later the Germans were faced with having to contemplate retreating completely from their African positions. After a lot of political maneuvering, our General Eisenhower had been chosen over Britain's General Montgomery to be the Allied commander in chief. Secret meetings between Churchill and Roosevelt, along with their military advisors, were taking place to decide the future course of the war. The general feeling was one of confidence that the tide was turning. In mid-March of 1943 I took the train to London, planning to continue to the town of Surbiton for a visit with a couple of married friends, Vick and Daisy. Vick was an airline steward friend of mine who carried "care" parcels over the ocean at my mother's behest. I had planned a visit for many weeks and work had always interfered until this day. En route to make my visit I walked right under my first serious air raid. It was a most amazing sight. I found it hard to believe that it was all in dead earnest. There is something insanely wrong about civilized men throwing hunks of blazing iron at each other with evil intent. The first unnerving thing is the terrifying siren that echoes right down into your boots. I kept hearing it hours after it ceased to wail. I could imagine how it must panic the children who had less understanding than adults did of what was happening.

Then comes the sound of the enemy aircraft right overhead where you cannot see them. This unseen presence seemed to frighten almost everyone but it enraged me. The strangest sight was all the ack-ack (antiaircraft fire) that went rocketing up into the sky and the brilliant lights that flashed when it burst. The searchlights, too, with their piercing beams playing the game of "I'll catch you yet" with the enemy bombers, were amazing to behold. When that raid started I was still in the train from Maidenhead, approaching London, where I would catch another train to Surbiton. I was pressed against the huge plate glass window in the train corridor. I stood, swaying with the moving train for a good half hour. Slowly it dawned on me that I was not charmed and that plate glass is not exactly the best shrapnel screen, so I stepped back from the window.

When I stepped off the train in London's Paddington Station, I had to convince myself that what I was looking at was real and not a dramatic scene from some motion picture. An unnatural silence prevailed although there were hundreds of people waiting for guidance. A woman's voice kept calling over the speaker system and directing people into the several air-raid shelters. The British were using their underground tube tunnels, what we call our subways, as air-raid shelters. There was some hesitancy on the part of the people to go down into the tunnels en masse because recently a woman had tripped and fallen on her way down the stairs. Before the wardens could stop them, dozens of other people piled on top of her and soon the entire staircase was full of people piled up in panic. When the disaster was finally cleared, an estimated one hundred seventy-three victims had died and another sixty were seriously injured. No wonder we all felt some apprehension when the air-raid alarm sounded and it was time to descend into the underground.

Down in the tube station, women with young babies took what seats were available. The rest of us sat on our luggage or on the floor. Volunteer wardens constantly moved among us with offers of water, blankets, and aspirin. Soon we heard the welcome "all clear" and we filed back up the stairs in an orderly fashion. Above ground the station was clearing gradually as people left for their homes or caught departing trains. On this occasion not much ground damage had been sustained and British ack-ack managed to bring down four or five of the raiding enemy bombers. I had a strong urge to be up above the fray instead of underneath it and I contemplated why there was so much opposition to women fighter pilots. If we women know our aviation stuff, why not let us fly and fight?

The Surbiton train was still running on schedule; the British prided themselves on not letting the Nazis disrupt their transportation schedules. I returned to the departure gates and boarded my train. Again on my train to Surbiton, I had to stand in the corridor for lack of seats and thus had an unobstructed view of the results of the attack on London. The searchlights darted frantically around the sky like a tangle of illuminated cat's paws chasing after a mouse. After a lull in the attack, the ack-ack would begin again against the unseen Nazi bombers; the ensuing explosions resembled dangerous fireworks. In a weird way, it was magnificent—perhaps not to the blitz-weary British, but to me because it was the first I'd experienced. When I arrived in Surbiton there was still one lone raider directly overhead. He created great tension when he dropped his lethal load, but his bombs fell on the outskirts of Surbiton, wounding no one. Shells were bursting all over the sky, searchlights were flashing hither and yon, houses were trembling with the repercussions, and I stood under it, quite awestruck.

Vick and Daisy were waiting for me with Mother's fat care parcel. We had a long evening together, what was left of it, while the lone aircraft whined around and around overhead. We did not feel comfortable getting into bed with the Lone Ranger overhead, so we sat and talked about our lives. The German plane finally droned away and we sighed with relief and hopped into bed. Soon he was back, this time with a few of his chums for moral support, and together they harassed poor Surbiton until dawn. I slept fitfully in a chair from 1:00 until about 4:30 in the morning, when the sirens went screaming again and the antiaircraft guns started booming wildly. In spite of being with warm friends, I confess I felt very much alone in the wide world at that dreary hour.

Daisy and Vick were determined to be hospitable hosts. They announced that they were taking me to see Hampton Court, which was nearby. In spite of our sleepless night, we all arose at an early hour and set out for some sightseeing. Hampton Court palace had been built in 1514 for Cardinal Thomas Wolsey as his home. When Wolsey failed to persuade the pope to grant King Henry VIII's divorce from Catherine of Aragon, he was impeached and his property forfeited to the king. The place had been built as a huge square around an ample center court. The rooms—so many they seemed countless—surrounded the inner court on all four sides. The other view from the rooms was of vast, rolling acres of lovely flowerbeds, green lawns, and grand old trees. I thought how impressive it would be to live always in a huge palace like Hampton Court. I wondered what the occupants, king or lord, did all day. In the evening Vick and Daisy took me to see what they announced as a "musical." It turned out to be a striptease routine. Vick told me it was most unusual to see such a show in England, but he seemed quite at ease with the nude bodies. I was embarrassed for the sake of the naked women. We ended our evening before Vick's and Daisy's fireplace, listening to the BBC war news, where we all dozed off.

I got up at 5:00 the next morning; gathered up my stateside loot of chocolate and silk stockings, mints, candied nuts, powdered milk, Mother's strawberry jam (how did the jam survive the voyage?); and caught an early train back to London amid colorful displays of renewed ack-ack aimed at unseen, high-flying raiders. It was all over by the time my train pulled into Paddington Station—for this time, at least.

I had just stepped from the subway car and was walking toward my Maidenhead train when Alice popped out of an incoming train. It was an unplanned coincidence. I had one more day of leave coming to me and Alice asked, "Would you like to spend it with me?" Our morning passed in frivolous shopping: an animal book in French for Vick and Daisy's daughter and another copy for little Suzanne, then gifts for Nita, Jane, and Mother. It felt good to earn a salary and spend it on those you love. It was harder to find presents for Dad and TC, and after awhile I gave up.

Alice took me to walk around Liberty House. The place was paneled entirely in dark wood and furnished with authentic antique pieces of mahogany and oak. There were extensive displays of exquisite Wedgwood china that would have delighted Mother, who had her own treasured Wedgwood pieces. On the business side, there were colorful scarves and slippers for sale. I wandered into their book department and was captivated by the old leather bindings. I told myself I would have a shelf full of leather-bound books myself some day.

We lunched, Alice and I, at the famous Trocadaro entertainment center and hurried off to a matinee. It was called *Best Bib and Tucker*, a musical with elaborate costumes and lovely performers. It reminded me of our Broadway productions. I realized going to the theater was one of the ways the British took their minds off those Nazi raiders overhead.

My last day as duty pilot on Barton-in-the-Clay aerodrome was not an idle one. It started out like a normal airport day and I was catching up on my stateside mail when things began to happen. Two Americans came breezing in with a beautiful twin-engine Beechcraft that made my mouth water. They were hopelessly lost, surprised to be dealing with a female duty pilot, but gratified to know they were still in England. They needed detailed directions to get back to their base. By this time in my career, I knew where all seven hundred aerodromes were located so I could put them on their route with little effort.

Next I was instructed to watch out for and report the landing of a Proctor. While waiting for the Proctor, I had to see that a Hurricane and a Walrus took off without damaging each other. Then a Magister took off and almost collided with a Hart that was weaving unconcernedly over the circuit and had failed to make radio contact with me. At the same time, a couple of engineers were taxiing Fairchilds back and forth on the tarmac and a mechanic chose to run up another Fairchild to full "revs" about two yards from my right ear. Into the other ear, a ferry flight officer with RAF authority was giving me further orders. My reaction was to nod in a friendly manner, keep my eye on the hectic traffic, air and ground, and, if someone crashed, be prepared to rush out and help pick up the pieces.

On a more serious note, we had lost another ATA pilot in that period. With so many losses, the ATA would have come out on the short end if it were not for the steady influx of RAF pilots into the ATA training program.

After that hectic day as duty pilot at Barton, Egbert informed me that he was making time to give me a final check ride and would I be ready at 2:00 that afternoon? I paced up and down all morning, dragging my parachute behind me, to be ready when Egbert was. But Egbert went into one meeting after another with the bigwigs from Luton. Time went by and it was a darkening 4:00 in the afternoon when Egbert came out of his final meeting. He looked at me standing there expectantly, parachute at the ready. From the look on his face I gathered that he had forgotten all about my check ride.

He announced, "I have to go locate a lost Luton aircraft somewhere up north. Come ride along with me. That is, if you wish. Two sets of eyes are better than one." As for my pending check ride, he made no mention of it. We piled into a waiting Fairchild and were off, searching the fields at low altitude until we passed right over the lost pilot. He was sitting on the wing of his Maggie and waiting our arrival, showing all the confidence of a new cadet. As we touched down back in Barton with the found pilot on board, I asked plaintively, "What about my check ride, captain?"

Egbert took his ever-present pipe out of his mouth, looked at me briefly, and replied, "Oh, you don't need any check flight. Pack up your kit and report to Luton in the morning." With no fanfare and with all the attention on a lost pilot who was found, I passed quietly out of basic training and into the more challenging secondary course at Luton aerodrome. Transferring my personal operations to Luton aerodrome was not a complicated proposition. I was able to continue living at my assigned billet, the Guys' best bedroom in Luton town. The aerodrome was a short bus ride from the town or a long walk, if Alice were in charge of transportation.

⚜ ⚜

The pace at Luton was markedly more accelerated than it had been at Barton. On the first day that I reported I was given a dual session on the Hart—a 500-horsepower, all-purpose, single-engine plane—and I experienced my first real forced landing. We had practiced forced landings so often that a real forced landing hardly stirred my pulse. My instructor, named Paull, had me in the air and we were well into our second hour on the beast with a combination of take-offs and landings and estimated course settings. Just as we became airborne after my takeoff, our exhaust pipe blew off with a loud "throo–bam." Paull grabbed the controls away from me, immediately dropped the nose and cut the throttle, banked to the left and managed a glide-in, dead-stick landing downwind on the strip, an impressive feat. Had I been solo, I think I would have opted to go barging on around a complete circuit, throttle wide open as long as the machine responded; I probably would have burned out the engine. The incident did not reflect well on our engineers. After all, an exhaust pipe is a big-ticket item to be falling off.

The next day, instead of humble cadet student, I felt like Master of the Universe. I soloed that big brute of a Hart. I liked Paull's method of putting his students entirely on their own. It inspired our needed self-confidence . . . although, now that I think about it, he did grab the controls when our exhaust pipe blew. I had figured out, more or less, what tames the Hart, which has a tendency to touch down reassuringly for a landing,

Scebeli, *the Norwegian cargo ship that took the author from New York City to Liverpool in 1942.*

Awaiting the Nazi invasion on a British road with all the signs removed and rolls of barbed wire ready to pull across the road.

The aircraft dispersal at Barton-le-Clay.

Scotty with his "toy" and the author with Peter's motorcycle.

Left to right: Ricardo Lussier Sicré, Jay Lussier Sicré, author, Penn Lussier Sicré, Emile Lussier Sicré.

Ready for a training flight in the "Maggie."

Ready to make a delivery.

The author's sister, Nita Lussier; Squadron Leader Emile Lussier, CO; and author, St. Hubert Airport, Montreal, Canada, 1942.

Vera Fleming Lussier, formerly Miss West Canada, and Suzanne, youngest of the daughters.

The author's sister, Jane Lussier Strong, in her uniform as a naval munitions inspector, Maryland, 1943.

The author and her sister, Nita Lussier, X-2, OSS, in their invented military uniforms, France, 1944.

Practicing for a shot the author never had to make, Pyrenees, France, 1944.

Practicing with Major Frank Holcomb for a parachute jump the author was never given permission to make, Thuir, France, 1944. (Nita and Mike are assisting.)

Ilfracombe down in Devonshire, with typical unfriendly flying conditions.

General Eisenhower visiting the Americans at Thurleigh to christen a Flying Fortress named after him. In the background is Colonel Putnam, commanding officer at Thurleigh.

The Île d'Oléron, off the coast of Rochefort, France, a Nazi holdout recaptured by French forces with the requested participation of X-2, OSS in May 1945.

then without apparent reason leap into the air again. At that point you will be looking at the end of your runway and still be three feet off the ground. If you have your flaps extended and you have eased back on the throttle, it is a mere matter of hauling back on the stick at the correct moment, holding it there firmly and letting her slap herself onto the deck.

One day we had been washed out all morning, but about 2:00 in the afternoon the sky lifted a little and Paull called for me over the Tannoy (loudspeaker system). He interrupted an animated game of ping-pong between Tony and me, during which I decided that I was emotionally several years older than Tony. He was able to envelop himself completely in a silly game and get genuine pleasure from it, while I never completely relaxed about our war.

When I reported to Paull, he asked me if I could manage a bit of solo, "just circuits and bumps?" I assured him I was ready to solo. Deep inside I thought frantically, "Is he crazy? After only two hours I am not ready for this big brute. I will not get it down all in one piece." But some stubborn inner force made me refuse to admit I was not fully capable and that this craft, a mere piece of machinery, could frighten me. So, with no hesitation, I bounded out to the 500-horsepower beast, chattered through my cockpit drill, and was away, away into the sky. I whipped around the circuit for an hour, and each time I landed it was textbook smooth. Paull knew better than I did that I was ready for the Hart.

The Harts got parked on the far side of the Luton aerodrome, a good mile from the watchtower. I was out there tying down my now-friendly Hart when Scotty rolled up in his Fairchild. He had been ferrying around pilots all day. He leaned out of his cockpit and yelled, "Taxi?" I slung my parachute into the back of the Fairchild and hopped into the copilot seat while Scotty zipped us over to the watchtower. I sat there in my navy coverall with my white silk gloves pulled on for warmth. Swinging my helmet between my knees, listening to Scotty's voice, I thought to myself how utterly otherworldly all this was and what a perfect way to earn one's bread and win the war. If my life could have stopped right there, taxiing leisurely around the 'drome at landing time, with the Hart solo under my belt, Scotty chattering contentedly in my ear, and all the finish-up-the-day activity passing before, overhead, and behind, why, I think I would have been willing to die without a murmur of discontent. Such moments happen so rarely. I chalked this one up alongside my last Huntingfield full moon with TC and my mid-ocean sunrise on the deck of *Scebeli* under the title of "never to be forgotten."

Although Corporal Kelly—Bill—had been moved to what appeared to be a "staging area" in southern England, he was still granted an occasional leave and we were able to meet up. Sometimes our organizational skills failed us and we did not connect. I received one ambiguous telephone message from him saying he was in London and I "knew where to meet" him. I did remember arranging to meet him somewhere, but where was it? The only place that came to mind was Grosvenor House, the hotel where the American military hung out, so I settled for that. After a mad dash "home" to get changed into going-to-London garb, I made the evening 6:00 train. It was raining when I arrived so I took a taxi to Grosvenor House. There was no sign of my "cousin" Bill. I telephoned all the other known American hangouts that I could remember, but there was not a sign of Kelly. I finally collapsed into a chair in the Grosvenor lobby and opened my copy of *Full Orchestra*. I had been there almost two hours when a lonely-looking American wandered over and asked meekly if he could sit down and talk to me. I was pleased to have the company. He turned out to be a first lieutenant bombardier from a Flying Fortress (B-17) squadron stationed just north of Bedford. Bill Colantoni was his name. We talked about our past lives like two old people rocking on the back porch. He was from Pennsylvania and had worked at the Maryland Beltsville laboratories where I had done tuberculosis tests on cows in one of the two jobs I had as a freshman. His squadron was currently on what was called "operational," and he had completed fifteen sweeps already. Thirty was the magic cut-off number at which point you were pulled off active duty, put on deskwork, and allowed to go home. His past missions had all been flown in daylight, which added danger.

He read me the following quote from a piece of paper that he took from his wallet. It was attributed to Enver Curry, a B-17 bombadier: "The nearest thing to being in the 'Chin Turret,' the bombardier site of a B-17, is the dream where you are walking down the road with no clothes on. You knew that the glass around you wasn't worth anything for protection. The smallest round or fragment would go clean through it. The man at the front has the best view of what is going on, but he pays for it." Neither of us mentioned fear or what we wanted to do when this war ended if we survived, yet I envied him his job of bombadier.

CHAPTER 7

Adventures and Misadventures on Land and in the Air

IN ONE OF MY DAD'S LETTERS, he asked me to call on an old World War I flying buddy of his and make a case for getting him over into service in England. It startled me, that request for help, because I had always thought of my father and everybody else's father as giving help, not asking for it. But on a day off, I went around to the Air Ministry in London and located Dad's friend, Air Vice Marshal Hubbard. I think he had stayed in the RAF after World War I. I made Dad's case, but Hubbard shook his head discouragingly and explained that Dad's age would be a great deterrent.

After my meeting at the Air Ministry, I met Scotty, who was quite drunk although it was only the middle of the afternoon. He was waiting contentedly for me to come and take charge of him. I did that by taking him for a long walk through Hyde Park and giving him several cups of strong black coffee. When Scotty could walk straight, we called on his tailor in Saville Row where he was optimistically having a Harris Tweed suit made. I was so taken with the beauty of Scotty's suit that I decided to be optimistic too and order one for myself, but the tailors claimed they did not have any more of the fabric. "Never mind," consoled Scotty, "I'll let you borrow mine." I wondered fleetingly if either of us would ever get to wear the suit when it was finished. Scotty was not as sober as I had assumed. Regardless, we set out on a relentless round of the available pubs.

At one point in our stroll, we passed Madame Tussaud's Museum, famous the world over for life-like depictions in wax of famous persons. Scotty, ever with an eye out for opportunities to advance my cultural development, insisted he had to take me on an immediate tour. I was startled to see how lifelike the figures appeared to be—Henry VIII and his six wives, Churchill, and Roosevelt. As I moved through the museum, I was startled to find myself staring into the clear blue eyes of a wax figure of handsome Jim Mollison, our ATA colleague at Luton aerodrome and the Commonwealth's most famous flyer, who held world records for distance and endurance in the sky.

When Scotty decided I had seen enough wax people, he dragged me out of the museum and back to the rounds of the clubs. At the Beaver and at the Eagle I had to wait outside because women were not permitted inside. The old rules had not yet been amended to accommodate women service personnel.

"One coffee," I cautioned Scotty as he went in "to inspect," as he put it. At both places he came back out in a minute so I took it that there was not much action behind the doors. We had better luck at the New Zealand club where we met so many of Scotty's cronies that I thought we would never escape. But we did, to a civilized dinner at the aloof Grosvenor House, amid all the wealthy American civilians. A small orchestra was playing; after some food, Scotty was in condition to dance to "If I Didn't Care." Next we visited the Savoy Hotel to listen to another band, and to have a few more dances. En route to the Savoy, we looked into a shady dive called Chez Moi, but it turned out to be too sinister even for Scotty.

We caught the late train back to Luton, and in the carriage Scotty burst out with the confession that he had fallen in love with me, that he honored my commitment to the invisible TC, but he just wanted me to know. After all the life Scotty had lived and all the women he had strung along, to get tripped up by an American farmer was sadly ironic. I listened to him politely, reached over and patted his hand in a sisterly way.

"Too much booze, Scotty, too much booze, and too many lonely nights."

It was time to take on the Fairchild, a five-passenger plane similar to our Taylorcraft, with a super Scorah engine, built at 125-horsepower and souped up to 140-horsepower for fully loaded ferry passenger service. I had been "steering" Fairchilds around the sky for several weeks for lazy ATA pilots, but I had yet to solo one. One morning I had spent another hour solo in a Hart. I had flown up Bedford way, wistfully surveying the many aerodromes en route and wishing I knew to which one Kenny Reecher was assigned so that I could pay him a visit. Kenny had been a student at the University of Maryland at the same time as Nita and I were and Nita was very attracted to him. He was now a B-17 pilot somewhere down below and we hoped to meet up in the future. In the afternoon an instructor named Brandt seemed to have inherited me. I often wondered on what criteria the instructors divided us up. He looked me up and down, standing there eagerly with my parachute in hand.

"Show me what you know," he demanded, climbing into our Fairchild in front of me and settling himself into the copilot's seat. Without one word of instruction I took off and made a neat circuit of the field, landing in a reasonable manner.

"You can fly this thing and you are just wasting my time," said Brandt. "Let's go play," and off we shot toward White Waltham, the ATA headquarters. Along the way Brandt spotted a lone bunch of kids standing in a road, grabbed the controls away from me, and took us right down over a telephone wire and in between two close-together trees. All the kids flattened themselves on the road and Brandt laughed wickedly. I imagined them telling their parents that evening how they were attacked by a maverick German airplane. From there, we found a train to tease and had a game of "aerial golf" on a golf course. Next Brandt ordered me to pilot him to London on an estimated course, with me doing the estimating. Our real destination turned out to be his own home. Again, he took over the controls and shot up his family house in a most hair-raising manner.

Something about my flying must have impressed Brandt because it was reported to me that he told a group of cadets, "There are only three women in the ATA I would consent to fly hands-tied with and one of them is Cadet Lussier." Made me feel useful. After Brandt finished showing off for his family, he let me fly us sedately back to Luton aerodrome, where he asked me to gain altitude and showed me how to play in the clouds. Those clouds were an amazing sight, billows on billows of heaping, fluffy whiteness. I had the urgent desire to fling open the door and step out on the clouds. I could have sworn they were going to support my weight—a wonderful feeling, if somewhat lightheaded. After I landed, Brandt clambered out of the plane and announced, "You go do it."

And I soloed.

While I was adding my Fairchild time to my flight log, I noticed that we were required to have three hours of dual instruction and five additional hours of solo before we were checked out and entrusted with the lives of other pilots. When I totaled up my time it came to one hour solo and about six shoot-up or showing off hours. Our CO would perish if he found out.

In the evening I pondered how I would ever get back to my old life after the war, hard work on the farm. I did not envision myself in any other job but farming, since so few jobs in aviation, my first choice, were open to women. Living alone you come to put a value on privacy. It occurred to me that I was supporting myself at this time and that I must be perfectly capable of continuing to do so for the rest of my life. That seemed strange to me after having Dad to lean upon on for all my young years. It was slowly dawning on me that I was able to take complete care of myself.

One morning I was assigned an easy cross-country, to Honington first with a landing at Cambridge, and from there a return to Luton. Scotty had been assigned a different route, but our first legs ran parallel and we planned to fly tandem. At the last minute Scotty's aircraft was U/S, so I flew alone. Up above Cambridge I was whizzing along right on track. The sun was blazing brightly. The sky was as clear as glass from recent rains. The land below looked like pictures of toys in a book. Quite suddenly I had the most glorious feeling and I gazed at the sky and the ground and, of course, at my instruments, and smiled quietly to myself. "These moments do not happen too often," I thought. I was back on base so early that the CO told me to wait around until he had time to give me the pep talk that he gave to all the cadets before they escaped from his clutches into the ferry pools.

He started out, "Now that you are a pilot. . . ." He even went into the details of my behavior away from the field. I decided he was preparing me for my wings and the donning of my uniform.

A letter from Ole that had been posted in Canada arrived one day. He tried to describe the horrible trip he had endured across the north Atlantic, but the censors had eliminated most of his efforts with a pair of scissors—except for the word "horrible." Ole wrote in Norwegian and it took me most of the day with my Norwegian dictionary to translate what the censors had left.

Scotty and I were sitting in the canteen one day when someone came over to our table and asked us something in a foreign language. Scotty looked blank and I translated, "He asks if you have a match," thinking all the time he had spoken in French. Later I realized he had been talking in Norwegian, so some of communicating with Ole had rubbed off on me.

One day the skies chose to make a display of England's capricious weather. First we would have a regular deluge of rain, then a sudden clearing of the skies with the sun popping out. More clouds would pile up ominously and, without warning, we would be pelted with hailstones. Another clearing, another shower, and so it went all morning. This changeable weather is one of the hardest features to become accustomed to as a pilot on this little island. If you can fly in Britain, you can fly anywhere in the world. Scotty swore all these "fronts" are deliberate exports by us Americans. Finally the CO gave up on any flying possibilities, declared a general washout, and released us for the rest of the afternoon.

A mad scramble ensued with almost everyone grabbing taxis and catching trains before the weather improved and the CO changed his mind. Scotty and I had planned to catch a bus and spend the rest of the day in quaint, nearby Whipsnade, but the rain was lashing us from all sides at the bus station, so we hopped on the first bus going past and stayed on it to the end of its run. We found ourselves in Bedford and took a foot tour of the town. We happened on the very place where John Bunyan had written *Pilgrim's Progress*. After having read Bunyan's book more than once, it was humbling to stand on the exact spot where he had written the work. I made a mental note to write my high school English teacher about this exciting event.

Tony's posting to the next conversion class at White Waltham came through, along with a day off. We said our goodbyes and he took the train into London to see his family. From now on, communication between us would have to be by telephone unless we ran into each other on our separate ferry flights. That arrangement would please my TC when I wrote him about it. He had always been suspicious about my relationship with Tony, wanting to but not quite believing my insistence that ours was a platonic relationship.

Scotty's birthday rolled around (he was not admitting which one), and I presented him with a pair of my precious Ray Bans. His billeter cooked a bang-up supper to which I was invited. We gorged on peaches with cream and shortbread as good as Mother's. Later, we went to a local concert, each wearing one of the mittens decorated with jingle bells that Mother had knitted for me. We kept jingling them just to be a general public annoyance. The sky was clearing rapidly and we agreed that we could look forward to serious flying the next day.

Against our optimistic prediction of good flying weather, it was miserable the next morning with an evil gale blowing across our runway. But the powers-that-be sent us up into the sky regardless. I started off cautiously for Ratcliffe. By the time I was over Leicester, I was in the thick of some pea soup fog. I should have landed, but had I set down, the local tower would have held me until the skies cleared and, in that case, I was looking at an overnighter in Leicester. Not for me. I did a 180-degree turn and scooted back to Luton, with that stuff chasing me on all sides. It was certainly no day for the lightweight Magisters to be up there. I was hanging on my straps most of the time and it was a constant battle with the controls to keep Maggie level with what little of the horizon I could see.

An earlier letter from TC described a similar experience with the weather on his cross-countries. He spoke of one classmate who ended up three hundred miles off course. If he had made such a mistake in England, he would no longer have been in England—France, maybe, or the Netherlands. TC also described practicing blitz landings at night with no guiding lights. I worried so about TC making it through the war alive. It seemed selfish of me to want all my special friends to come out alive. But how could they? And who would be the lucky ones?

I did not plan it ahead of time, but one day I finally paid an air visit to Kenny Reecher's aerodrome that I now knew was at Thurleigh, very close to Luton. I was breezing along on my assigned cross-country. It was cold as blazes. I was being meticulous about staying smack on course, aided by the railways. I fell to reflecting how interesting my position was, compared to being back in Baltimore on this same day a year ago. My anxiety to be on the continent was subdued for the moment and I was completely happy to be flying over beloved England and studying the many intriguing features of the countryside. I whipped around my route from Luton to Cambridge to Cranwell, a big new double aerodrome, where I landed to refuel. I went on to little Rearsby, with a look at Radlette on the way. Into my last leg back to Luton, on a whim I cut over to Thurleigh, only forty miles off my assigned course, and did a mild shoot-up of the control tower. I knew from a letter that Kenny was in the hospital with a kidney infection, so I did not set down. I returned to Luton flying low all the way, skimming hilltops, streaking in between trees, swooping down into open fields. It was the first time since I had started flying in England that I had been so frivolous. I was getting very familiar with the Maggie and I wanted to test my skills.

One evening after supper at Scotty's billet I walked home alone. The sky was neither black nor deep blue, but rather that very soft, velvety color women wear to "first nights." There were thousands of bright stars. Then I heard the droning of a few enemy planes in the distance and the searchlights slid up into the stars. The beams looked like carefully made strips of white gauze stretched over the velvet. Two of the search beams came up from one side and two from the opposite side. They went creeping about the sky like moles in the daylight trying to find each other. Finally they met and became one, then swept about like soldiers on the march. One battery of beams went up together. It reminded me of the times in math class when we were asked to draw dozens of lines all intersecting each other at the top. That is what those beams reminded me of: a school kid's doodling.

I strolled into ferry flight one morning, expecting to pick up a chit for yet another boring Magister cross-country route. To my astonishment I was posted for ferrying. This would be my first solo ferry flight. To make it more harrowing for me, it all took place down in the remote shire of Devon. Ordinarily I would enjoy seeing a new part of the kingdom, but starting the next day I had been awarded some leave; all the ferry jobs in England were not going to make me spend it stranded in distant Devon.

Another American pilot, Betty McDougall, was accompanying me. She was one of the "older women," at least in my eyes, whom Jackie Cochran had brought over from the States. With an impressive number of hours racked up in her flying log, she worked with a relaxed, ho-hum attitude. I did not tell her this was my first day on the ferry job. Our trip started out ominously when our assigned taxi plane, a twin-engine Anson, went U/S and we had to wait for a replacement. It was noon before the replacement turned up and we could take off. By rapid calculation I figured it would be about 1:30 in the afternoon when we got to our destination in the Anson and picked up the two Tiger Moths awaiting us. I groaned inwardly as I saw my leave time fading away.

Once in the air, though, I forgot my worry about getting back to base and admired the scenery. We flew above the clouds all the way south and I dozed off to sleep as the sun made everything warm and cozy. We broke through the cloud cover and there below us was the Bristol Channel with the white breakers rolling in on a gray-white beach. Several cliffs added that painted-there-on-purpose look to the scene. In between two imposing cliffs our destination aerodrome was sprawling out like a lazy spider with flattened legs. It was a Wimpy (Wellington bomber) air base and all the

Wimpys were painted white because they were assigned to Sea Scout duty, which took the daily patrol over the water.

Our Anson dumped out the Other Betty and me with little ceremony and scooted off on its next mission. I tried to impress the ground staff with the urgency of releasing us and our Tiger Moths before dark. Other Betty did not seem to care.

"What's the hurry?" she asked me, stretching out on a couch in the flight room. She did not have leave coming the next day. We did get off at 3:00 in the afternoon, due entirely to my insistence. We set out together, the two Bettys, but our routes soon parted, partly because I was revved up to maximum in order to get back to Luton before last landing time and Other Betty was poking along at her leisure, slow as the Second Coming.

Just to be perverse, the weather was miserable all the way and my eyes took a fierce beating without the protection of my goggles, which I had lost ages ago. I made a perfect, if I do say so myself, three-pointer at Reading on the Woodley aerodrome, right behind my Fairchild taxi craft that had come to fly me back to Luton. By being sweet to the "consignor," I was able to get rid of my Tiger Moth in record time, hop into my waiting Fairchild taxi, and get back to Luton before darkness descended and closed the aerodromes for ATA landings. I handed in my chit, completed, at operations and started the long train ride to Maidenhead and my leave time. The irony is that at 5:30 that evening I had been right over Alice's house in Maidenhead. If I had been thinking, I could have asked to be dropped at nearby White Waltham aerodrome and thus have eliminated hours of train time. On the other hand, it had been a big thrill for me to hand in my first ferry chit personally.

Alice prodded me awake the first thing in the morning with that inevitable cup of tea and inquired what I intended to do with my leave day.

I produced a wide yawn and said, "Ohhh, just loaf."

Alice was stymied for a moment—but just for a moment. "That is fine. It will do you good to relax. That is what you need, complete relaxation. So why don't you come up to London with me and we will see the pantomime?"

Alice won; we went up to London. Before going to the theater, I dragged Alice into Austin Reed's for the final fitting of my ATA uniform. Finished, it still looked like the uniform of the street cleaning force. I was able to jazz it up somewhat by selecting a peaked cap to wear with it instead of the more common side cap. Alice clucked her approval and we swept on to the theater.

The pantomime is strictly a British type of theatrical entertainment. It involves loud music, slapstick comedy, and topical jokes with very little dialogue, hence it is a "dumb" show, or pantomime. Gestures take the place of words, and they are set to appropriate music. From an American point of view, the whole proceedings are shockingly disorganized with nothing remotely resembling a plot or an overall theme or even any meaning. Once I surrendered my need for structure, I enjoyed the colorful costumes, the banging music, and the silliness.

I went back to flying the next day in marginal weather. My assigned route was so skimpy that I could almost see around it: over to Monton-in-the-Marsh, up to Wellesbourne (past Stratford-on-Avon, the home of Shakespeare), and back to Luton. I found myself on the Luton leg and it was only twelve noon. Twelve noon—too early to go back to my base. The devil took hold of me and I decided to visit Kenny's aerodrome at Thurleigh. I had already located it at forty miles off my assigned course. "I will go in," I said to myself, although I knew that Kenny was still in the hospital. "I will just touch down, ask after Kenny, and get on back to Luton." It was not to be.

No sooner had I touched down and taxied off the active runway than a jeep loaded with American GIs came tearing up to me. They jumped out and swarmed over my Maggie, inspecting the pathetic little engine, the meager instruments, and marveling at the open-to-the-elements cockpit. They enticed me with an invitation to a typical Yank lunch: pork chops, roast potatoes, carrots, beans, and peaches for dessert. Because it was raining ever so slightly, offering me a legitimate excuse to tarry, I accepted the invitation. After lunch, I half-heartedly attempted to leave, but Flying Control got together with Bomber Command—that controls all landings and takeoffs—and between them they refused me a clearance. They even called Luton and reported, "Cadet Lussier could not take off; maybe in the morning if the weather clears up." Of course, there was the matter of why I had to land in the first place. With all this tomfoolery, the weather did close in and, with a clear conscience, I could spend the night at Thurleigh. I was supplied with a room and a bath, a jeep, and the services of two "batmen," the English phrase for helpers.

After another delicious meal, the CO, Colonel Putnam, rounded up some of his men and took us into the American officers' club in nearby

Bedford. I had not worn my uniform that morning, so I was still in my sloppy slacks and aging, green, oversized shirt. No one seemed to notice. The colonel steered me from table to table and introduced me to various lads, explaining their outstanding traits. Ray was pounding the piano. He was an exceptional pianist and Putnam leaned against the piano watching Ray's hands. While he watched and listened he told me how he had been in a tight spot over Holland not long ago, surrounded by bursts of flak and unable to escape. Ray had been Kenny's navigator. I was introduced to Putnam's own navigator, too. The colonel complained rather weakly, "The kid is very informal for an Air Force officer, but he always seems to get us where we want to go." The colonel, being twenty-seven, considered himself an old man among so many twenty-one-year olds.

I was awakened bright and early the next morning by the inevitable "cuppa," only this time it was coffee instead of tea, the difference between British and American stations. After a breakfast of pancakes, I insisted I had to get back to my base, but again Putnam intervened and proudly took me for a jeep tour of his base.

If I had gone to Thurleigh air base by land I would have taken a typical English country lane from Bedford, winding in and out among old trees, deep-rutted from wagon wheels, passing quaint thatch-roofed farm houses, and green meadows with now and then a placid cow grazing. When the road got to the base, a completely different world began. A bar blocked the entrance and would not be raised until the visitor was identified. Suddenly a concrete road began; on either side were neat rows of up-to-date buildings, officers' quarters, barracks, a mess hall, a Red Cross building, and endless hangars. There was even a theater.

Colonel Putnam was one of the original American staff, as was Kenny, to come over to England the previous year, 1942. He showed me through the Flying Fortress with which he had led the first U.S. raid onto the continent and many subsequent raids—Lille, Lorient, Saint-Nazaire, Wilhelmsburg. Then he drove me around the perimeter of the base. I was not sure I should be seeing all this secret stuff, but I took it in anyway. Again, as I was insisting I needed to get back to work, another former University of Maryland student, a Lieutenant Lambert, offered me a hop in his Fortress. My resolve to get back to my base suddenly faded. I grabbed my parachute from the Maggie and joined Lambert in the dispersal area.

Lambert's "baby," as he called it, was carrying a full bomb load, but he had decided to risk a short practice run rather than take the time to offload his cargo. There was endless labor in getting such a huge machine airworthy and his crew worked like beavers for almost an hour. Eventually we climbed into the craft, rumbled along the taxi strip out to the end of the active runway, and took off. What a thrill for me. I was impressed. Both Lambert and his copilot handled the great plane with extreme skill. I hung over the backs of their seats, observing everything they did. Lambert demonstrated for me how the PDI (power distance index) and the autogyro instruments worked. The English may be aces in engine production, but Americans outproduce them with ingenious instruments.

"Where are we headed?" I asked.

"To Luton," echoed the crew. "We want to see where Betty hangs out."

I was reluctant to agree, considering how insignificant my dirt strip looked compared to their rolling acres of concrete. But I politely agreed to navigate us there. By now I knew this landscape like the palm of my hand, even without a map. Lambert declined my help, insisting that he wanted to follow the headings that his own navigator "phoned up from his desk full of maps."

"He is really good," Lambert declared.

I watched our compass headings and the familiar landmarks below as the big Fortress drifted farther and farther off the course that would take us to Luton. I thought to myself, Lambert's navigator was not being "really good" today. I said nothing until first the navigator, then the copilot, and finally Lambert admitted they were lost and asked me to navigate. I was delighted. I slipped into the copilot seat, swung the great nose of the heavy ship back on course, and, to everyone's astonishment, took their ship due over Luton aerodrome. One discreet circuit of the field so I could brag later, "That was me," and back to Thurleigh. Although I felt I had earned the right, Lambert firmly refused to let me try a landing because of the bomb load we were carrying: six one-thousand pounders. We did not tell CO Putnam about our adventure.

"Now I must leave," I insisted.

One of the noncommissioned officers, a corporal, needed to get down to Luton and asked for a ride. Since I had broken so many regulations already on this visit, I stuffed him into my front cockpit and took him along, without a parachute—yet another broken regulation. I made the corporal squeeze down out of sight when we landed in Luton and taxied over behind a hangar where he could hop out undetected. My conscience was bothering me because of my absence from work so I requested another aircraft for the rest of the afternoon and was shoved into an old Tudor for an hour of British circuits and bumps. Following my glorious flight in the Flying Fortress, the "bumps" in the Tudor were a miserable comedown.

After operations shut down and we pilots were headed into Luton on the bus, I tried to tell Peter and Scotty about my great day.

"Did you see the Fortress that circled Luton this morning? That was me doing the piloting."

They snickered. "Oh, yeah, Betty, that was you all right. Don't you wish?"

I never did get to brag about my adventure.

CHAPTER 8

Accidents Will Happen

SCOTTY WAS CURING HIMSELF of being in love with Cadet Lussier. He had arranged a real date with a real woman for the evening. At the last minute he tried to weasel out of it, but Peter and I forced him to attend. I wanted him to spend more time with other women and possibly get interested in one special woman. He needed to branch out in his social life.

An item from the close-call column: The day after Other Betty and I made our deliveries to Reading aerodrome, the Germans bombed the place to smithereens, killing many people. At the time of the attack Jim Mollison was passing over with a load of taxi passengers. His Fairchild was raked with machine gun bullets, but there were no casualties in his plane. What happened to us personally in this war seemed to depend so much on happenstance, where we were at any particular moment. If Other Betty and I had been delivering our planes one day later the war would have been over for us.

One day Scotty and I took our day off and headed for London. We had a dual purpose: I was meeting Florence Searle, the passenger I'd met on *Scebeli*. It would be our first get-together since we had landed in England. Scotty was meeting one of his innumerable New Zealand buddies. Because we had missed the most convenient train and it was not raining for a change, we decided we should hitchhike. Our uniforms usually assured us a ride from some softhearted civilian with gasoline coupons and a car. During our first hour we just about kept pace with the train and a bus that alternated passing us and us passing the bus. We got one ride from a lad who was testing a truck and ended up in another truck that took us right into Piccadilly Circus in the heart of London. The road transportation gave me a fine chance to study the English scenery at close range; it was quite a contrast to the sky view. Scotty joined Florence and me for dinner at the Normandy, as he had intended all along. "Well, maybe he will like Florence," I thought, ever optimistic. When Florence had reported to the Ministry of Labour, she had been hoping for an assignment to a photographic unit, which would have made use of her experience as a script continuity worker in Hollywood. But, along with all the other women from *Scebeli*, she was stuffed into the Women's Auxiliary Air Force and sent to the south to drive military vehicles. She reported to us that she felt preparations were under way for an invasion of the continent. After dinner, we scoured all the likely places for Scotty's friend, but we never did turn him up.

I was due for a check ride in the Fairchild. One of the instructors at Luton took me up and carefully checked out my skills: stalls, straight and level, turns. Then suddenly he ordered me to fly him down to Thame, a town in Oxfordshire. The instructor seemed satisfied; at least, he did not correct me at any point. When I got us into the air smoothly and looked over to see how the inspector was reacting to my piloting skills, I saw that he had dozed off, sound asleep on a check ride. Well, maybe it is a hard life, being an inspector. I waggled my wings abruptly to wake him up and he remarked, not in the least embarrassed, "That's the highest compliment I can pay your piloting." It was not really my flying that put him to sleep: he was most likely tired from a long day at the desk.

I wore my uniform for the first time that day and felt awkward. My new peaked cap caused a flurry of fashion excitement among the women pilots, and Other Betty said she was determined to buy such a cap for herself.

One evening Kenny Reecher called, his voice strangely different from our University of Maryland days. He had been released from the hospital, was back in Thurleigh as squadron operations officer, and was anxious for us to get together. We agreed on a weekend meeting in London. However, the next morning I was assigned to fly Luton–Cranfield–Wittering–Duxford–Luton. The route took me temptingly close to Kenny's base and, on a whim, I veered in that direction and landed in Thurleigh. "I will say hello to Kenny and get right back to work," I promised myself. As I rolled to a stop, one of the mechanics grabbed my wing to steer me toward a hangar.

"I'm not staying," I shouted over the noise of my Maggie engine. "Just want to say hello to Lieutenant Reecher."

The mechanic shook his head. "Lieutenant Reecher just took off to go visit you in Luton."

Kenny and I must have crossed each other somewhere in midcourse, Kenny Luton-bound and me Thurleigh-bound. Later I learned that Kenny did indeed land his huge Fortress on the tiny Luton aerodrome, using up most of the available runway and causing a great flutter of emergency activity. The fire truck and an ambulance raced out to meet him, sure that they must have witnessed a forced landing. The Luton duty pilot and duty crew watched as all the American boys climbed out, one, two, three, four, five, six, and then the pilot, Kenny.

"Is this a forced landing, sir? What services do you require?"

Kenny looked mildly surprised and answered, "No services, thanks. We came to visit Cadet Lussier."

Nothing harsh was said to Lieutenant Reecher about his unorthodox visit, but when I returned CO Wood gave me a serious dressing down. He had been much too polite, too British, to say anything to the Yank, but he felt he could blame me for the visit and he did.

Another day, on my route Luton–Canfield–Halton–Luton, all of which are aerodromes you can see at the same time from two thousand feet on a clear day, I had deviated to Thurleigh in a Magister to give my new friends and Kenny a friendly shoot-up. I led behind me one of the RAF cadets in his trainer plane because he had been assigned my same route and two planes zooming around is more impressive than one. Once we were both in the air, I regretted my invitation because the young RAF pilot seemed to be insane. He almost rolled his wheels on the top of the control tower and raked the entire runway only about three feet off the ground. I knew I would be blamed for that. We tried playing follow-the-leader, with RAF leading. He chose to dive on a train; after it passed he kept along over the train tracks at zero feet. All of a sudden ahead of us some high-tension wires loomed up, crossing our path. I pulled up to a safe distance, but RAF did not. He was so intent on keeping on the ground that he was not looking ahead as he should have been and he did not notice the cables. He was heading right into them at 120 miles an hour. It made me sick to my stomach and I quickly selected a field to land in so I could go back to gather up the pieces. No more than one second before he would have struck the wires, he spotted them. There was no time for him to climb to safety, so he ducked underneath. A narrow escape. My hands were shaking all the way home. When we landed at Luton there was a message for both of us to report to CO Wood. We were trembling in our boots because we were sure someone had seen our high-tension cables episode and had reported it already. Instead, it turned out that CO Wood was annoyed because we had landed at Luton too close together.

"This is dangerous," he admonished us.

RAF and I stole a glance at each other. If CO Wood only knew what else was dangerous.

One morning, as soon as I got to the Luton aerodrome, I went into the operations room, as was customary, and checked out the station operations board. The board contained a permanent list of all the ferry pilots and student pilots who were assigned to Luton, myself among them. Each morning before our arrival the flight dispatcher would pencil in after our names our individual assignments for the day, our destination aerodromes, and the specific aircraft we would be flying. This day I had been assigned to pick up a Magister in Sywell and deliver it to Prestwick, Scotland. Although my group was in student status, occasionally we were assigned a ferry job. It was usually for the practical reason that ATA deliveries were falling behind schedule, but it also served to test our skills and stretch our abilities.

My assignment pleased me because the skies were clear and I had never been to Scotland, let alone flown into the Prestwick aerodrome. I scanned the list of my fellow pilots to see if any of them would be flying the same route or, at least, going in my direction part of the way. Usually two or three planes would be headed for the same destination on the same day and we always hoped for compatible pilots on our routes. It made for a pleasant lunch stopover and provided help shoving our planes around for refueling. Sometimes we could even switch assignments so that at the end of our day's work we would have friends to hang out with until we were picked up by the Anson or one of the Fairchilds being used to collect pilots.

To my pleasure that day Jim Mollison had the identical assignment, destined for the Prestwick aerodrome. Although we were both assigned to Luton, we had not become friends. Maybe it was the age difference or Bill Haines' ominous warning about Jim's charms with the women. Maybe in a subconscious way he was still mourning the loss of his wife, Amy. Although they had been divorced for several years when she was killed, pilots who knew Jim well said her death was a shock for him.

From the meteorology desk I picked up the latest weather forecasts for the area of my route and hurried into the pilots' lounge. I got out the proper maps with the intention of plotting my course. Mollison was in the lounge already, working on his flight plan. This was a pilot who, at thirty-eight years of age, had more than 5,370 flight hours recorded in his logbook. On top of that, he had been raised in Scotland. He could have flown from Luton to Prestwick with his eyes shut. Yet here he was, working out a meticulous flight plan.

Then I made my big mistake. After admiring Mollison's businesslike work habits, instead of following his good example and setting to work on my own flight plan I thought to myself, "Why should I make out a flight plan that would take me, an inexperienced pilot, a considerable amount of time? Why do that when the great Jim Mollison with those five thousand flight hours under his belt is making out his flight plan? Why don't I just follow Jim up to Scotland?" The sky was clear that day. We had been assigned the same model aircraft so we would be maintaining identical airspeeds. It seemed logical to me. I flopped into a chair near Mollison, as near as I could get without being intrusive, and fiddled around with my maps and the weather forecast, the winds, and cloud bases. Mollison glanced up at me and I took the occasion to remark that we were both delivering planes to Prestwick and was it not a great day to be flying? He grunted in reluctant acknowledgment and intoned that a pilot should never trust a sunny morning in England.

"Up there," he raised his eyes, "could be different," and he went back to his flight calculations. When he finished, he snapped his notebook closed, stowed it away in the knee pocket of his flight suit, and left the pilots' lounge with a nod of "See you later."

In a very few minutes, we were loaded with other pilots into an Anson and dropped off at Sywell aerodrome where our delivery planes awaited us. I located my aircraft, a Magister, down the line and ran my exterior check. I swung into the cockpit and ran my cockpit checklist. I cranked up and sat there, engine revved up, until I saw Mollison taxi out to the runway, take off, and establish a compass heading that would take him northwest. I intended it to take me northwest also.

For the next two hours we winged our way across industrial England and over Lancashire. In spite of Mollison's pessimism, we were meeting with ideal flying conditions. At this point, it seemed to me that we should be thinking about refueling soon and picking out an aerodrome where we could land for fuel. I scanned below for choices. Manchester had an inviting strip. That would have been my choice, but apparently our leader was sailing right over. I craned my neck forward to see what Mollison intended to do. He was no longer in front of me, nor to the left nor to the right. He and his Magister had disappeared. Maybe he had reversed his course while I was not looking and had landed back at Manchester. Whatever his thinking, he was not there in front of me, serving as my guide. I throttled back my speed, hoping he would fly past me. For some unexplainable reason, I did not return to Manchester to refuel, but opened my throttle again and barged on northwest. Maybe I thought I would overtake Jim. Soon I could see water and, although my map was somewhere unreachable on the floor and useless to me, I knew where I was. I identified Morecambe Bay and, contrary to an aviation dictate, I cut right across the open water. "Always skirt a body of water. It may add a few more minutes to your flight time, but it is easier to make a forced landing on land than it is on water."

Here I was, in the middle of Morecambe Bay, still looking forlornly for my intrepid leader, Captain Mollison. Somehow, I thought he would pop up in front of me, but soon I left the Bay behind and found myself over the National Forest of the Lake District. Trees, trees, and more trees, with no sign of a refueling oasis. There before me was the Solway Firth and right across the middle of it I went, with no regard for staying over dry land. From Solway I took a course out of my head that was a few degrees to the west of Mollison's original route. Over the Southern Uplands I went with no relieving aerodromes in sight. Suddenly I spotted more water ahead, the Firth of Clyde, if I was in luck. And I was in luck—and found I was passing right over the Prestwick aerodrome.

I scooted directly in without contacting the control tower, landed on the active runway and taxied to the dispersal area. A mechanic came out to help me tie down the Magister.

"Will you please check my fuel level, sir?" I asked him.

He put his stick into the wing tank, took it out, and held it up before my eyes. It was absolutely dry.

"Must have landed on fumes," he commented.

There was no sign at Prestwick of Captain Mollison. Suddenly I remembered that he was a Scotsman and this was his home turf. Surely he had stopped en route to visit an old Scot friend and spend the night. Or did he know all along that I was lurking behind him and he disappeared to teach me a valuable lesson: "Do your own navigation"?

The sky was darkening as I caught a bus into the Prestwick train station, bought a ticket, and spent a long, jarring night getting back to where I had started that morning. It was uncomfortable, but at least I was not worried about running out of petrol.

One day I was up in the sky, finishing my required solo flight time on the big old Hart and was preparing to sit down on an aerodrome with no wind sock displayed. Since I had no radio communications with the field control tower and could not ask for confirmation as to which air strip was in service, I landed on the strip indicated by the ground "T," a big wooden contraption used to show pilots which strip is in use. This "T" had been erroneously set cross-wind and a Hart does not like to be landed cross-wind—who does? Over on one wing and into a vicious ground loop I went, with those 500 horsepowers rearing straight up in the air above my face. "When in trouble, cut your power," so I did, and clambered out with embarrassment to confront the alert fire truck. A small patch on my wounded wing and I was cleared to get back in the air, looking forward to another lecture from CO Wood, and having to file an official accident report.

CHAPTER 9

The Seeds of Discontent:
No Continental Service for the Women

TO THE INTENSE RELIEF OF those on the ground, Luftwaffe raids on internal British targets were occurring with less and less frequency because the Germans felt pinched by the Allied bombing of their fuel sources. I did meet up with some of them on a cross-country that took me to Bristol. I watched two or three Messerschmitt 109s strafing the barrage balloons that protected the city. It was scary for me to think how easily they could bring me down if they spotted me. I knew that in the Maggie I could descend to below treetop level and fly around barns and haystacks until I was out of danger—or so I thought. I never understood why a powerful Messerschmitt would want to come after a putt-putting Magister trainer; the trainer would never be doing any harm to the fighter plane. Perhaps it was a matter of showing off your superior power without being in any danger yourself.

Just seeing the 109s at close range was scary for me. The next day, I was compensated for my fright. I was flying along in a slight haze when suddenly I flew right out of it. All below me the mud-colored haze covered the ground, but at two thousand feet the haze stopped as though someone had sliced it across with a huge butcher knife. There the clear air started, blue and pure and clean as a new baby blanket. Above me the sun was hot in contrast to the cool wind in my face; I was flying in an open cockpit. For those few moments I would not have wanted to be any other place in the world. Then the haze thickened, the sun went behind the nearest cloud, my hands became icy cold, and I felt quite normally miserable again.

Kenny and I finally engineered our historic first meeting on the European side of the Atlantic Ocean. We met in London. Kenny came accompanied by several of his Air Force buddies, those who did not believe there was such a thing as a female pilot in service. I do not know how I looked to Kenny, who had last seen me crossing the University of Maryland campus with a load of books in my arms, but he looked as he had in the old campus days, except he was thinner and his dark eyes reflected a new sadness that his fifteen completed missions must have put there. We all had dinner together at Maxime, where Chinese food was a specialty in spite of its French name. From Maxime's we repaired to the Coconut Grove, a service hangout, where we giggled about our aerodrome mix-up that had brought the wrath of my Luton commander down on my head. Then we danced the night away, fueled by many plain lemonades. Kenny and I stayed up until 3:00 in the morning, recalling all our campus episodes. We were like two little old people, reminiscing about their childhoods. We discussed our separate love lives. I told him about TC. He told me that he had no special girlfriend, that he still longed for my sister, Nita, but had the feeling that she did not long for him. I assured him she was still interested and the news cheered him up.

"When will she be joining you?" he asked.

"It's not looking too good right now, but we haven't given up on getting her over here."

As to our personal relationship, we agreed to try hard to be platonic friends, ignoring the fact that we were attracted to each other. It was fulfilling to talk to an old friend from home. New friends in a strange country are never the same as old friends from your own beloved country. Three hours later, having had only three hours sleep, I departed on the 6:00 train to make it back to my 'drome in time for flight duty.

On one of our London leaves, Scotty and I roamed through the Victoria and Albert Museum in Kensington. We were both aware of the museum's worldwide fame, but at that moment in history there was not much of value on view. Large sections of the building had been closed off and the artifacts moved to hiding places in the countryside where they would be safe from Luftwaffe air raids. The wrought iron exhibit was still open, with caskets and gates from the past. There were plaster reproductions of many of the famous statues that were in hiding and more reproductions in miniature of trains and aircraft; there was even a perfect miniature period dollhouse, fully furnished. I was awed by the realization that even in their hour of extreme danger the British authorities had taken the time and trouble to produce and display replicas of their treasures while hiding the originals in a safe place where the Nazi bombs would never find them. Why would the British do that? I suppose they knew they were facing a long and painful war, but they wanted their citizens to continue to have access to their culture.

For lunch Scotty and I stopped at the Cheshire Cheese, an old inn. It was the very spot where essayist and politician Joseph Addison and fellow essayist, politician, and playwright Richard Steele, cofounders of the periodical *Spectator*, met to carry out their famous discussions. Maybe we sat at one of the tables they had gathered around.

To lighten the atmosphere at the end of the day, we took in a movie, *Tomorrow We Live*. In fact, it did not lighten our spirits, being about the grim and futile efforts of the Free French.

⚜ ⚜

One day I was called in by the school adjutant and reprimanded for wearing a multicolored scarf with my uniform. How was I to know? It had never occurred to me that brightening up my somber navy blue garb with a little brilliance was a bad thing. Thinking it over more carefully from the point of view of the authorities, I suppose a colored scarf does defeat the purpose of a uniform, but it seems a big fuss to make over such a detail. Instead of yelling for me over the Tannoy, why couldn't the adjutant stop me when we passed in the hall and just say quietly, "Take that thing off." The adjutant also reminded me to keep my blond hair pinned back out of sight or cut most of it off. Since several of the RAF pilots had asked me particularly not to cut my hair, I opted for the pinned-back solution.

As I was exiting his office, the adjutant called out, "And where is your gas mask? I don't see any gas mask. This is a war, you know, Get one."

"Yes, sir," I replied.

That was the latest bugaboo—a fear of the Germans dropping poison gas on Britain out of sheer frustration as the war turned against them. It was rumored that the Nazis were manufacturing some types of poison gas. Gas masks were still hard to come by, and once again I made a mental note to locate one.

⚜ ⚜

There was some good news, news that was more important than my hair length. Our Allied positions were looking more and more favorable. In Africa, Operation Torch had been under way since November 1942, with successful landings accomplished in Morocco at Casablanca and in

Oran. These landings were manned mainly by U.S. forces. The British under General Montgomery were busy wrestling Tunisia out of Field Marshal Rommel's hands; by the end of January 1943, the British had captured Tripoli. There was much fighting back and forth and a surrender was achieved in May, after the Axis forces had been forced to retreat to the shores of the Mediterranean Sea, with 250,000 Italian and German troops becoming prisoners of war. Field Marshal Rommel was not among those prisoners. He had been whisked, somewhat in disgrace with Hitler because of his retreat, to northern Italy, where he took charge of German and Italian troop movements. General Hans von Arnim replaced Rommel in North Africa, but he was unable to stem the retreat. Later in 1943 Rommel would be transferred to the Channel coast and put in charge of preparing the coastal defenses against an anticipated Allied invasion. He became a key person in the battles to keep Europe in Nazi hands. Farther west, in Russia, Hitler had taken a huge gamble by attacking Stalingrad (now Volgograd); the Germans had suffered a disastrous defeat there.

We pilots of the ATA were gratified with the progress of our forces. We had been promised the chance to volunteer for service on the continent as soon as the essential aerodromes were liberated from German occupation, cleared of mines, and opened to Allied traffic. We looked forward to it with nervous anticipation. It would be the culmination of our many months spent hauling planes around an England made dreary with war. We could then finally feel we were a real part of the war effort, a contributing factor to an Allied victory. We did feel some trepidation because we would be flying in danger. The Luftwaffe pilots were not likely to see any difference between unarmed ferry planes and armed-to-the-teeth fighter craft; we would only count as another addition to their total score of downed planes. So Scotty, Peter, and I made it known to our CO that we wanted to be the first volunteers for continental service after the troops landed in France.

My work at Luton aerodrome at that time half consisted of taxi pick-ups, as the pilot of the five-passenger Fairchild, and half of trundling around England on those familiar practice route courses, getting ever more familiar with those seven hundred aerodromes. On the days I was ferrying pilots, I had to stick strictly to my schedule of dropping pilots off where they needed to be to make their pick-ups and collecting other pilots where they should be waiting if all had gone well with their delivery flights. Any variation from my assigned schedule was a setback for the entire day's routine. On the days I was assigned to fly practice routes, my schedule was a whole lot more relaxed: nobody was depending on me and my Fairchild to appear at any set time.

One day I was assigned a route that took me south to Westonzoyland, then farther south to Warmwell, back to Gatwick and Odiham, and so home to Luton. I had never seen the southern coast of England, having disembarked from *Scebeli* in Liverpool far to the north and west, so I was taken by the sight of the beaches and glimpses of the English Channel. Seeing the Channel brought to my mind how close we were to our enemy—just over the narrow strip of water. Southampton lay sprawling in and out of the surrounding hills. The town looked quaint, but it was sadly battered from the many bombings it had suffered. I was hoping to see one of the storied Nazi raiders who were rumored to patrol the English coast on their way home from battle in the English skies, looking for strays and innocents like me. It seems a contrary thing to me to have done—to seek out a powerful enemy—and it is hard to find any sense for doing so. Perhaps I felt that if I flew low enough I would be safe from sight and I could still get a look at a Messerschmitt 109 in flight. I circled around the area for a time, scanning the horizon, but the air was empty of all activity and I headed back to Gatwick. When I got within sight of Luton, I checked my watch. It was only 4:00 in the afternoon. Temptation beckoned. I scooted over to Thurleigh. Kenny had asked me to give him some dual time on my little Magister. In return, he dangled the promise of some time for me on his Fortress. How could I resist and let that chance go by?

As soon as I landed, Kenny came bounding out of his squadron operations office. He told me that early in the morning the squadron had been out on a mission. The target had been Wilhelmshaven, located in Germany off the North Sea.

Kenny said, "The antiaircraft gunners must have their master's degrees in gunnery because they were so accurate."

All the participating Fortresses took some damage. One of them had not returned, shot down over Germany. Observers had counted parachutes ejecting from the damaged ship, but could not agree on how many crewmembers had made it safely to the ground. Some of the crew were now prisoners. It made me ashamed that I had been hanging around the south coast that morning, looking for enemy fighters for fun. We mutually decided not to talk any more about the raid.

Kenny climbed into my forward cockpit and took over. I was amazed to find him smooth and gentle on the controls. I had imagined that with all his B-17 training he would tend to be ham-fisted on a small plane. He was doing so well that I held both my hands up in the air to indicate that he had complete control. He circled his airfield twice and zoomed down too close to his mess hall. After a time, I waggled the stick to indicate that it was time for us to land. The open cockpit made it too noisy to communicate by voice so Kenny gave me a roger sign with his thumb and I settled back peacefully, arms crossed, to watch his approach. The Maggie proceeded gently across the aerodrome, getting lower and lower. "Aha," I thought, "Kenny is giving me a demonstration of his close-to-the-ground technique." Just as the Maggie passed over one of the Fortresses, she dipped her wing and took a dive for the ground. I had withheld interfering as long as I could because it is bad manners to back-seat fly with another pilot. Finally, I could not stand the suspense: we were about to hit something, like a Fortress. I grabbed the stick in one hand, pushed the throttle wide open with the other hand, and climbed her up to safety just before the wing touched. I was thinking, "This is my Maggie and I am responsible." As soon as we touched down, I started giving Kenny a lecture about foolhardy flying. He looked mildly astonished. "I thought you signaled that you wanted to make the landing."

Maggie had flown all the way across the aerodrome on her own. If we had crashed, what a scandal it would have created.

I should have learned from that incident to be more cautious when Kenny was in my aircraft, but no. The very next time we were up together Kenny started making peculiar motions with his hands. Assuming he was signaling that he wanted to have the controls to himself, I raised both my arms in the hands-off sign and went to watching the landscape. Abruptly, I found myself upside down with my maps and gloves flopping about the open cockpit and my eyes full of dust. I clutched frantically at my much-too-loose-for-this-sort-of-activity safety harness and screamed at Kenny to right us. My poor little trainer was beyond the age of graceful aerobatics. At that point the engine gave a feeble cough and died, as I knew it would because Maggie did not have a carburetor adjusted for slow rolling. Dead silence followed, upside down with the blue sky below us and all the green hills above. A few more seconds passed while Kenny snapped the Maggie back and put us into a glide and the engine picked up again.

Kenny's comment on climbing out of the cockpit unharmed was, "My four engines spoil me for depending on one engine only."

I wondered how happy his Fortress would have been, flying around upside down.

Later that day I paid for my transgression by having to make an emergency landing at Lichfield aerodrome with a dead engine. Four engineers and three hours later still had not put the Maggie engine back into service. I felt guilty not telling them about our slow roll that was surely the cause of the problem. Eventually they got me able to fly back to my destination, Barton-in-the-Clay.

Raiders struck Luton one night. I do not know what they were after because as far as I knew there was nothing strategically important in our area. Maybe the Luftwaffe was acting on some bogus intelligence. One of the bombs hit so close that the Guys' house shuddered all over. Mrs. Guy came dashing into my room and awakened me from a sound slumber to tell me that I better get dressed and stay alert for the rest of the night, just in case we got hit.

I muttered an unenthusiastic, "Uh huh," and dropped off to sleep again. I had to fly in the morning. Mrs. Guy was not to be put off. She yanked open my blackout curtain to scare me awake. By rolling over on one side and opening an eye, I could see the creepy searchlights sweeping about the sky, the brilliant bursts of British ack-ack fire, and our own aircraft batting across the sky amid the blam . . . blam of an occasional bomb. It was dramatic and harrowing at the same time, but I dropped off to sleep; I had to go to work in the morning. When the sun rose, our house was still standing. We had been lucky one more night.

When I told my ATA gang about my near calls with Kenny, they came up with some incredible parachute tales, stories to send shivers up and down my spine.

Just before I joined the ATA a young pilot jumped out of a bomber on a practice exercise and neglected to snap on his 'chute first. He fell from two hundred feet at least, and broke only one leg. Then there was a Russian who bailed out at 20,000 feet; he had on his 'chute, but it failed to open. He landed in a huge drift of soft snow, dug himself out, and walked away, so the Russians swear. An RAF pilot forgot to take his 'chute along on a mission, hard as that is to believe. When his engine conked out and he was forced to ditch, he glided to within twenty feet of the ground, turned his aircraft over and allowed himself to fall out unhurt. Would that even be possible?

Myrtle, a cute American pilot from New Jersey; Tanya, the English beauty; and Other Betty provided me with much-appreciated female company. Myrtle had come over to England the year before with Jacqueline Cochran. Myrtle was posted to Luton where I saw her daily. Tanya, of course, was in my cadet class and paralleled my progress through the training, although she already had many flying hours recorded in her logbook. Other Betty was on ferry duty and dropped in frequently. She often stayed overnight so we could eat together and exchange experiences. Kenny's CO, Colonel Putnam, started calling on us to attend the dances he arranged for his officers at the officers' club in nearby Bedford. Sometimes it took adept juggling to meet our social obligations and keep everyone happy. The colonel was clamoring for dance partners one afternoon and Ole, my gunner friend, on leave between *Scebeli* voyages, was in town to visit me. After work, I had Scotty tell Ole I had been caught off base for the night, then I met Myrtle at the Red Lion pub and took the next train to Bedford. The colonel whisked us to the club in his car. Other Betty was already there and numerous other service women had been rounded up. We danced and danced and consumed huge hamburgers and chicken sandwiches. Kenny's navigator, Ray, took over the piano and boomed out "There's a Fortress That's Leaving Bombay." Soon all the boys were gathered around Ray at the piano, singing lustily, drinks in hand, arms draped cozily around their partners for the evening. Someone started the Army Air Corps song and it became a moment for me to remember, those too-young fliers singing their hearts out, not knowing if they would still be able to return the following evening.

I wanted to spend the night at the air base, but Myrtle said, "I've got my check ride on the Hart first thing in the morning and I need some sleep," so we caught the last train back to Luton.

The next day after work I did see my patient friend, Ole. Peter, Scotty, and I took him for a tour of Luton, mostly the pubs of Luton. When I was saying goodbye at his hotel, he gave me an irate speech about not needing "those two nursemaids" all our time together. He knew that word in English and he was referring to my pals, Scotty and Peter. He said he wanted to be taken seriously as a suitor. That was never a possibility—TC stood firmly in the way. I patted him on the cheek in my sisterly fashion and said goodnight.

One day it came time for Kenny to pay me back for the Magister flight time I had given him. The day before his squadron had suffered a horrific midair collision between two B-17s. The planes were total washouts, about half a million dollars worth, but no lives were lost, which is the most important thing. It must have been raining parachutes in Thurleigh for a few moments, fourteen of them. I wonder how the British dealt with all that sensitive and secret debris?

I was assigned a Fairchild to deliver over at Thame aerodrome in the morning, a short hop. Since I would not be picked up for the return to Luton until the afternoon, I stopped en route for my Fortress dual time with Kenny. When I set down in my Fairchild taxi, causing some curiosity because I usually showed up in a Magister, Kenny was about to test fly a Fortress that was fresh out of the repair hangar. Her name was Sweet Pea. I joined Kenny on board. At first I hung around the cockpit, leaning over Kenny's shoulder, watching his instruments and commenting on his flying style.

"You have a look-at-me-Mama expression on your face," I told him.

With Kenny's permission, I followed the catwalk back into the bare fuselage, then dropped down into the glass nose where I stretched out on my stomach and watched the landscape swish past; at one thousand feet, I could see all the details. Cows were visible in their pastures and the narrow country roads cut through the countryside. I thought, "Wouldn't my father get a kick out of this?" And this crew would be proud to have him as a passenger with his illustrious past. In his photograph album, he had many shots of World War I bombers. I wondered if he had ever hopped a ride in a bomber on his airfield in France. Or in Canada— had he ever hopped a ride? I threaded my way back to the cockpit, put on a set of earphones and listened to some jazz music. There we were, one thousand feet in the air, behind those four huge engines, a warring England underneath, evening lurking overhead, and we were listening to "I Met Her On Monday." Whenever I have heard that tune since then, I remember my ride with Kenny and his crew and hear once again that quip from the tower to the refueling crew, "Do you have time to refuel a Fairchild for a fair child?"

When I got to Thame and delivered my Fairchild, Peter was there, having delivered another Fairchild. Together, we stretched our legs by touring the little town of Thame. It was a quaint hamlet, all old stone houses with thatched roofs. The streets were narrow and twisted like the letter "S." Hardly any cars were in view; instead, there were many horse-drawn wagons. We finished off our tour by pacing the 'drome perimeter twice before our ride picked us up. Still, we were back in Barton so early that I was assigned to deliver another plane, this time to Luton, "On your way home," as the dispatcher put it. One RAF cadet was doing the same job, so we tucked our wings together and formatted neatly the short distance to Luton aerodrome.

I had overnighted at Thurleigh base, my Maggie in the hangar with a U/S tag on it. While a Yank mechanic worked on my plane, the day stretched before me. Ray offered to give me an hour of instruction on the Link trainer used for learning to fly on instruments. He loved that Link trainer and wanted all of us to use it as much as possible. Naturally, the cockpit was the bomber type and the controls responded differently from those I was accustomed to. What a show I put on, up and down and all around. Ray, monitoring my lesson from an earthbound cockpit, called out for me to execute a 180-degree turn. After I had turned about 400 degrees, he inquired politely if I ever intended to stop.

There was a mission over Europe scheduled for later that morning. I could tell by the dull hum of the Fortress engines warming up, a hum that pervaded the mess hall a mile from the aircraft dispersal sites. I could tell also by the tightness around CO Putnam's mouth and by the stopwatches propped up in front of everyone's morning glass of tomato juice in the mess hall.

I spent a half-hour vainly trying to persuade one of the pilots into taking me with him over Germany or France. I wanted to experience what those pilots did. After listening to one hundred reasons why I would only be a hazard at 30,000 feet, I accepted that I was not wanted and wandered off to the top of the control tower to watch the takeoff with Colonel Putnam.

As the minutes ticked away, the hum of activity began to die down. I examined the sky; the weather was still open up above. However, the condition of the English sky is no indication of conditions in the German sky. It turned out that the continental weather was closed in, making precision bombing impossible. The impending mission was scrubbed.

Just as the aircrew began to relax, energetic Putnam called for a practice mission. His new order sent the crews scuttling back to their ships. Sensing a new chance, I again presented my plea to be included as crew.

"What can happen?" I begged.

CO Putnam relented and grudgingly agreed that I could ride along in his Fortress, the target ship. I pulled a pair of khaki overalls over my navy uniform and we were soon jostling along the aerodrome perimeter track to the dispersal site. We jerked to a stop in the shadow of a Fortress wing. The CO was lost in the sheath of papers on his lap.

The driver of the jeep leaned back and asked in an awestruck voice, "You aren't going to ride in that thing, are you?"

"Of course I am. Why not?" I answered.

"Oh nothing, nothing at all, except I wouldn't be caught dead up there if I didn't have to go. You be sure to take your 'chute along."

The ground crew looked at me with the same you're-condemned-to-die expression on their faces. I began to wonder if I had left my last will and testament in good order. Just then Putnam came out of his cloud of papers and swung his lanky frame into the fuselage of the Fortress. I scrambled after him, following along behind on the catwalk, and climbed into the copilot's seat. Putnam had promised I could fly. We buckled our safety belts and were soon rumbling along the perimeter track and turning into the wind. I still like the sensation of rolling down the runway faster and faster and the thrilling moment when the aircraft leaves the ground. We hovered over the aerodrome until the flight had formed above us. The planes banked one by one and headed cross-country toward the North Sea. Opening our throttles, we surged along after them. Putnam explained to me that his group had been working out a new formation bombing technique. It seemed to solve many problems on paper, but it needed a trial in a practice run before they could use the method with confidence in combat. Putnam planned two runs—one at a low level, the other at altitude. We would be on the altitude run and piloting the tow ship, an old model "E" B-17 named Emma. To make Emma faster in the air for her target-towing duties, she was stripped of all her heavy armament except for the waist and belly-gun turrets. The lower formation consisted of twenty of the newer "F" model Fortresses. After all the Fortresses had lumbered into the air, we joined the lower formation, throttled back, and flew wing tucked into wing for half an hour, all the way to the Channel coast.

I took the wheel while Putnam gave his attention to judging his pilots' formation technique. In combat, perfect formation is necessary to survival; every minute spent achieving it on a practice mission is a minute well spent. Without warning, the entire flight disappeared before us in a bank of clouds. The next instant Emma plunged in after them. We peered anxiously into the all-enveloping white vapor. I waited for Putnam to take over the controls, but he had left me in charge. A slight break in the white cloak revealed a Fortress rudder perilously close to our wing. The CO made a nervous downward motion with his hand. I pushed the wheel forward and we descended one hundred feet to lessen the danger of collision. Another tense moment and we emerged from the cloudbank into the sunshine as suddenly as we had entered it. Ah, English weather. The sea now spread out before us in placid serenity with the sun making lovely shadings of blue and green on the water. The Fortresses swung into tighter formation again and I throttled back Emma so we could see the bombs fall.

Putnam yelled above the roar of the engine, "Follow along below and behind the formation, please. That way I can observe the maneuver. After the bombs are away, we can climb up with them and reel out the tow target. Then the fun begins."

I recalled the sympathetic faces of the ground crew and smiled weakly.

Putnam was anxious to see how his newly designed bombing pattern would work out in practice. The flight made a dummy run over the chosen area and dropped aluminum paint, which is something like mercury in that it holds together more than ordinary paint would; it serves as a target. It struck the water and spread over the waves in a huge circle, throwing back the sun's rays. Still in good formation, the Fortresses made a circuit of the area, then flew directly over the paint target. "Bombs away," and, like rows of disciplined matchsticks, the bombs dropped out of the open bays. They seemed to hang suspended in the nothingness for a second. A moment later they were clustering on the paint blob and throwing up plumes of spray. Colonel Putnam smiled. His new technique must have been a success.

I, too, had a moment of feeling absolute nothingness, soul-filling nothingness, the beautiful blue sky, the silvery sea, the shining, relentless Fortresses. Up there, like that, it was hard to reconcile the heart-stopping beauty with our grim real purpose.

A word into the intercom and the crewmembers in the tail began to reel out the tow target. I felt Emma surge forward with an increase of throttle; Putnam was at the helm again. We climbed out of our position that the crews call the Purple Heart corner and started romping back and forth in front of the formation, through it, over it, under it. The tail guns of the formation Fortresses flashed red. The belly guns opened next and the top turret gunners joined in as we swept by them. I could see tracer bullets plainly spitting out. One tracer went past our wing too close and the crew ducked behind their armor plate and stayed there. Since I would never have an experience like this again, I did not duck behind the armor plate. Instead, I dashed from one end of the Fortress to the other, first down in the navigator's nose, then up for a spell of piloting, then down in the tail to watch the "drogie" (the tow target) drawing all the fire, then into the waist position. We made one more pass at the formation, meeting them head-on and climbing steeply above them. Their guns blazed away and suddenly the drogie whipped off into the wind, a direct hit.

A final dip of her great wings and Emma turned back toward the English coast, losing half our altitude so we could speed up and land ahead of the formations. Putnam allowed me to do all the flying and buried his nose in his notes, never making any corrections to my piloting and navigating. He said he had heard rumors that I could fly this big thing and he wanted to see for himself if it were true. He took over the controls to land and we lingered on the taxi strip to watch the formation peel off, one by one, and come in to land.

I stayed for supper with the officers; while I was washing up in the colonel's quarters, I saw his Distinguished Flying Cross (DFC) that the British had awarded him for leading the first American raid over Germany. Putnam also had the Silver Star and the Air Medal. He was only twenty-seven years old, but to Kenny and me he seemed like an elderly gent.

After supper I caught a train back to Luton for the night. After my day in the air, the train seemed so slow. TC once wrote me, "I bat across the sky all day at four hundred miles an hour, then spend five hours trying to hitchhike the paltry sixteen miles into town for the evening."

Back in Luton, Peter and Scotty were still awake and strolling the town. I tried to tell them about my unbelievable day over the North Sea.

"Piloting a Flying Fortress all by yourself, towing a drogie through a twenty-plane formation, of course you were. And we are Winston Churchill."

When I thought about it again, that is exactly how I had spent my day. Only the bit about Winston Churchill was exaggerated.

After I was alone that night, I looked at the ceiling and tried to understand why I should have all the skills to be a passable bomber pilot or a fighter pilot and still not be allowed to serve in combat, only because I am the wrong gender.

CHAPTER 10

A Well-Deserved Break

PETER WALSHE WAS ALWAYS my favorite flight companion. He did not seem to have any nerves or fear. We flew some hair-raising routes together. Our reputation must have spread because the dispatchers in Ferry Flight seldom assigned us taxi jobs or even practice routes together. One morning Ferry Flight slipped up and sent us out together. We were a lethal combination in our navy blue uniforms and jaunty caps—tall, lanky Peter and short, stocky Betty. The route that the dispatcher sent us off together on took us to Brize-Norton, Colerne, Andover, and home to Luton. We agreed that Peter would lead the way going out and I would command on our return flight. We scooted along in our Maggies, about one hundred feet off the deck all the way. Down into the fields we went, between challenging trees, romping beside haystacks. I pushed my throttle full forward and cut right over in front of Peter's propeller wash, not remembering the slipstream effect. Later he told me that I had almost caused him to clip a wing on the ground. On arrival in the vicinity of our first landing aerodrome, Brize-Norton, we needed a signature to verify our presence there. Peter pointed out the landing strip and motioned for me to take the lead. I wondered why he was signaling me, but went ahead and landed, with Peter following close behind. As we rolled to a stop, we both realized that we were not in Brize-Norton at all. We were in a little aerodrome called Hullavington. Peter had lost his map in one of our crazy dives at a haystack. I must have been flying low myself because I was zipping along in the rear of Peter's plane, gasping at the way he was skimming objects, when it dawned on me that I was looking up at his fuselage. My plane must have been lower than Peter's.

Scotty and I coincided on another of our days off and together decided we should do some more serious sightseeing. Our last target had been the Victoria and Albert Museum and we needed a new conversational subject for our pub-crawls. After we got to London, we started our tour in Petticoat Lane. Neither of us was particularly interested in the Lane, but it was the point of constant queries: "Have you been to Petticoat Lane yet?" and "You must see Petticoat Lane." Hidden away in an old quarter of London, Petticoat Lane is known for its variety of vintage clothing on the scruffy side alongside current fashion. The vendors hawked their wares vigorously, exploiting the desire of the visitors to make off with a piece of old England.

"Look at this stone, will ya. It's straight from Windsor Castle," or "Queen Mary of Scotland herself wore this very pair of gloves."

Scotty and I resisted the temptation to buy Queen Mary's gloves or to become the owners of a piece of Windsor Castle. Since it was an unusual, bright day, we walked ourselves over to the Tower of London, hugging the shore of the Thames River. I could not see why they called it a "tower" when it looked more like a great fort with a large, dry moat wrapped around it. It was dotted with thick-walled turrets that enforced its fort-like appearance. We were remembering all the innocent and not so innocent royals who had been imprisoned and died there, going back almost a thousand years. Adding the human touch, beside one of the ancient turrets some enterprising person had strung up a clothesline from which shirts and pants were drying in the rare sunshine. It was a twentieth-century prop in an eleventh-century setting.

After our exhausting sightseeing, we treated ourselves to tea in Stanmore, with its tiny gardens and thatch-roofed houses, where we met up with some friends of Scotty's. Our pleasant day ended back in central London. Scotty went off with his rowdy New Zealand friends and I went to find Kenny.

Kenny and I had made plans to meet and dance the night away. At the hotel there was a message from him. He would not be joining me for the evening. One of his Fortresses had not returned from the mission that day and Ray was on board as navigator. My heart contracted. I wandered around my silent room, feeling utterly useless. Below me was Oxford Street, usually crowded and busy all night. Now it was ominously deserted. Just beyond was the famous Marble Arch, looking drab and dreary under its wartime grime. I had a flash of Ray banging away on the piano, shouting out the lyrics of "There's A Fortress That's Leaving Bombay," and standing in front of me in the mess muttering, "Mmm, nothin' but nice." That was his approval statement. From that day to this, he had become a prisoner somewhere in France—if his luck had held up, if his parachute had opened, if he had landed alive. The Germans had been known to machine gun American and British pilots in slowly descending parachutes. Ray had just been appointed to squadron operations the day before and this was the thirteenth raid for him. Kenny, who had chosen the crewmembers, said he had been reluctant to send Ray out, but operations could not come up with a replacement so Ray had filled in.

Now Kenny had the excruciating task of notifying Ray's parents that he was missing. After a certain time went by with no further news of Ray, he would pass to the status of missing in action and presumed dead. Then Kenny would be contacting Ray's parents again.

Kenny telephoned me. "I hate this job," he said, "choosing the men who might not come back."

He was close to tears. I retired early in my hotel room because Ray's loss put me in a down mood. Then, too, I had to get back to my post first thing in the morning. At 1:00 in the morning my telephone jangled once again. It was Scotty, shivering out on a bench on the Embankment, unable to find a bed in any hotel.

"Come up and sleep in Kenny's room," I offered, having forgotten to cancel it when Kenny called that he would not be coming in to London. Up Scotty came, past the grumpy night porter who snickered suggestively to see that the two rooms were conveniently connected with a door.

"It must be the English way of discreetly accommodating us service people," I observed, but I did not bother to explain that Kenny and I did not use that door. TC was always between us. Scotty and I were still standing in our connecting door and talking when the shrill air-raid siren sounded.

Scotty groaned, "No more sleep tonight, but at least I will be warm."

We switched off our lights, drew back the blackout curtain, and threw open wide the window, leaning out over Oxford street to watch the spectacular show. A huge Nazi bomber droned overhead in plain sight while our searchlights frantically felt around for him. They first caught up with him right above our hotel, and flak went up in amazing quantities. Brilliant bursts in the sky and ear-splitting explosions all around us. There was a regular rain of metal coming down. The bomber passed on to the south of the city, lurching crazily from side to side in an attempt to evade the searchlights. Eventually the raider must have been shot down because there was the sound of a sizeable explosion a few miles south of the city and the sky lit up as though it were ablaze.

Scotty and I had pulled up chairs in front of the window and continued to sit there in the dark, watching this dramatic war scene unfold before us as if it were on a stage. We attempted, without much success, to find any reason for this to be happening. Here we were—Scotty all the way from New Zealand, me from the United States—and up there in the sky was someone from Germany, with the two of us trying to kill the German, and vice versa. And what would be the end? War is insane, we decided, and went off to our beds for the few hours that remained before our train left for Luton and another workday began.

※ ◎⤻

The Tannoy had been nagging us all day. "Wear your full and formal uniform tomorrow and report at 9:00 sharp in the morning, not a minute later," it droned, repeating the same message throughout the day. We pilots speculated on what they had in store for us. I suggested that William Stephenson might be going to review us, because of his flying background and his continued interest in flying services. I knew he was expected in London any day now for a visit and that he was considered an important link in the war machine, being the head of BSC in the United States. But I also knew from Alice that the great man had not arrived in England yet. They did bully us into compliance, though, and when we all turned up before 9:00 in the morning, looking tidy, trim, and businesslike, we were herded out to our largest hangar and lined up in some imitation of the military. We had never practiced formation, so we were ragged.

A hush fell over the space. The hangar door was rolled back all the way and our mystery visitors walked in. They were a middle-aged woman and two teenage girls. But this was not just any trio of English womanhood: it was Queen Elizabeth, wife of George VI, with their daughters, the princesses Elizabeth and Margaret. They had come to review us. When the bombing of London had begun, the royal family had been offered asylum in Canada, as had the royal family of the Netherlands. The family from the Netherlands accepted the shelter. The English royalty did not. I imagined them talking it over in Buckingham Palace, King George VI and Elizabeth, the queen consort. I imagined her opting to remain in residence at the palace. I imagined it thus because when Buckingham Palace was hit by a bomb, Queen Elizabeth was known to have sighed with relief and remarked that now they were in the same situation as the rest of the Londoners: vulnerable. She had not been born royalty. She was what English law calls a commoner. She could empathize with all those Londoners enduring the nightly bombings. Now she stood in front of the ATA pilots, passing us in review. Queen Elizabeth probably had requested this assignment. She must have been curious to see a group of women performing a so-called man's job, piloting planes.

Queen Elizabeth was a tiny woman. She looked barely five feet tall. She was dressed in a drab, dark suit, thick wool stockings, and serious walking shoes. On her head was a no-nonsense hat; she wore a modest brooch on the lapel of her suit jacket. It looked as if she had on two sweaters under her wool jacket; maybe the palace was drafty. She started down the line of pilots to greet each of us personally. The two young princesses—sixteen-year-old Elizabeth and her younger sister, Margaret—followed dutifully after her. Elizabeth was very somber. We had read that she was serving currently as a subaltern in the Auxiliary Territorial Service, but I had never seen a photograph of her in the uniform. Margaret, being younger, was less serious. She nudged Elizabeth in the back to hurry her along and get this chore over with. They both wore little dresses and woolly hats. All three of these royal persons had the extraordinarily translucent complexion achieved only by living in England's foggy, foggy air. The Queen gave a short speech that she read in her high-pitched voice, thanking us for offering our lives in patriotic service to England. She seemed to know that many of us were foreigners. With a final gesture, taking in all of the pilots, she and her daughters swept out of our hangar and were gone. Did that really happen? It seemed so much like a dream. Peter, Scotty, and I looked at each other in disbelief.

While I was still in a magical palace mood later that day, I saw a beautiful sight. I was making a close-by Fairchild delivery. The sun was shining brightly, and the haze had just cleared. I was flying at two hundred feet above the ground when suddenly a hill sloped up ahead. Right on the top of it was a massive, sprawling castle. There were numerous wings stretching out from the main structure, all with impressive turrets and huge leaded casements for windows. Then a vivid green lawn flashed into my view, rolling away from the castle walls, down to a gully with a peaceful lake. It was like a picture from my history book: the incredibly green-blue water with groves of carefully planted trees all around and the banks of the lake dense with flowering shrubs. The scene went by in a flash. I was so mesmerized that as I swept past I kept staring over my shoulder, imagining myself back in the days of King Arthur. I would not have been surprised to see a steed gallop up the graveled road carrying a knight in shining armor on his back. As I was still daydreaming, I turned my head forward in time to see a murderous Spitfire zoom across my flight path. The contrast was so sharp—the old, romantic castle, invoking past centuries, and the streamlined, vicious Spitfire hell-bent to its murderous task.

When I landed back at Barton after flying Kimble–White Waltham–Luton, I was paged to the flight office for a cablegram. The sickish feeling filled my stomach again. I crossed my fingers: Make it not be Dad, please. Nor TC, I implored. It turned out to be a cheery greeting from one of my Maryland friends, hinting that he would be seeing me soon. England was indeed filling up with Americans.

Peter passed his final check and was awarded his wings. He had survived several months of supervised service, sometimes cross-country flights, sometimes ferrying pilots to their destinations. I could not have been any more elated had it been my own wings. To celebrate the big occasion, we invaded the Green Man pub after supper at our various billets. We drank a few toasts. We had to do without Scotty's presence because he had involved himself in a minor accident at Gatwick aerodrome and had to spend the night there having repairs effected.

The day after Peter got winged I was called in to Flight Captain Harry Woods' office. F/CCO Woods was our commanding officer. He was sitting behind his desk toying with a small model of a Spitfire. I was tempted to tell him that when I was a youth I used to make those models, but I held my tongue. He rose to his feet and, with no ceremony at all, leaned across his desk and pinned my own golden wings onto my uniform jacket. In ATA you started out as a lowly cadet no matter how many flying hours you brought with you. When you received your wings, you were designated a third officer. From that rank you passed to second officer, where you were assigned to handle faster, more-powerful aircraft. Finally, as a first officer you were qualified to fly almost any model with wings and an engine that came down the pike. After all those months of being Cadet Lussier in my plain uniform, it felt good to look down at those golden wings and know that henceforth I was Third Officer Lussier. The CO gave me what must be his routine pep talk with lots of cautionary advice. It made me feel discouraged for a moment, but when I thought about it I realized there would be no gain in our instructors encouraging overconfidence in newly minted third officers. Better to keep us wary and ready for the worst. As if to cheer me up after his lecture, the CO ordered me to fly him over to Thame and back, my first official flight duty as a third officer.

Scotty finally came home through a thick haze. He had been out for five nights. He could not stand being out another one. It was already 7:00 in the evening when he landed, well after the allowed landing time. Scotty had received his golden wings before he went out into that fog. To celebrate our three pairs of golden wings we all supped together in a newly opened restaurant, with dessert afterward at Scotty's billet—peaches, cream, and coffee from New Zealand, unheard-of luxuries in England.

My first thought the next morning when I woke up on the first day of my three-day wing leave (time off allotted to all pilots after completing training) was, "What shall I do to celebrate the momentous occasion?"

By the time I was dressed I had decided to whistle up to Thurleigh and demand some exchange time on Kenny's Fortress. He owed me time and I had never had practice with oxygen at altitude.

I took the train to Bedford and walked around until I spotted an Air Corps uniform who, sure enough, had a jeep and was headed to Thurleigh.

"Could I hitch a ride?"

Yes I could, and the uniform dropped me at the control tower office. As we got near the tower I detected the bustle of unusual activity. I bounded up the stairs, burst into the little glass-enclosed observation room, and asked what was going on. In one corner an operator bent over his wireless set, sending terse directions to aircraft far out of sight. In another corner, an officer frantically conversed on three telephones at once. At an open window another officer stood behind a pair of binoculars. The man behind the binoculars looked up long enough to inform me that the mission of the day was about to begin. He added that there was a better view of the takeoff from the edge of the runway.

I dashed down the tower steps, begged a ride from a nearby driver, and leaped into his jeep; we tore around the perimeter track to the head of the takeoff runway. Half a dozen other vehicles were parked there. Colonel Putnam motioned me to join him where he stood in a group of officers. I did so. They were all glancing in unison, first at their watches, then at the sky, and finally at the waiting bombers on the tarmac. What a majestic sight those bombers were. They waited on their individual sites like great, impatient birds of prey. Their propellers turned over in warm-up setting and the noise of the engines filled the early morning air with a tremendous drone. It was to be a daylight raid, far more dangerous that the usual night raids, and Kenny was flying.

If I see a thousand more takeoffs I will never lose the vivid impression I have of that scene. The English weather had relented enough to produce the perfect day for a high-altitude, precision-bombing mission. The sun was just climbing into the sky and shone down through a ground mist, making everything look unreal. One by one those great ships trundled awkwardly to the takeoff position, wheeled around, and, gaining momentum, rumbled down the runway into the morning mist.

The ground crews around me made attempts at lighthearted comments, but I could hear the strain in their voices. A young pilot pointed to a bomber turning into the wind.

"There she goes without me for the first time and I'm glad of the rest."

He was grounded because of the wounds he had received on his last raid. I could see his knuckles go white when he clutched at the side of the jeep and his eyes never left his ship as she passed out of sight in the sky.

"There's Scarlett. Her pilot named her that because his name is O'Hara," another pilot explained.

"Look at Sweet Pea. Her crew adopted a British war orphan and named the child after that plane." Sweet Pea was the Fortress Kenny had flight tested with me on board.

"Watch the Banshee. She's a veteran. She will account for her share of enemy fighters before she comes home tonight. That's Tally-Ho right behind."

Finally, Maryland My Maryland pulled up smartly onto the runway and I could see Kenny leaning over his controls. He might have been strolling across the campus at the University of Maryland again, so calm and nonchalant did he look. I waved, trying to be casual, but inside I felt very left out of what mattered.

The last aircraft, the eighteenth, rolled down the runway and swept into the sky. One by one they circled and climbed to 20,000 feet and formed into the familiar Vs. Their smooth, gray fuselages blended well into the English sky, but the sun reflected on the bristling gun turrets and turned them into sparking targets for Nazi raiders. As they passed out of sight toward the coast, they were still climbing steadily to their final ceiling of 30,000 feet.

The air suddenly grew too quiet and we who had been left behind on the ground looked vacantly at each other, not wanting to converse. Slowly everyone wandered back to the work of the day. Colonel Putnam seemed to understand my nervousness. He had always assumed that Kenny and I had a romantic relationship going and no amount of denials from us both would change his mind. After he nodded at my new wings and expressed his pleasure, he took me in hand and herded me off to lunch. Food always cheers me up and I realized I had forgotten to eat breakfast.

After a delicious lunch I retreated to Colonel Putnam's quarters to get out of his way while he toured the visiting generals, General Ecker and General Andrews (the "stars," we called them), around his base. The squadron had taken off at 11:30 in the morning and could not be expected back until late afternoon, 4:00 or 5:00 at the earliest, but I could not stop myself from checking my wristwatch every hour. Mentally I flew with the squadron as they droned over the coastline. Another hour and they would be over the continent. One more hour and they would be deep over enemy antiaircraft fire. I left the lounge quickly at that point and took a long walk around the aerodrome perimeter with my thoughts still on the mission. No one thought of anything else all day. This waiting on the ground was far worse than being in the air. Only a few half-hearted attempts at conversation were made. And the wristwatch checks continued. Along about mid-afternoon, someone remarked, "They are on their way home now." It would be at least seven hours from takeoff to landing. Faces brightened because soon the tense waiting would be over. A nervous youth snapped on a radio.

What seemed like years later, an excited sergeant dashed up the path, flung open the door of the lounge, and announced breathlessly, "They have just been reported recrossing the English coast."

A curly-haired lieutenant grabbed the sergeant's arm, and asked sharply, "How many?" The sergeant pulled away from the lieutenant and started back down the path to the control tower and, still moving, called over his shoulder "Can't tell yet, too high. Should be over here in twenty minutes."

We jumped to our feet and scrambled out of the lounge, getting in each other's way at the narrow doorjamb in an effort to see the Fortresses as they returned. Going up the control tower steps, I collided with Colonel Putnam headed in the same direction. He nodded his blond head abruptly to mean, "Follow me," and together we climbed to the top of the tower. From there we commanded a full view of the entire aerodrome and could sweep the sky in all directions. "Put" paced nervously back and forth, back and forth, across the confinement of the platform. Putnam, at twenty-seven years old, was little more than a youth, though he was a seasoned veteran of many missions. Now he seemed like a father awaiting his sons' return. We all strained our eyes northward for a first glimpse of the bombers.

A faraway humming became audible then gradually grew louder. Tiny specks of gray appeared in the sky. The humming turned into a drone and more gray specks came into sight. I glanced at the colonel. He had his fingers crossed. I drew a deep breath, crossed my fingers, and began to count specks. Three–six–nine, that group was all back and in perfect flight formation. Twelve–fifteen–eighteen. Relief. They were all accounted for, but number seventeen was slightly out of formation, indicating some minor engine trouble—although engine trouble in the air is never minor.

Putnam gave a cheer and I half expected him to turn a handspring in relief. Instead, he snatched me around the waist and waltzed us across the platform. Then he became the serious CO again and barked orders at his men. There might be wounded on board, especially in number seventeen. Lives might depend on minutes. The crash crews lined the active runway with their trucks. The ambulances were standing by and the doctors were ready.

The sun had dropped behind the trees and the soft mist had begun to rise as the first wing of the squadron swooped over the control tower and peeled off in perfect formation to execute their landings. There was something defiantly triumphant in those graceful gray birds as they alighted on the runway, one after another. The men beside the crash trucks and ambulances milled about anxiously, but no red flares to indicate first aid urgently needed appeared from the cockpits of the bombers as the last wing landed. We breathed sighs of relief and turned to watch the other wings sweep home.

As manifested by its erratic flight, number seventeen had seen trouble. Immediately after landing, ship number seventeen veered off the runway with one engine smoking ominously. A crash truck sped out to her aid. The rest of the squadron taxied slowly past the control tower and on to their dispersal sites some distance away. Weary gunners and wireless operators poked their tousled heads through the hatches and managed tired grins of triumph. They had been aloft for seven long hours. Some of the crewmembers were singing. I went over to the operations office to intercept Kenny, but ran into such a throng of weary men wandering around in various stages of undress that I beat a modest retreat. I did stay for supper with a tidied up and freshly dressed Kenny and learned that the day's mission had been against the industrial center at Vegesack, near the German city of Bremen. Aside from the shot-out engine on bomber seventeen, only a few of the other planes had been raked with bullets from enemy fighters or from bits of flak. It had been a successful mission, but the crewmembers knew they all would be called the next day to take part in a similar harrowing experience.

I stayed overnight on the base, savoring my wing leave time, with no need to get to work early. The next day I took Kenny down to Maidenhead to meet Alice and her family. On the way, we stopped in London and had lunch at the Cheshire Cheese. The place was crowded, mostly service people, so we shared a table with an Air Corps officer and his wife. They turned out to be from Catonsville, Maryland, where my TC lived; it further turned out that they knew TC's family well. The world is a small place indeed. I hoped the officer did not report to TC that I was lunching with such a handsome officer.

After lunch we took in a musical comedy, *It's Foolish but It's Fun*. It was light and amusing. It did not appeal to me—I prefer drama—but

Kenny thought it was hilarious. He embarrassed me several times with his peals of laughter, sometimes in the wrong places.

Later we sought out Lee McCardell, the *Baltimore Sun* correspondent in London. He had asked us to stop in and submit to an interview for the paper. He was tucked away behind a desk piled high with papers in a musty office on Fleet Street. When we arrived, he was pounding on a battered typewriter, but he stopped, grabbed his notebook and pen, and began to interview the two of us, soliciting as much information as we were allowed to divulge about our respective jobs. By the end of the interview, we had covered our work, our ideals, and our impressions of England. We stayed off the subject of our plans for after the war because who knew if we had futures.

In Maidenhead Alice was home, David was still awake, and their niece Carole appeared to meet Kenny. We had a quiet evening sitting around the fireplace and talking. It must have been good for Kenny to spend time with a family now and then. He must have been thinking about the contrast between being with this English family and where he had been that morning. After I was comfortably tucked into my bed, I heard Kenny call my name from his room. I jumped out of bed and went padding down the cold hall in my bare feet to see what he needed. What he needed was for me to shut off the light switch in his room so he would not have to get out of bed again. His mother must have given him lots of attention as he was growing up. Since I was standing right there by the switch, I did turn off his light for him.

⚜

Having returned from Maidenhead after my last day of wing leave, I awakened early the next morning and went bounding out to Luton aerodrome, full of exuberant spirits and good intentions of being a keen pilot on my first day of assignment to Ferry Flight Pool Number Five. The heavy morning fog never did lift and by 3:00 that afternoon we were scrubbed for flying. Tommy Warner had wended his way over from his army base in Rushdan. He was more a colleague and friend of my sister, Jane, than of mine but on the theory of any port in a storm, he had asked to spend his leave time with me. I dug him out of a dreary service canteen in Luton and we spent what remained of the afternoon together. Entertaining anyone in Luton seemed to consist mainly of eating and walking. We started out with tea at Kingsfare. Peter came along with us at my request to lighten the atmosphere. Next we took a long walk in the park. When we were sufficiently hungry again, we retired to a place called the Hollywood for supper. Tommy already had consumed a huge dinner with me at the Guys', so he would not be hungry for days to come. We kept off the subject of our uncertain futures and talked mainly of home and how much we missed it, both of us. He saw this present period of his life as a waste of good years, with his old life, the one he wanted, standing still. I could not agree with his point of view. Maybe it would be a waste as far as instruction and practice in destroying life and property, but he could make use of the time by getting around to various parts of England on his leave and really seeing the country. Instead, like most of the American service members, he spent all his off days in the middle of London or with familiar American friends who were living his same life, or with old friends like me.

CHAPTER 11

Ferry Pool Number Five

SO MY FIRST DAY ON ASSIGNMENT to Ferry Pool Number Five passed. My second day was more interesting. After hoping all morning for a total down day so we could depart from the field and head for London, we saw the fog lift about noon. Third Officer Mead, one of the ferry pilots, had a Swordfish to deliver. He invited Peter and me to tag along with him over to dispersal. There he treated us to half an hour of fascinating cockpit instruction. Neither of us had seen a Swordfish before.

As soon as the sun penetrated the ground fog, I was sent helter-skelter down to Hatfield with a Fairchild full of Mosquito pilots. Mosquito pilots were the cream of ferry pilots and we lesser pilots were in awe of their skills. To be entrusted with a handful of them was indeed an honor and a responsibility for me. I got them safely to Hatfield and went on to Halton to pick up a pilot who had delivered a Dominie there. That was another plane I had never seen at close range. This pilot was half an hour late, but I waited patiently for her arrival.

When I delivered her to Luton, a lull in my schedule allowed me to sit in the lovely warm-by-now sun for a spell. At 5:00, late in the flying day, I was ordered out to Bradwell Bay, right on the English Channel, to pick up a passenger. A most peculiar overcast hung over that aerodrome. It was a layer of cloud right on the deck. It had some holes in it here and there, and I was determined to come down through one of them. The control officer must have had other ideas because he kept firing warning flares at me. I sensed one of his flares striking my Fairchild. At the impact, I took the hint and whisked myself back to Luton without my passenger. Dusk was falling as I landed so the dispatcher released me. Peter and I went around to Scotty's digs to reprimand him for overstaying his leave by one day. In defense, he produced two dozen incomparably beautiful eggs so we stifled our criticism and asked his billeteer to cook us each an egg, please. And two for herself.

***

The next day would be a typical Ferry Pool Number Five day: some glitches, some smooth sailing, variable weather, and at least one breathtaking moment. Early on I flew out to Bradwell Bay to pick up the pilot I had left stranded there the afternoon before. When I landed, he had wandered off somewhere and was an hour late returning. Some practice maneuvers were in progress that no one wished to explain to me. Hordes of Mosquitoes, Blenheims, and Spitfires were continually taking off and landing. Without prior warning—which is how they always occurred—a gas raid took place. Someone released a tear gas bomb, in an accidental friendly fire incident. The stuff leaked into my Fairchild, where I was sheltering from the intense traffic. It made my eyes burn and smart. My passenger appeared at that moment and approached me, properly clad in his gas mask.

"Where is your gas mask?" he inquired.

I realized I must find a gas mask.

This pilot needed to go to Cambridge so I left him there and continued alone to Duxford for my next pick-up. This next pilot also was hours late, but I had been instructed to wait for him. In the meantime, one of the ground crew took me out to a hangar on a distant dispersal strip and let me examine a captured German Messerschmitt Bf 109 (ME-109). It had been captured intact and was a beautiful piece of workmanship, which is what you would expect from the German engineers. I ran my hands along the smooth finish, hopped in the cockpit, and studied the instruments at close range. I knew there would be no use bragging to Peter and Scotty that I had been sitting in an ME-109. "Nobody gets near an ME-109," they would declare.

As we were walking back to the control tower, a shot-up Fortress came in for a forced landing, about as forced as a Fortress could get— three engines shot away, one wing full of flak, the tail-gun turret blasted to eternity, taking the tail gunner along with it. I would never have thought that a plane so large and bearing all that heavy armament could fly anyplace on one engine. If I had not witnessed the exploit with my own eyes, I would not have believed it. But here was Butch from Bassingborn coming in, literally on a wing and a prayer. It left us ferry pilots in deep awe. It was one more scene I would never be able to sell to Peter and Scotty.

━◌　◌━

It was early winter. There was a gale blowing up from the south and an abundance of dirty weather all around us, so the dispatcher discreetly kept Peter and me on the ground. We were the juniors in Ferry Pool Number Five so we merited this protection. Our entire day's effort consisted of being driven to dispersal in the field car, walking twenty-five yards, hopping into two Fairchilds, and taxiing them gingerly over to the pool through the gale without winging them over. If the wind died down enough to be classified safe, other, more-experienced pilots would make the pick-ups that same day. Peter and I spent the rest of our day in the pilots' lounge, with the required intake of coffee and tea. We managed one walk around the aerodrome perimeter in the howling wind, clinging to each other to prevent lift-off.

In the evening we sat through *Desperate Journey* to watch Errol Flynn's antics as our hero, the bomber pilot. How the technical errors of Hollywood stand out when you have been flying awhile.

My sister Nita, the one serving with the Canadian Women's Auxiliary Air Force, was still looking for a way to get to England. I had spoken about her to our adjutant and Nita would have a good chance to be taken on as a cadet in the ATA. But the risk of crossing the ocean with the U-boats so dominant was still great. Kenny and I agreed that she was much safer serving out the war in Vancouver, watching for attackers.

The day was a total washout at the ferry pool. We welcomed an unscheduled day's rest once in awhile, but when the weather cleared up the unmade deliveries that had piled up while we were idle made us work at double and triple our normal pace. Since I could see that it was to be a down day, I took my notebook to the aerodrome, intending to do some writing. With a radio blaring "There Are Such Things," the ping-pong ball constantly ping-ponging, and Tanya incessantly chattering noisily and excitedly to whomever would listen, writing turned out to be an impossibility. At 3:00 in the afternoon, visibility still down to zero on the deck, CO Wood called a general release. Peter and I scurried down the road at a fast pace. We had nowhere in particular to go, but we liked the feeling of being on the loose. We wandered around Luton shopping for odds and ends, needs that had piled up during our busy days: a shoehorn for Peter, a new paper supply and some Band-Aids for me, and a handful of pencils for our taxi sign-in sheet. We walked two or three miles into the countryside to look at a tea set that I was hoping to buy for Mother. I had seen it advertised, but the owner was not at home.

The unflyable weather held over into a third day. The day before I had completed the writing of an article for the *Baltimore Sun* but could not locate a typewriter to put it in legible form. As Peter and I sat in the lounge, First Officer Last walked by, carrying his own personal typewriter. I eyed it enviously. He retired into a small adjacent room and we could hear the click-clack of the keys.

Peter suggested, "Why don't you borrow his typewriter?"

I shook my head. Last was known to be a historical scholar. Probably he was working on a book of Roman civilization, or at least some business correspondence. When Last emerged from his seclusion an hour later, he triumphantly showed us a sheet of paper. It was a list of silly popular song titles typed up to form one long sentence that made sense. So much for a history of Roman civilization. And First Officer Last flew Mosquitoes.

The sky cleared briefly in the late afternoon and I was sent hell-bent-for-leather off to Bradwell Bay to collect Captain Roche and First Officer Last. They had gone off before me to pick up and deliver two Mosquitoes. They were late getting into Bradwell Bay and the sky was lowering. I had my Fairchild revved up and waiting on the edge of the runway so they could leap out of their Mosquitoes and into my Fairchild for the mad dash back to base ahead of the weather. On the return flight I settled down contentedly into a back seat. In the ATA, the senior pilot on board always had the option of flying the plane. Captain Roche was one of those who chose to fly. I thought of how fortunate I was to be a pilot with the ATA. I considered the possibility of returning to the States now, maybe returning to a factory job, and I knew I could not do it. I could take my body back home, but my heart would stay here, flying the English skies until England was out of danger.

The following day I was handed a chit that took me down to Devonshire on multiple deliveries. It would be my first foray into Devon and I looked forward to it. Planes were piling up all over England. It had to do with the relentless preparations for the coming invasion of the continent. We delivery pilots were very much in demand. We were doing double, sometimes triple, duty. This was a glorious morning and our ferrying chits were given out early. It would be a long day. There was much laughter and ribbing when the other pilots discovered that Peter and I were assigned together to pick up Tiger Moths near Salisbury and deliver them to Barnstaple in Devon. Although Peter and I were now flying more sedately since we had been awarded the golden wings, our reputation for being dual daredevils had never faded. We left Luton by Fairchild and were dropped off at Old Sarum, a small aerodrome near Salisbury. We picked up our assigned Tiger Moths there and delivered them to Llandow. We did not wait long there before another Fairchild picked us up and whisked us over to St. Athan, still in Devon.

On the St. Athan strip, a Wellington bomber was all revved up, awaiting our arrival, so we caught a ride over to Barnstaple. I marveled at how well our dispatcher coordinated our flights. We complained about him and criticized his performance, but just look at us: getting around the county so smoothly and doing our deliveries. The hop in the Wellington was marvelous. I was allowed to sit up in the glass nose on the bomber-airman's cramped armchair. From there I watched the scenery whip past. The sun was still hot through the glass. The compass was just below my feet. For half an hour I had the feeling of commanding the whole world, at twenty-one years of age.

The Wellington dumped Peter and me out at Barnstaple and my Walter Mitty dream of commanding the world from a bomber chair ended. Our luck ran out there for getting back to base that night. By the time we had wasted half an hour walking over to the small Atlantic Coast Airlines strip, everyone had gone home. There was nothing to do but stash our flying kit and get ourselves into town on a bus. Peter had made previous deliveries and pick-ups in Barnstaple, so he steered us to a hotel he had stayed in. His choice turned out to be pretty dismal, but we were exhausted from our day of flying. We ate whatever they put in front of us in the dining room and sleep came like a great, heavy blanket.

In the morning we made our way back to the aerodrome, expecting to check out our assigned Tiger Moths and be on our way. The weather in Devon had other plans for us. It was not going to cooperate. The haze was right down to the ground and fronts were gathering all along the Atlantic coast. In spite of the gloomy forecast for the entire day, we hung around the aerodrome until well after lunchtime. There must have been a plant nearby turning out Tiger Moths because a test pilot, Ken Rayffe, was at work on a Tiger Moth, and he invited me to come along in the plane while he tested it in the air. It was too windy up there, but Ken was a skilled pilot and he practically turned that Moth inside out. I had a horrible sensation of nausea and fought not to throw up. Being sick would have ruined my reputation, I thought, so I pretended I was enjoying all the loops, spins, and snap rolls, and even our vertical dive at the ground. I was grateful when Ken returned the Moth and me to solid ground. Since the weather was obliging Peter and me to spend another night in Barnstaple, Ken kindly recommended a small inn he knew near the aerodrome. We made reservations over the phone and presented ourselves later with our bags. It turned out to be a charming place with better-than-expected food.

***

Some people consider that Devon in the southwestern corner of Great Britain has the prettiest landscape of all the kingdom. I was seeing it in early winter, so it was hard to judge, but it certainly has an untamed beauty. Before this war, it had been a favorite place, along with Cornwall, for Londoners to spend their summer vacations because of the warm, sunny weather and the sandy beaches on the coast. We did not see any vacationers during those days—only a few service people, like Peter and me, caught down there while doing their jobs. I had read that the clay used to make the famous English chinaware is from this area and that there are tin mines—probably devoted to war work in that period.

The region is steeped in history, too. Farther east is Stonehenge with its mysterious standing stones and, at Glastonbury, what is purported to be King Arthur's burial site. Between there and Bath were many reminders of the Roman invaders. The best way to get around this area is to use your own two feet. Peter and I did plenty of that. Even though Peter had been here before on delivery assignments, he did not know the area, so we hiked all over the Barnstaple hills together.

I even kicked off my shoes and waded around in the mud of a creek in my bare feet. It reminded me of being barefoot on Huntingfield Farm back in Maryland. We lolled on top of the highest hill we could find overlooking the town, the river, and the aerodrome, absorbing the ancient, mysterious beauty of Devonshire. We discussed at length our differing philosophies of life—me expecting everyone to be honest and everything to become perfect, and Peter more pragmatic and accepting life as it presented itself. I knew Peter had become fond of me because, although he never said anything very personal, he always hung around. This day, up there in the hills, the two of us alone, I waited for Peter to say he loved me. I was prepared with my usual "TC" defense, but Peter never got near the subject of love—English reserve, I concluded—and to my relief we remained on our platonic basis.

A third day of unbelievable weather dawned in a shut-down Devonshire, precluding any long-distance flying. Peter and I went to locate a well-known china and pottery works and I bought some pieces: a mug for my little sister Suzanne, and a little brown jug for Mother. I could envision the jug filled with ice and lemonade sitting on a table out under the trees in Maryland during a coming summer.

When we returned to the aerodrome to read the meteorological forecasts, Scotty was there. He had arrived by train to pick up another of the Tiger Moths awaiting delivery. Here were the three musketeers together again. What a slip-up at operations. Surely the dispatcher did not realize what he was doing when he assigned Scotty to join Peter and me. Since the forecasts were still not flyable and Peter and I had seen enough of Barnstaple, the three of us took a bus out to the coastal cliffs, to a town called Ilfracombe. This was the most popular of the seaside resorts because of its sandy beaches. The view was breathtaking. The cliffs ran straight down and dropped into the Bristol Channel. There were hiking trails all the way to the very top of the cliffs. We three idle pilots spent hours climbing around the cliffs before we took our bus back to Barnstaple at the end of the day.

The next day brought us another weathered-in day. Desperate for activity, we announced an eating contest and astonished those watching us by devouring platefuls of the famous Devonshire cake or crumpets, accompanied by tea and toast. Third Officer Lussier won the contest hands-down with a total of two slabs of toast, a big blob of strawberry jam, two cups of tea, and seven cream cakes and fruit tarts. That is correct—seven cakes and tarts. After the contest, we all felt ashamed and remorseful at putting on such a display of greed in a hungry England. It had happened because Devon was remote from the war scene and its trials. We went in search of some horses to ride to help us shake down all that food, but none was available. I wondered if the scarcity of horses had anything to do with the horse steaks on the menus of the London service clubs.

On the fifth day the offending front finally passed over and we were able to take off in our respective Tiger Moths, with the test pilot, Ken, urging me to come back soon. He did not extend his invitation to Peter and Scotty. Once in the sky we three flew in trim formation as far as Bristol. There, Peter and Scotty peeled off in the direction of Scotland. I continued into the Midlands to the Sywell aerodrome. I had decided not to stop for refueling and found myself on edge the last part of the flight. I landed on my reserve tank and silently promised myself never to take that chance again.

After I made my delivery and while waiting for my taxi pick-up, I talked to a Free French pilot who had helped train the Lafayette Squadron during World War I, and who remembered my father and his reputation as a fearless fighter pilot. The world of flying is a small place indeed.

CHAPTER 12

Kenny, Cousin Jack, Scotty, and Stephenson

THE FIRST THING I DID when I got back from Devonshire to my billet at the Guys' house was flop into a bathtub full of hot water for half an hour, then gouge grease and oil from under my fingernails and Devonshire mud from under my toenails. Next, I sorted through a dozen letters that had accumulated, three of them from TC, full of his training adventures and his excitement at being posted to England soon with his fighter pilot unit, or so the scuttlebutt said—no pilot could know for certain where he would be assigned. There also were telephone messages: Alice had called to tell me that Stephenson had arrived at last in London and I should plan to spend some time with him.

That evening in March 1943, Kenny came to visit. When I emerged from my long bath and came downstairs, wearing a dress, Kenny was surrounded by the guests of the Guys. Every British citizen was convinced that every American in uniform knew the exact date of the coming Allied invasion of the continent and that after enough proffered tea and crumpets the date would be divulged. Contrary to this conviction, I believed that nobody knew the date—not Kenny, not Kelly, not Eisenhower, not Churchill. I believed none of these authorities knew because I did not think the date had been set yet.

Kenny and I made a polite withdrawal from the Guys' living room and I whisked Kenny down to the Red Lion for what I thought would be a quiet dinner alone. Tanya and Myrtle were at the pub; after one look at handsome Kenny they invited themselves to join us. For once loquacious Tanya was speechless, listening to Kenny's Fortress chatter, in which Myrtle was able to participate. She must have flown Fortresses back in the States. Tanya was awed by Kenny's dark good looks more than by the shoptalk. She stared at his handsome face. I could tell that she was holding back from any serious flirting for my sake. I made a mental note to tell her it was all right to flirt with him if she wanted because my heart was back in Texas with TC.

I never was able to have that private talk with Tanya. The next day, on a routine delivery, Tanya met her death. It was an ugly end for vivacious Tanya, with her long blond hair, her cornflower-blue eyes, and her sunny nature. The engine of the Oxford she was to deliver cut out on takeoff. She had no speed to attempt a dead-stick, straight-ahead emergency landing. The Oxford went engine first into the ground and exploded. Just days before her accident, we pilots had been sitting around our ready room comparing flying notes. Tanya had told us that she tended to be careless about preflight checklists.

"I expect the ground crew to get the planes ready to fly. Then I step in and do the flying."

She described a few close calls she had survived in her civilian flying experience. There would be an investigation and we would be told officially what happened to Tanya in the Oxford, but the consensus was that Tanya did not take the necessary time to warm up the engine before takeoff and the ground crew had not done it for her.

During the days just after Tanya's death, nobody smiled at the aerodrome. I went home to my billet that evening and wrote a serious note to Alice, giving her my "in the event of death" details. Whenever another pilot gets killed, you realize that it could have been you, and next time maybe it will be.

As if to make up for our idle five or six days in ethereal Devonshire and after we endured the expected ribbing about our "paid vacation" in the west, Scotty, Peter, and I entered into a period of intense work in the air. Either we were ferrying pilots from dawn until dark or we were delivering planes all over England. In the next three days, I was in and out of Kemble and over to Havington. While waiting there for my taxi plane to return me to Luton, I met another American woman pilot, Mary Hooper, who was posted to Ratcliffe aerodrome. She also was waiting for a ride and we had time to discuss our varying impressions of our host country. Mary held the view that the English resented the Americans. I tried to explain how in this time of great uncertainty in their lives and the amount of stress they lived under we came off as overbearing and too sure of ourselves. Besides, we had so much money to spend. I knew the English were grateful to have us there and would never forget our gesture, but they would not be human if they did not envy us our Everything.

When several pilots had piled up in Havington, a ferry plane arrived and we were whisked back to Luton. I was shoved off again, up to Warby. Warby was a Lancaster operational 'drome. It was awe inspiring to see all the Lancasters lined up being armed for an operation that night. From there we flew to Watton to pick up a Polish female pilot. She was one of the few women pilots who had escaped from the Nazi invasion, and she had joined the ATA immediately.

Another day, it was up to Bigglewade to drop off a pilot, then over to Sywell to drop off another. Returning to Luton from Sywell, I flew within sight of Thurleigh and was sorely tempted to stop and check on Kenny, but we had too much flying to do at ATA. No sooner had I touched down at our home base, Luton, than I was off to make more collections at Snailwell. There I picked up a pilot who had delivered a Typhoon. He needed to be flown to Hatfield, and because I had not refueled recently, we were running unnervingly short on fuel.

"Let's stop and get petrol," I suggested.

As the senior pilot, he was in charge. "Naw, we can make it," he guessed, and slapped the toggle over onto our reserve tank. Every pilot knows you never use your reserve tank except in an emergency, but you also never correct a senior pilot. He had guessed right and we did make it to our destination.

The following day, I must have set the field record for trips to Hatfield. I flew down there three separate times during the day. I began to feel as if I could fly that route with my eyes closed. I picked up Captain Roche again in little Henlow. I seemed to have taken on the role of Roche's personal pilot—he kept asking for me—and I was grateful for his professional manner.

One evening I rushed up to London to connect with Kenny. After a survey of the hotels and clubs where he might be hanging out failed to uncover him, I remembered that weeks ago we had planned to make this an evening shared with Ray. He had been looking forward to it also. We had promised to find him a piano to pound. With Ray still missing and presumed dead, surely Kenny was feeling depressed and preferred to be alone. I respected his privacy and called my Canadian cousin, Jack Fleming, who had come from the wide plains of Alberta, Canada, and was "staging" somewhere in the east of England. It would be our first meeting since I was thirteen years old, when our mother drove us daughters from Maryland to Alberta to meet all our Canadian relatives. We met at the Park

Hotel. He was still quiet and handsome. I must have looked all grown up if he was imagining the thirteen-year-old girl of years ago. We decided to go have dinner, since we both confessed to being hungry. It wasn't long before we were talking together like old friends. We laughed at each other's accent, his Canadian "aboots" and my Maryland "y'alls." We stayed off the subject of the war because we both knew the time was winding down to D-Day and all it implied.

Jack, who was serving in the RCAF, brought the same news as Kelly had: troops were piling up near the Channel coasts and an invasion could not be far in the future. My heart beat faster and I imagined myself winging over France, ferrying a badly needed aircraft to a fighter pilot. After eating, we went to see the movie *Star Spangled Rhythm*. It was light musical entertainment. We followed it with yet another movie, *Immortal Sergeant*. That one was heavy drama and not the best fare for a soldier who was preparing for war, but I got wrapped up in the plot.

When we ran out of movies and the clubs had closed down, we said our goodbyes and I found myself a room at the American Red Cross. Although I knew I had to catch the morning 6:00 train to get to work on time, I lay in the dark, staring at the ceiling and worrying about my friends who would be making the invasion, and wishing I could share their burden.

The next morning, although I reported to the aerodrome on time and ready to fly, the weather was socked in miserably. I used the down time to seek out Myrtle from New Jersey and tagged along while she did some shopping. I envied her the fat American salary—I was on British wages—and sighed to see all the stuff I would have bought if I had her paycheck.

"Might as well spend it," Myrtle excused herself, seeing my obvious envy. "Who knows if we will still be here tomorrow?"

After Myrtle finished spending her money and went on to another rendezvous, I made my way to Piccadilly Circus where I met my cousin Jack again. We had a last cup of coffee together and said our goodbyes, then he left for Portsmouth.

It was time to seek out Stephenson. He was installed in the luxurious Claridge Hotel. I threaded my way through the considerable security that protected him; when I knocked, Alice herself opened the door of his suite, playing her role of the efficient, discreet secretary, screening access to an espionage chief. She fitted effortlessly into the scene. Stephenson and I must have talked to each other for an hour. I brought him up to date on my flying and my family news, especially Dad, his old World War I squadron buddy. He told me what he could of his intelligence activities, but there was not very much he could share.

He flabbergasted me with remarks like, "I had lunch with Lady Mountbatten yesterday. Louis could not join us because he has the flu," and "Noel sent me a copy of *In Which We Serve*. I enjoyed it. You should read it yourself. If I remember, I will leave my copy with Miss Green for you."

And, of course, he was having daily meetings with his friend and boss, Winston.

He asked if there was anything he could do for me and at first I answered "No," feeling I had managed alone this far and did not want to be obliged to anyone. A few moments later, after rethinking his offer, I relented: "I would not mind if you asked for me as your pilot for your trip around the country."

I knew from Alice that he planned on making an inspection tour to several sensitive war plants up north, and I knew the ATA was assigned to fly him, because he had told me so in New York.

He smiled at my request. "I can ask for you, but don't hold your breath."

I smiled, too, knowing it would never happen. Why would the British government trust their most valuable intelligence officer in America to a Third Officer with a Fairchild?

When Scotty and Peter got to know me better, they were both appalled at how uneducated I was—big on Roman and medieval history from my high school classes, but sadly lacking education in culture and the arts. I think they made a pact behind my back to bring me up to snuff. That would account for Scotty dragging me into London to the Victoria and Albert Museum and nudging me over to a tour of the Tower of London. It was Peter's turn now. When our days off next coincided, Peter told me firmly we were going to visit famous Cambridge. Scotty was hoping for rain so he could come with us, but it was a fair morning and he had to go to work in the sky.

Cambridge is north of Luton. We started out in that direction on a local bus. When the bus seemed to have come to the end of its route, we did a spot of hitchhiking. We were wearing our uniforms so everyone stopped for us. Mrs. Guy had made up some sandwiches for our lunch, which we ate as soon as we were out of her sight, wandering down the road.

Peter had attended Trinity, one of the Cambridge University colleges, where he had studied law. I could tell he was proud of his college as he told me all about Cambridge tradition. He made me feel how grand it would be to attend classes there, but I quickly realized that women students were the lowest form of life on the totem pole. Peter showed me one of the colleges where women were allowed to attend and it was about a mile out of town. He gave me a tour through the chapel at King's College. It was magnificent, majestic, and impressive. King's had been constructed in the fifteenth century, long before the Europeans had colonized America. It was difficult for my American mind, accustomed to all things modern, to visualize such antiquity. The various other colleges were scattered throughout the town. They were built using the same scheme as King's: a courtyard in the center with the two-story halls surrounding it, some of them dating back to the fifteenth century.

Before the war, Cambridge had been a quiet university town. The only worry then was whether you would be run down by an overenthusiastic student on one of the hundreds of university bicycles. That was before the coming of the Yanks. Now the King's subjects had to take greater care lest they get in the path of a jeep tearing through town or a GI pedaling his bicycle on the wrong side of the street.

Peter said the shops still looked much the same as they had when he had been a student there: they were on narrow, winding streets, with a natural preponderance of bookstalls and printers' shops. The big change was that the customers were nearly all wearing khaki. There were constant clumps of American soldiers looking longingly into the windows of the sports shops for which Cambridge was famous. Were they thinking of what would happen after the war, of shedding their uniforms for the sportswear they saw in the windows? The old marketplace, Peter explained, had taken to the new life style reluctantly. For more than a thousand years farmers had trooped into the spacious square on foot or in pony carts to sell their produce. To accommodate the American invasion, the square had been marked off into efficient parking slots. Businesslike Army trucks and jeeps were pulling in and out of the square all day and all night.

The university itself also had felt the effects of our friendly invasion. Some of the buildings had been completely taken over for the quartering of troops while some buildings were being used for the soldiers' classes. We saw signs saying "No Entrance" over several ancient stone archways, much to Peter's disapproval.

"Do you have to take over our universities, too?" he chided me.

Through the forbidden archways, troops could be seen drilling in the courtyards.

The beautiful little River Cam is the centerpiece of Cambridge. It winds its way peacefully through the town between vivid green banks and frequent bursts of tulips and daffodils, below the ancient stone walls bordering the college grounds, and under an occasional bridge. I could never have done any studying if I had been a student there. There were so many Americans paddling along the Cam in canoes, rowing energetically in boats, and struggling awkwardly with the traditional British punt, that I begged Peter to take me out on the water. He complied. Being British, he chose a punt and handled it like a professional. I tried to imagine him punting on the river on a spring day with his college sweetheart. When I suggested such a scene to him, he turned pink and refused to speak about it. He was 100 percent reserved British.

We returned to Luton as we had come, combining a bus ride with some hitchhiking. After supper in our separate billets, we met again and took in the movie *Random Harvest*, a heartbreaking, realistic story.

The Clothing Ration Board sent me thirty-three more clothing coupons to see me through until spring and maybe pay for the tweed suit that I was having made. Also, the ATA was now issuing us a chocolate ration with each ferry chit we completed. If the three of us, Scotty, Peter, and I, pooled our rations, we could accumulate a good chocolate reserve for the future. This was a good example of how fair the British tried to be, even with something as insignificant as chocolate. Who but the British would have included ferry pilots in the distribution of chocolate bars, growing ever larger as more Allied ships made it though enemy-infested waters?

Scotty had been sent over to Thame to put in his time on the Hart. He was almost ready to solo so Peter and I did not see much of him. In his absence Peter and I had another overworked day. It reflects the intensified preparations for an invasion. I compared the mood of the country that spring with that of the mood the previous year when I first arrived in England. The previous year the emphasis was on the defense from a possible Nazi invasion of Great Britain's beaches. In 1943 all the emphasis was on the preparations for the Allied invasion of the continental beaches.

Our intense day started by being flown in an Anson to Cowley, where we each picked up a Tiger Moth and delivered it to High Ercall. From there we were Ansoned over to Derby, where we picked up Magisters for delivery to Woodley. Woodley aerodrome was teeming with aircraft of all types. One peculiar model was being air tested as I landed. I could not believe my eyes. I vow the plane got itself airborne from a standstill: it seemed to leap straight up into the air. It reminded me of a similar model on the Dundalk airport back in Baltimore. After landing we rushed over to get a better look at this model, but none of the RAF pilots or ground crew would talk to us. "We can't talk about it," they said of the plane.

Our taxi Anson was waiting for us in Woodley, so we were back in Luton in very good time. It had been such a glorious day, weather-wise, that flying had been a pleasure.

Scotty had returned from Thame, all checked out on the Hart, about which he said, "I hate it." Well, everybody did. It had so many bad habits.

There was still plenty of sunlight left, so we three took a bus out to Dunstable, had our drink in a local pub, and began the seven-mile walk back to Luton. Along about 10:00 that night, halfway through our long march, the sky began to fill with a dull sound, like rolling thunder in the distance. The sound grew louder and louder. Aircraft began to appear as far as we could see. The first planes we could identify were the British bombers, Lancasters. They spread out in the sky for miles. Behind them came Halifaxes and behind the Halifaxes were Sterlings. On and on they rolled. Standing there in the dusty road, we could look up and see all these aircraft silhouetted against the sky where the sun had just gone down. It was an awe-inspiring sight to see all those black specks, to hear that heavy drone, and to know that they were on their way to create some devastation someplace in a matter of hours. Those black specks must have slid across our piece of the sky for an entire fifteen minutes; at least two hundred of them passed over our heads. Even cynical Scotty was rendered speechless after this experience. We walked in silence the rest of the way to Luton.

≈≈ ≈≈

The first time all our days off coincided, Peter took Scotty and me on a guided tour of St. Albans. He showed us the cathedral for which the town is famous. It is a lovely old structure—at least the Norman part is. It is a mixture of early English (before the Norman Conquest), Norman, and Victorian. The Victorian section is extremely ugly and seems out of character next to the quiet brick of the Norman tower. Listening to myself describe the cathedral, I sound exactly like our tour guide, Peter, who is the authority on these things.

Peter next took us to inspect the remains of a Roman town, Verulamium, that had been excavated. The park in St. Albans was built around the ruins, and there are many stately trees on the site. It amazed me that the Romans ventured more than a thousand miles from their homes in Italy and set up these structures—settlements at that time—that evolved into towns. Reflecting on the existence of Verulamium made me feel insignificant.

～⊚ ⊚～

For two days running that spring I spent more time in the air than on the ground. It was taxi duty time for me again. My first hop was to Castle Camps to pick up competent Mrs. Crossley who had delivered a Mosquito there. I believe she was an English pilot, although there was no time for me to talk to her; the giveaway was her lovely complexion. Later I flew up to Sywell for another passenger. When I dropped him off, I took on another woman pilot and delivered her to Hatfield. From there I went to Henlow to pick up my favorite passenger, Captain Roche. I thought he was probably the best pilot in our service, on a par with our record holder, Jim Mollison.

I was looking forward to an early evening, but one of the local Maryland contingent, Tommy Warner, was waiting on the Guys' doorstep, bearing delicacies for the group. I could not say no to some socializing. We had dinner together and went to a movie, *Once on a Honeymoon*. My friend departed to catch his train and I no sooner had returned to the Guys' house than the air-raid siren went off with its sinister wail. There was no sleeping for any of us until after 1:30 in the morning. We had been informed that the Nazis were suffering from fuel shortages and conducting fewer air raids, but they still managed to disrupt our sleeping patterns.

The second day of my nonstop flights started out by my having to take a passenger around in my Fairchild. For a goodly time, I trailed him from aerodrome to aerodrome, picking him up after his delivery and dropping him again, at Cowley, at Lyneham, at Witney.

In Witney we met Pat Billington, who was picking up a Hurricane. At the sight of company for lunch, he pulled off his parachute harness and joined us. From there I flew alone in my Fairchild to Colerne with orders to await the arrival of two pilots bringing in Typhoons from Scotland. I astonished the dispatcher crew in the watchtower by stretching out full length near the Signals area, propping my head on a book, *Pattern for Survival*, by John H. Bradley. It was very popular reading that year, but it served as a pillow for me and I promptly fell sound asleep. The dispatcher crew did not know about my heavy social life and the air raid the previous night, or they would not have been so surprised. About 6:30 that evening an order came to me from Luton to return to base without my intended passenger pilots. They were weathered in somewhere south of Prestwick, Scotland.

After I parked my Fairchild in dispersal and dragged my parachute back to storage, I went into the lounge and dropped like a stone on the couch, scattering my gloves, maps, helmet, and goggles all over the floor. Peter was there waiting for me.

"Oh, Peter, I cannot entertain the U.S. Army tonight. I just do not have the energy for it."

Peter went about patiently picking up my things as I dropped them and said very quietly, "I've called Mrs. Guy and told her you were stuck out until late. She promised to tell the Army."

Peter was a real friend and my social secretary in the bargain.

I had a sudden let up in deliveries so Officer Kempter, also assigned to Luton, invited me to be his copilot for the day. We were flown to Croughton by Anson and there picked up a Master. It was a Number III model with a Mercury engine. I pulled out my handling notes and whipped through the Master cockpit drill several times, familiarizing myself with the strange cockpit. Kempter let me handle the takeoff, then let me fly to Shawbury and land there by myself. The Master was quite a change from the toylike Magisters and Tiger Moths. We cruised at 180 mph, and there was a broad array of new gauges to look at, although our ATA training forbade us to fly by any of them—just the old compass and gyro for us. Leaving the Master at Shawbury, we caught another Anson ride to Harwarden where a Whitley was waiting to be delivered to Brize-Norton. The Whitley was the March V model with two Merlyn 20 engines, the same engine used in the Spitfires. I was getting closer to the big stuff. Again, Officer Kempter let me do all the flying and I was in heaven, pushing all that power around in the sky. Eventually we ended up back in Luton and I thanked the captain for a most instructive day. Thinking back on our schedule, it was a typical ATA pilot day: we were expected to handle three different types of planes with just the handling notes to help out.

I was technically on taxi duty, not ferry duty, when the dispatcher came racing into the lounge and informed me that I was to deliver a Magister to Kirkbride. Kirkbride is on the Solway Firth, which divides Scotland from northern England. The change of plans occurred because the assigned ferry flight pilot had not reported for duty that morning. The dispatcher handed me the Magister chit and shoved me into an Anson on ferry duty that happened to be going to my destination, Cliff Pypardway over to Cliff Pypard. All the heavy expert pilots seemed to be going there too—our own CO Woods, Captain Roche, and Kempter, of our instructive yesterday. There were ten of us altogether. The others had orders to pick up Spitfires and fly them to the south coast where the build-up for the invasion seemed to be taking place. Eight brilliant pilots hopped into eight waiting Spitfires, took off smartly, and headed to the Channel coast. There turned out to be two Magisters to deliver, so CO Wood jumped into the second one, took off, and went to his heading. I took off right behind him in my Magister. As I had not had time to do any routing before they shoved me into the ferry Anson, I tucked myself close behind the CO and made our entire flight without losing track of him. As we got farther north, passing over breathtakingly beautiful hills, I kept expecting the CO to sit down somewhere so we could refuel; I assumed he knew that we needed to do so. But no, he must have known our fuel capacity better than I did because he kept relentlessly flying north. The last twenty minutes I pushed my map onto the floor, clutched the stick with both hands, and prayed for a nice convenient aerodrome, one of those seven hundred that exist in Great Britain, to loom into sight when I ran out of gas. When we finally landed in Kirkbride I am sure I had not so much as a gallon of fuel in my tank, and I wondered what the CO had in his. Suppose some overworked mechanic had not topped our tanks that morning? Where would we have forced-landed among all those trees? And how stupid of me not to have landed comfortably when I knew I needed to refuel. My hands were still trembling when I signed over my Magister to the Kirkbride dispatcher. I never said a word about fuel levels to the CO. We piled into an Anson that had come to collect us and had a smooth flight back to Luton, with ample fuel in the tanks indicated, so I could enjoy the majesty of the hills.

Peter and I were assigned to ferry together for a day. It was always less like work and more like entertainment to fly with Peter. We were Ansoned over to Cowley where we each picked up a Tiger. According to our assignment chits, we were to deliver them to Feltham, an aerodrome in the Greater London area. We agreed to fly together. En route, we had to pass quite close to Reading, so we detoured slightly in order to shoot up the house of Peter's cousin. Our flight was about an hour long so we flew beside the Thames River, past Maidenhead and right into the city, a new and frightening experience for me. We had to thread our way through the corridor that made a path around the barrage balloons. It was tricky flying and called for careful attention.

The Feltham aerodrome had been a lovely little prewar private flying club. After the dispatcher took possession of our Tigers, the staff invited us to join them for lunch at the rambling old clubhouse, now serving as a mess hall and offices.

Peter and I returned to base so early that I got to my billet in time to meet the Guys' guest, a young Oxford student. So that is what one looks like, I thought: tweed jacket, open-necked shirt, tennis shoes, and a joyful attitude. Good-looking, too. For a moment I secretly envied his carefree, eighteen-year-old student life and wanted to change jobs with him.

⚜ ⚜

The long-awaited flight tour with Stephenson had finally arrived. "Can she be my pilot?" Stephenson had asked. "No," the ATA had replied. But as a compromise he was allowed to have me as his copilot.

I was allowed to return to Maidenhead for the night to get my uniform in perfect order. The ATA did not want me to reflect badly on them. They were puzzled enough in the first place as to why Stephenson would ask for me as his pilot, even though I tried to explain the old sentiment he had with my father dating back to World War I. The next day our tour started. A long, black limousine drove right up onto the taxiway and William Stephenson, a small, modest-looking man, stepped out of the limo and immediately into the Dominie, officially known as a De Haviland 89A, that had been chosen to transport him around. Captain Fairweather himself, one of our senior bosses, was to be Stephenson's pilot. I was sitting in the copilot's chair, but Fairweather made it very clear it was only to please Stephenson. He emphasized that I was to keep my hands off the wheel.

"Don't touch the wheel, you understand?" he said.

The weather was not favoring our flight, but then, when did the English weather ever cooperate?

Our first stop was at Ringway, near Manchester, and Fairweather took us through some stinking weather. He impressed me by not using a map. At Ringway, Stephenson met with a colleague from his intelligence world, while we, his crew, had coffee. When Stephenson was ready, we headed through the lousy weather over to Oxford, gaining altitude until we were flying above the rain clouds in a bright blue sky. I was dying to do some piloting, but I knew better than to beg. I could only keep my hands folded and look at the scenery.

We landed at Kidlington where Pressed Steel Ltd. was located. It was one of Stephenson's enterprises before the start of the war. Now he had given over supervision of the plant in order to take up his duties in the intelligence world, a job he had volunteered for at no salary to himself. He told me I could take a tour of the plant while he was having a meeting with the manager. I had been angling for several months to get inside one of these production plants. Alice had convinced me it could never happen because security was so strict. I wanted to compare British methods and equipment with ours at Glenn Martin's in Baltimore, where I had worked before coming to England. This plant was using a considerable amount of American machinery and the layout was quite similar to ours. The main difference seemed to be the great variety of assemblies being turned out at this one site. We saw Lancaster wings, Wellington tail assemblies, Typhoon cowlings, and, in an adjacent building, several types of shell casings. When Stephenson had finished his meeting, we flew him down to Brooklands, where he told me he had plans to meet with Lord Beaverbrook.

On the way there, the weather having cleared partially, I got my first view of the famous Windsor Castle from the air.

It was quite an education to watch Captain Fairweather thread his way through the barrage balloons and into the corridor that led onto the aerodrome, which was located in the oval horse racetrack. The balloons were anchored all around the perimeter of the track and they swayed diagonally over the center of the runway, making it seem impassable. Fairweather explained to me that there were certain landmarks a pilot could watch for and these would lead him safely through. The captain was doing it all in his head—no maps. We landed smartly and Stephenson stepped out of our plane and into Lord Beaverbrook's waiting car. Taking off in our Dominie was not too healthy because of a stiff crosswind on the lone runway. Once in the sky, though, we passed over Belvedere Castle, known to be the favorite hideaway of the Duke of Windsor's, and skirted the famed Ascot racetrack.

Stephenson called me that night to tell me how much he had enjoyed our flight together. That had to be a big fat lie because of all the bouncing around the weather had given us.

CHAPTER 13

D-Day Nears

IN THE EVENING, after a tiring day on delivery duty, Peter took me to meet the cousin we had been buzzing with our Maggies for weeks. The cousin turned out to be a charming young man who had served in the Fleet Air Arm. He had been a pilot on board a cruiser for two years of overseas duty. On his last run his ship had been torpedoed and had sunk in what he swore was nine seconds, carrying most of the crew to the bottom of the sea. He was lucky: only eight crewmembers survived to be rescued and he was one of them. When I met him he was awaiting the assignment of his new posting. It was hard for me to imagine the courage it must take to get on another ship after his experience.

"His uniform is smarter looking than ours," I remarked to Peter.

The Fleet Air Arm was the service Peter had been in before volunteering for the ATA. I often wondered what disaster he had lived through in his previous service that resulted in his flying with me. No amount of prodding or trading—"If you tell me, I'll tell you"—would get him to talk about it.

~⊚~ ~⊚~

Kenny's squadron had been hit hard the past two weeks of nightly raids. Practically all the crews had to be replaced because they had been wounded, fatigued, or killed. In one recent raid twenty Fortresses took off from Thurleigh but only ten returned. Ten of them lost—one hundred men. How could I hear of such a disaster and still be satisfied to flip around in a Fairchild? Why could I not do more?

~⊚~ ~⊚~

While carrying out my full load of taxi duties and plane deliveries, I was spotting an impressive number of heavy aircraft and getting a goodly amount of time in on many of them. On a taxi trip to pick up a pilot in Marlask, which is way up on the East coast, close to the hostile European coast, I identified Spitfires, Typhoons, Bostons, Masters, Lysanders, Mustangs, and, from the ground, a stray Fortress passing overhead. This was renewed evidence that the Allies were preparing an unbeatable invasion of the continent.

I tried to envision what the southern part of England must look like, if viewed from 30,000 feet. I thought it would resemble a vast staging area; it *was* a vast staging area. Besides all those thousands of planes, bombers, fighters, and observers, there were endless camps with thousands upon thousands of Army foot troops like my "cousin" Bill Kelly and my friend Tommy Warner, all cleverly camouflaged and hidden among the trees and brush of southern England.

We heard intriguing rumors of unusual activities closer to our home base, over near Tempsford. Tempsford was a modest village on the narrow road west of Cambridge. If you were not alert, you would pass right by its few buildings without noticing that it was a village. Just after the road forked for Bedford, there were a series of pastures or meadows given over to rural purposes. In one of the pastures, the crop had been shaved off in an unnatural way and a grassy runway had been opened up. Maybe it would have gone unnoticed to the casual observer, but pilots know a runway when they see it and this was a runway. There was a barn in the meadow and we noticed the door had been widened to double the normal width. There, we figured, was the hiding place for some type of aircraft. We were never able to get close enough for a serious inspection because there were always British Army types on guard and they would hustle us on our way when we tried to linger. But in the local pubs there was much speculation. Those who claimed to know avowed that flights were made after the sun went down, with both takeoffs and landings in that field. The flights taking off all went to the east and landing flights came from that direction, too—from Europe.

On one of our visits to the local pub, Peter and I learned the reason for all the secrecy. Tempsford meadow was the focal point for drops into Europe. Supplies were being flown to the French Maquis, the Resistance arm of French civilians. We had seen them in Hollywood movies: spies with radio sets being parachuted into occupied France to make contact with the Resistance fighters and to set up information networks for the coming invasion. It was one part of the vast invasion plan and it was happening right in front of us. I was intrigued, excited, and scared, all at the same time.

I arose one morning that spring with the sunshine blazing in my window. If I so wished, I was entitled to a leave day. The sun so seldom shone at that time of year that I opted for the leave and I decided to make it an outdoor day. Peter had brought his motorcycle to my billet some time before and had taught me the fundamentals of riding it. I dubbed his machine the Black Beetle. Inspired by the sunshine, I mounted the Black Beetle and whooped up to Thurleigh, another busman's holiday. There was some question of whether I had enough petrol in the tank to make the drive. I avoided that potential problem by not looking into the tank. If I stalled, at least I would not have to force-land in some trees. On arriving at the Thurleigh base, I slipped into the motor pool to mooch a petrol handout. The mechanics were delighted to see this reminder of home. They descended on Beetle and me like a swarm of bees. They made me prop up the Beetle on her stand and then the fun began. Two lads put in the petrol, two others topped off the oil tank, someone changed the ragged battery wires for me while a few more fixed the U/S horn. There must have been twenty youthful airmen swamping the Beetle. To the mechanics, it was a distraction, taking their minds off the serious business of war for a short time.

Although Kenny was back in the hospital because of his kidney infection and Colonel "Put" had been transferred out to a unit that was planning the invasion, I made my way to the control tower and scrambled up onto the roof to get a good view of the afternoon takeoff. The Fortresses lumbered into the air with their heavy bomb loads just skimming the treetops, banked around, and eased into formation. They swept over the aerodrome three times. On the last sweep they had attained an altitude of 10,000 feet and were still climbing. Later I was told that two hundred of them went out that day and that the target was Wilhelmshaven. I shuddered for the innocent civilians who would be caught in that raid. After the Fortresses passed out of sight, I clambered down from the roof of the control tower and headed for the Mess to have some lunch. At the door, I crossed paths with one of Kenny's ground crew. He put his hand on my shoulder and I immediately expected some bad news.

Instead, he said casually, "Have you heard? Ray and the rest of the Maryland My Maryland crew have been located, all alive and unwounded. The Red Cross found them." What a feeling of immense joy and thanksgiving I felt. After their Fortress had been crippled by enemy fire, they had been able to parachute out and were captured by the Nazis when they landed. The German army moved them around several times, which was why they had not been identified sooner. Later the Germans left them in a prisoner-of-war camp that the Red Cross was monitoring.

Somehow all this time I must have felt Ray would be a survivor because I had not thought of him as dead at all. Kenny would be so grateful. Besides having his friend and navigator safe, he would not have to write that final letter to Ray's parents.

Along with the good news of Ray's survival, they gave me the news that Kenny had been awarded the Distinguished Flying Cross. It was awarded for his leadership on the Bremen (Vegesack) raid. When I wrote to his hospital to congratulate him, I suggested that the award was because Colonel Putnam was grateful to have at least one of his squadron return and it was face-saving for Kenny. We had to insert some lightheartedness into our lives or we would all go crazy. This is how the citation read:

First Lieutenant (since promoted to Captain) Kenneth A. Reecher, for heroism, extraordinary achievement, and performance beyond the call of duty while participating in a mission dispatched April 17, 1943, to bomb enemy installations at Bremen, Germany. . . . While en route to the target the formation in which Lt. Reecher was flying encountered repeatedly concentrated attacks by squadrons of enemy fighter planes. The leader of his squadron and two wingmen were shot out of formation and, as leader of the second element, Lt. Reecher's plane was hit several times. One direct hit set his No. 2 engine ablaze, while another shell entered the navigator's compartment and exploded, fatally injuring his navigator. Another shell exploded in the bomb bay and several direct hits on the right wing completely severed the main spar. Displaying courage, resourcefulness and skill, Lt. Reecher succeeded in putting out the fire and feathering his No. 2 engine. He then took over the lead of his squadron and managed with extreme difficulty to keep his almost uncontrollable aircraft in formation. He continued to the target, dropped his bombs and, with great difficulty, brought his crippled aircraft back to a friendly base. By heroism, extraordinary achievement and devotion beyond the call of duty, Lt. Reecher contributed materially to the success of a vital bombing mission, to the safety of his own aircraft and personnel and to the destruction of enemy installations, thereby reflecting highest credit on himself and on the armed forces of the United States of America. (Citation, Kenneth A. Reecher, author's collection)

Sometime during the course of my stay in England, Stephenson had introduced me to one of the de Havilands, Gwen. The de Havilands were a famous aviation family. At the time we were introduced, Gwen was working in intelligence and invited me to visit her at home. I set off on Peter's motorcycle during a leave day. I avoided the main roads as Gwen had recommended and stayed on the country lanes that wound in and out among the fields. There were thick hedges of what the English call "may" on either side of the lane; it is a white, flowering bush. The road was quite deserted, but occasionally a curious-looking English cyclist passed me. That is, they looked curious to me. Of course, I must have looked curious to them, too, in my red plaid skirt, fuzzy socks Mother had knitted, a too-big sweater, and a yard of silk scarf streaming out behind me in the breeze. The English cyclists always wore very professional-looking brown shorts and white sweaters with the old school jacket, a combination of clashing colors, on top. To complete the picture, they wore cumbersome knapsacks.

Farther on I had to pass through one of England's most historic villages, Ayot St. Lawrence. It consisted of one church in ruins, one pub in excellent operating condition, three houses, and the de Haviland estate. In approaching the village, I came on the church first. It was only a shell and wild flowers were growing along the crumbling, moldy walls. The story is that centuries ago a duke who lived in Ayot St. Lawrence decided to tear down the church because the Romans had built it. He began the destruction, but the king ordered him to cease, hence the half-and-half condition.

I next passed a huge, ugly, old brick house, completely hidden by a high hedge. A formidable looking iron gate barred the front entrance. Behind all this imposing camouflage lived none other than the illustrious and grouchy George Bernard Shaw. The villagers had an amusing story they told to unsuspecting visitors. A curious American was snooping around trying to get some gossip about Shaw from a villager.

"Just what sort of a man is this GBS?"

"Well," answered the villager sharply, "He minds his own business, which is more than I can say for some people."

The pub was next, then the other two houses. The road led from there into the de Haviland place. It had impressive stone posts and a little gate house that was very much out of repair. The manor house itself was lost in a jungle of lovely shrubs and small trees. It was as big as a hospital, and ugly. It was hard to see why someone would design such an uncompromising structure. The cottage was farther along the entrance road, much smaller and fitted with up-to-date fixtures. It was here that Gwen lived.

Gwen told me an amusing story about the estate. One of the eccentric old lords who had lived in the manor built a huge Greek temple in the middle of the estate. It was a large temple with two tall columns in the center, one on either side. The lord had himself buried on one side and his unloved wife on the other. The explanation he offered was this: he hated his wife so much he wanted the church that had joined them in life to separate them in death.

CHAPTER 14
Time for a Change: Resignation

WE HAD A NEW operations officer at Luton. Roy was his name and
he was addicted to cigarettes. When he found out that I had friends in
Thurleigh air base, he took to assigning me as many taxi and ferry jobs as
possible that would pass over that base. He would look the other way if I
landed there, and in return I was expected to come back with cigarettes. It
seemed a fair exchange.

"Aetheris Avidi" (Eager for the Air) was the motto of the ATA. At
the time I joined, I did not know that. When I received the official notice
that I had been accepted by the ATA to be a pilot, I knew very little about
the organization. Apparently I was not the only uninformed person. It
took the British Air Ministry about two years to officially tell the RAF
that an ATA existed, what type of work they were doing, and the high
degree of collaboration they required. Until that time the RAF must have
thought that those thousands of aircraft appearing on the tarmac at their
operational aerodromes had been dropped there by magic or maybe by the
factory test pilots on their way home from work. The first time I had heard
there was a ferrying service had been in 1941 in Baltimore when I went for
an interview with Jacqueline Cochran, hoping to come to England with
the group of pilots she was recruiting. She had mentioned at that time
that her recruited pilots would be flying for some vague civilian outfit,
servicing the piloting needs of the RAF. Beyond those bare facts, Cochran
had offered no details and never named the organization for which we
would be flying. Nor, on my arrival in England, had the people at the UK
Ministry of Labour been any more informative when I announced my
intention to enlist as a "ferry pilot."

When reporting for duty at the ATA headquarters in White Waltham,
it had become apparent to me why Cochran back in Baltimore and the

Ministry of Labour in London had been so vague: the ATA was being invented literally from one day to the next, according to the urgent needs of the RAF and calling on the organizing skills of its founders.

To return to the beginning, in late 1938 and early 1939 a director of the British Airways, Cdr. Gerald D'Erlanger and a colleague of his, Cdr. F. D. Bradbrooke, had come up with the concept of assembling a group composed of civilian pilots and those RAF pilots who were physically unfit for combat service. D'Erlanger himself, at thirty-two years old, was considered too old for active military duty. As the founders envisioned it, these pilots could be assigned to the duties of patrolling vulnerable English coastlines on the lookout for intruding raiders and hostile submarines, and of maintaining communications between the various ground units and headquarters.[1]

D'Erlanger and Bradbrooke took their idea to the RAF higher-ups. The RAF cited their model because, starting back in World War I, the RAF squadrons always had done their own "collecting," as they dubbed it. They had what was known as a ferry pool, with as few as ten assigned pilots in all. The pilots lived in a certain London hotel and went to and fro from the job by train or road, according to which transportation was available. These pilots were largely unsupervised; much valuable time was wasted at both ends of the deliveries by unreliable transport and the failure to supervise the pilots. In addition, because there were only these ten designated pilots assigned to ferrying, by 1939 the undelivered planes were backing up at an alarming rate. To help alleviate the backlog, some twin-engine Ansons were assigned for the transport of the ferry pilots. This more-rapid transport helped to some degree, but the backlog persisted; new fighter planes sat idly on the factory tarmacs when they were needed desperately by the squadrons on the line at the operational aerodromes.

Something drastic had to be done. The RAF decided to resurrect the model that commanders Bradbrooke and D'Erlanger had proffered in the past. They had come to the realization that it was "the only game in town" and they grabbed at it as the one chance they had to free up fighter pilots. From there on, D'Erlanger became the chief manager and Bradbrooke his close assistant. D'Erlanger himself is thought to have come up with the apt name "Air Transport Auxiliary."

As of late 1939 there still was no plan for the ATA to assist the RAF in delivering warplanes, only the clear intention of freeing up more RAF

---

1. Information on the ATA in pp. 154–159 taken from Flight Captain Stewart Keith Jopp, *Aeroplane* magazine, Parts I and II, November 30, 1945; Part III, December 7, 1945; and Part IV, December 21, 1945.

pilots from noncombatant work. D'Erlanger contacted a list of possible pilots, a list that he had assembled with foresight. These were pilots who would be willing to carry out communications and patrolling work for the RAF. There were twenty-six names on that original list. The choice of using White Waltham as the ATA's headquarters seems to have been based on these facts: D'Erlanger knew the CO. The first facility offered the ATA for their use was a rickety wooden hut on the edge of the tarmac, but before many months had passed ATA had begun to encroach on the other buildings at White Waltham. It was like the camel that first sticks his nose in your tent to keep warm and ends up with his entire body inside.

There is a funny story that goes like this: When the new outfit arrived at White Waltham and requested space from the RAF, they were treated with suspicion and distrust at the hangar level and assigned some insufficient room in a hangar, clearly marked by a newly painted white line. The RAF indicated, "That side is yours. This side is ours." The ATA accepted their limited allotment politely, but, so the story was told to us, each evening after the RAF had gone to sleep they moved the dividing white line out a foot or so. Like the cuckoo bird that takes over the sparrow's nest, the ATA ended up with all of White Waltham and the RAF found itself being sent elsewhere.

Flexibility was the key word for ATA operations in the first months of its existence. D'Erlanger recruited pilots to fly communications duties only, but it soon became obvious from the huge backlog of undelivered aircraft at the factories that they were needed to make deliveries, at least as far as the depots, which were the collection points. At the urgent request of the RAF, the ATA pilots slid gracefully into making factory-to-depot deliveries. To the astonishment of the skeptical RAF, these new duties rested lightly on the shoulders of the seasoned pilots that D'Erlanger had recruited. They flew flawlessly.

It was only a few weeks later in 1941, during the Battle of Britain, with every fighter pilot desperately needed to repel the Nazi air attacks, that the RAF pleaded with the ATA to help out with deliveries from the depots to the squadrons. The ATA pilots again gracefully complied and "help out" turned into a permanent task. When I took up duties with ATA, my fellow pilots were covering the country from north to south, east to west, flying every type of aircraft operational in Great Britain, an amazing feat. The number of ferry pools had expanded from the one first housed in the rickety woodshed at White Waltham to twenty-two ferry pools located pretty much all over Great Britain.

D'Erlanger continued as the commander of ATA until the end of the war. He was a brilliant tactician. Those skills, combined with his pleasant public manner—he was able to keep the peace between all the clashing personalities—made him the perfect choice to manage chaotic, temperamental ATA. Bradbrooke, the co-creator of ATA, was chief ferry pilot until his early death in a plane crash in Scotland in August of 1941.

While the Battle of Britain was still raging and after a depressing string of unflyable days, the ATA found itself with one thousand aircraft that had not been delivered. In a panic the ATA called on RAF Ferry Command to help. Ferry Command sent seventeen of their young fighter pilots over to White Waltham. Assuming they must be seasoned pilots, D'Erlanger put them directly to work clearing up the backlog of undelivered planes. Of the seventeen starters, eleven of those RAF pilots crashed their first aircraft. This performance emphasized for our bosses that ferry work is sensitive and special and requires special training before it is undertaken. Out of this experience grew the ATA training school and the invaluable "White Books." These were a collection of notes on each aircraft that ATA pilots developed to help transit from one type of aircraft to another and another. These White Books proved so useful that they became much in demand with the RAF pilots themselves. I believe they were eventually reproduced almost verbatim for RAF distribution. With the passage of time, many other aspects of the ATA training school also were copied by the RAF for its own training.

An ingenious technique that D'Erlanger worked out early in the life of ATA was a system of keeping track of the ferrying that needed to be done. It sounds like an obvious task and it *was* obvious, but figuring out how to achieve it was complicated. ATA set up a central control unit in Andover. At the end of each working day—working days being Monday to Sunday, sunup to sundown—the factories would inform the ATA control unit in Andover how many planes they had ready to be moved out on the following day and to which storage depot they were destined. At the same time, the active squadrons would inform the control unit what they would need to replace their losses of the day. Sometimes, after heavy casualties, these would be simply wish lists, without much chance to fill them. Regardless, members of the control unit would work through the night to coordinate all this information and come up with a smooth, workable schedule for the next day's ATA activities, a schedule that would send us pilots all over Great Britain. It entailed an enormous amount of juggling pilots and aircraft, but, with practice, it became a highly successful system. In the early hours of each morning, when we pilots stepped up to our operations desk, put out our hands, and received our work chits, we took it for granted that while we slept Mother ATA had figured out how best to use our talent for that day.

To give an idea of the volume of air traffic that accumulated, approximately 125,000 planes were manufactured in Great Britain during the war, in addition to the 17,000 delivered to England from Canada and the United States. Between 1940, when ATA got into full swing, and 1945, when the organization was disbanded, it is estimated that a total of 440,000 flights were made to get operational aircraft from the factories to the depots, and from the depots to the active squadrons. At least 340,000 of these deliveries were made by ATA pilots. It adds up to the ATA pilots making more flights than were made by the combined members of the RAF squadrons, their own ferry pools, and the Fighter Command—an awesome body of work.

When ATA closed up shop in 1945 it could claim to have employed 1,515 aircrews and to have sustained 153 fatalities. Of these fatalities, 142 were pilots, and 14 of those pilots were women; 7 were flight engineers, including one woman; 1 was a nurse, also a woman; and 1 was a cadet, our beautiful Tanya.

One of the most remarkable facts about ATA aircrews was their diversity. Besides being of both sexes, our pilots and engineers came from twenty-eight different nations: Argentina, Armenia, Australia, Belgium, Bermuda, Britain, Canada, Ceylon (Sri Lanka), Chile, Cuba, Czechoslovakia, Denmark, Ethiopia, Iceland, France, Holland, India, Malaya, Mauritius, New Zealand, Norway, Poland, Russia, South Africa, Spain, Switzerland, Thailand, and the United States. The largest number of foreigners came from Poland, perhaps because the Poles were driven so emphatically from their homeland at the start of the conflict and were able to travel overland, through still-unoccupied France, and so escape to Great Britain. One half of the members were British. My own closest companions were Scotty, from New Zealand, and Tony and Peter, both from England. It was remarkable how we all meshed together on a daily basis and worked toward one common objective: to get that aircraft delivered where it was needed as fast as was feasible.

The ATA doctors showed a great deal of flexibility in reviewing pilots who had sustained disabilities. They gave more weight to a pilot's experience and the number of hours he or she had flown than to the injury that took the pilot out of combat service. Eventually, competent pilots were in the air daily for ATA with the following medical problems: 5 were missing legs, 2 were missing arms, 3 were missing fingers or entire hands, 5 had partial paralysis, 9 had stiff joints (ankles and elbows), 5 had serious spinal conditions, 3 had only one eye, and more than 170 had weak eyesight. The overall flight record showed that these pilots with so-called handicaps had better safety records than the general body of pilots with their full faculties. Perhaps they earned this reputation by being extra careful in order to compensate for their disabilities.

From the beginning, the workload in ATA was carried equally by women and men pilots. It was a joy for me to be treated in such an egalitarian manner in a time when women were usually pushed aside, however gently, in favor of men. In fact, except for the constant and real dangers of war, it was like working in heaven. By the time I joined the ATA, the pay scale also had been equalized: pilots and engineers of the same rank were paid the same salaries, regardless of their gender. It made the ATA one of the first civilian organizations to recognize that gender should have nothing to do with salary.

The RAF always had been admirers of our U.S. get-things-done methods, so when some ATA pilots complained that we were not being allowed to take off from American-commanded aerodromes at our own discretion, they asked the RAF to intervene. The RAF liaison officer paid the usual courteous visit to the headquarters of the U.S. Air Force, explained the problem, and was assured that the orders would be changed. Four months passed with no easing up on the restrictions to ATA takeoffs from U.S. bases. Now the clever but desperate liaison officer sent off a polite letter and a small matchbox to U.S. headquarters. The letter reminded that the ATA pilots were still not able to take off when they judged it expedient and called attention to the contents of the matchbox. When the box was opened, out crept four live snails, one for each month since the request had first been made. The Americans got the gentle hint. It took only three more days before all American aerodromes received orders to permit ATA pilots to take off when they wanted to.

Of course, for me personally, it meant that when I wanted to stay overnight at Kenny's aerodrome and raid the PX (post exchange) I could no longer count on the U.S. operations officers to ground me there for "deteriorating local weather conditions." This new ruling meant that I had to be the one to decide if the weather permitted me to get back to home base.

The overall performance of the ATA, from conception to organization to full-throttle-ahead operation, should have been hailed and lauded as one of the great achievements of World War II. During its existence it became the powerful and indispensable right arm of the RAF, first in beating back the Nazi invasion of Britain, and second in supporting the preparation and undertaking of the Allied return to Europe. There are many experts who say that the RAF could not have repelled the Nazi onslaught without the daily presence of the ATA pilots. These same experts lament the offhand way, unnoticed and unsung, that the ATA was dismissed at the end of the war, without proper recognition for the extraordinary job the pilots and the ground crews did. Only a few ATA pilots were decorated, despite their long and perilous service to the RAF; the outfit as a whole was never cited. Flight Captain Stewart Keith-Jopp, who wrote extensively about the ATA after the war, noted that the ATA, except for a few formal letters of thanks from the authorities, died as it lived, unnoticed and almost unknown. And I could add, unappreciated.

It was TC's birthday, his twenty-third. I sat myself down before Peter's typewriter one morning with intentions of composing a really in-tune letter to him. As I sat there, fingers poised above the keys, I could find nothing to say to him. Anything I could have written seemed so trivial and inadequate when what I should have been doing was standing opposite him in person and extending my arms in a loving, best-wishes gesture. It was more than a year since we had said goodbye on the telephone. Although we had both written faithfully every few days and TC had cabled most of his Air Force pay away, our correspondence had taken on somewhat the air of a competition.

"I just checked out on the P-47," from TC.

"Well, I soloed the Hart and it's got 500 h.p.," from me.

"I flew solo all the way from Texas to Long Island."

"I flew London-Prestwick with only ground references."

During the long separation, both of us had built up new lives, involving new relationships. TC's last letter informed me that he had invited what he described as a cute girl. When I read that news, I felt a pang in my heart, but I reminded myself that I had what TC would call dates almost nightly with members of the opposite sex: Peter, Tony, Kenny, Scotty. I did report all my encounters to TC and expected him to accept them as platonic friendships. So why did I feel so stricken when he invited a cute girl to his dance? Yes, I definitely had strong feelings of ownership there and feelings that TC was a lamb straying from the fold. Or he was more like an eaglet, leaving the nest finally. Fed up, maybe? I quickly put away those feelings of jealousy and typed some words of devotion and remembrance, reminding him of our last weekend together, a day at the Catonsville swimming pool, a day at the granite quarry, sunshine and youth, to hold in our hearts. I told him we would be together soon. Before I waxed too sentimental, I switched to describing the aircraft that were passing overhead, dozens and dozens of every model. The invasion must surely be soon, although I did not write this because the censor would cut it out. The guilty wish passed through my mind that the invasion would happen before TC arrived with his fighter pilot unit, so he would not have to fly bomber escort on the first invasion wave.

Preparations for an invasion were more obvious each day, a frenzy of aircraft passing overhead, my ground forces friends with less time to visit. I was chilled, but secretly thrilled, that soon our ferry flights would be taking us to France. Thus, we settled into a comfortable, more-or-less predictable pattern, making our assigned deliveries of an ever-increasing variety of aircraft models, ferrying pilots the width and breadth of Great Britain to make drops and pick-ups of fighter and bomber pilots. That was our work.

We came to understand why we had been so meticulously trained to recognize every foot of the ground below us, to anticipate and predict the weather in the sky—which were the safe conditions for us to challenge and which too risky. We were waiting impatiently—at least *I* was waiting impatiently—for the day when the Allied troops would storm ashore on the French beaches and we ATA pilots would be called on to make our deliveries of aircraft and fighter planes to the frontline aerodromes. I was excited.

Imagine my dismay and chagrin when, as D-Day approached, our ATA supervisors casually announced to us that, yes, ATA pilots were going to see service in Europe, but only male ATA pilots. All female pilots, regardless of qualifications, would remain in Britain. Only male pilots would fly across the English Channel to make continental drops. There was no recognition of the superb job women had done and were continuing to do in ATA, no acknowledgment of the better-than-average record we had compiled, and the fact that women pilots were flying every type and model of aircraft the RAF was using. There were some lame excuses aired with reasoning that sending women into a combat zone would be contrary to the British tradition of protecting women. And they mentioned the inconvenience of the "separate needs of mixed crews," as they worded it.

When we received this momentous news, Scotty and Peter shrugged their shoulders and voiced the equivalent of no big deal.

"You will just have to stay put in England, Betty, while we look over the scene in France. We'll bring you a bunch of souvenirs," they told me.

They were not in the least sympathetic to my distress.

I felt let down and betrayed by my beloved ATA. All those months while the invasion was being planned and mounted we had served patiently behind the lines and waited for our day of action to come. Now, without even consulting us, the big decision had been made: women pilots would be left behind, sidelined once again in favor of male pilots. When I had absorbed the full import of this edict, I stormed into our CO's office with my complaint.

"You cannot leave us behind," I insisted. "You promised me we would be going to Europe."

"Mind your place, Third Officer Lussier. I did not make this new ruling, but I will obey it to the letter and you will do the same."

"No, I will not!" I shouted. "I will resign before I'll stay behind while you send men pilots to France."

"No, you won't. You won't resign because you love flying too much."

That was the end of our conversation. I determined to consult with Stephenson as soon as possible. Maybe he could get the ruling changed. I was sure the ruling had come right from Churchill's office and perhaps Stephenson could talk to him. Dream on, Third Officer Lussier, dream on.

As soon as Stephenson could fit me into his charged schedule, I poured out my disappointment with the recent ATA decision. First, he refused my ambitious request to talk to Churchill. Then, to my surprise—he was always surprising me—Stephenson came right up with an alternative. He told me that the Americans were organizing a first-ever intelligence-gathering service, that already agents were operating in the continent, on both sides of the front lines, and that they were badly in need of recruits.

"You go out and think about making a change that serious. Come back in two hours with your decision made and we will talk again." He shooed me out the door of his suite at the Claridge Hotel.

I met Scotty and Peter downstairs and we went to a movie together. Those two laughed and giggled about what was happening on the screen. I sat looking intently at the screen, but my eyes went right through it and my mind was at war with itself. For me, the problem was that I was wild about flying and I wanted badly to add the Spitfire and the bombers to my flying log, but I also wanted badly to serve on the continent in a more active way. Here was Stephenson offering me that chance, but in exchange I would have to give up my dream of flying Spitfires. I made my decision. When I met Stephenson back at the Hotel Claridge, he already had contacted the head of the new American service, the Office of Strategic Services (OSS). He put me on the telephone with him and we made our deal.

Alice and Stephenson helped me word a letter of resignation to Commander D'Erlanger, a letter in which I made it clear that I preferred to continue flying with the ATA for the RAF, but felt diminished not being allowed to do all the flying for which I was qualified. That included flying in Europe after the troops landed. The commander's father had just died, so it would be several days before I received a formal reply. I returned to my flying duties while I waited for the reply.

That night I wrote a long, careful letter to TC. He was due to land any day now in England with his fighter pilot squadron. He had been bombarding me lately with cablegrams hinting as much. If I were not there to greet him with open arms, he was going to faint dead away with disappointment. I had to make him understand my feelings about participating in this war. Our whole lives stretched ahead of us. If we still so chose and were lucky, we could spend many years together.

Then to tell my two main pals, Scotty and Peter. Scotty would be easiest because he had recently given up pursuing me and now was madly in love with an attractive young woman. Peter and I had trouble getting Scotty's attention. This particular afternoon, I insisted. Armed with our accumulated mass of chocolate (Remember the arrangement where we got a ration of chocolate for each delivery? We had been making a lot of deliveries . . .), we climbed up to the top of the local golf course. We had wanted to take this walk for some weeks. After we were all stretched out on Scotty's coat, eating our slabs of chocolate, I made my confession. Scotty thought I was joking, but Peter knew right away. His face went pale. We launched into a serious discussion and I could sense that they had both been caught unaware by my news, that they were shaken and somewhat annoyed at not being consulted. All three of us had become so accustomed to each other that my abrupt departure would be like tearing apart a family.

A parcel came from Mother: a crazy little black knitted hat, a pair of fuzzy ankle socks, and a pair of sea boots, knitted by my father for Ole. Ole would be touched. I needed to tell my family not to send any more parcels. My address would be a rolling one for the next many months.

The adjutant bellowed for me over the Tannoy one morning. When I reported to his office, there was my resignation letter opened on his desk. He was very upset with me. I explained once again that I intended to serve out the rest of the war on the continent, with the armies, and not in the Luton pilots' lounge.

He said, "I did not make the ruling and I can understand how you feel."

Then he gave me all the information I needed to get cleared.

The flying schedule for the day had been made out so I asked the CO if I could fly one more day. He was agreeable to my request and off I went for one last fling. An Anson took eight of us, Peter included, down to an aerodrome on the east side of London where we each picked up an Austre. An Austre is pretty much a Taylorcraft with a British engine mounted in it, the Cirrus Minor pulling 90 horsepowers. It handled like a Piper Cub, but responded sluggishly. For a last fling our flight was a wild exhibition. Peter and I just about wrote ourselves off a dozen times. We shot up a long line of frightened soldiers, skimmed haystacks, tractors, and cars, charged between trees with no real room for our wings and dropped down into fields below the roads. We did this for an entire hour and a half before landing at our destination, Aston Down. As we landed, Peter's Austre cut out, indicating that he had no petrol. I wondered how much I had left. After lunch, Peter and I caught a ride with Captain Roche, who was delivering a Lancaster and would be picked up in an Anson that we could share to get back to Luton base. We two stretched out full length in the bomb airman's comfortable hatch and actually snoozed as Captain Roche maneuvered us through several rain showers. For my last day at saving the British from the Nazis it was a fine experience.

I must admit to some reluctance at handing over my uniform, parachute, and aerodrome pass on that day in early May 1943. It felt like I was shutting the door to a garden and retiring to the cellar to mix chemicals that might save a few lives that no one was ever going to hear about. Walking down the street that evening, it crashed down on me that this indeed was a momentous move. I was cutting clear of something I had spent a lifetime yearning for—daily flying in all types of aircraft—and I was blindly walking into a thankless, dangerous job on the ground. What would make me do such a thing? Something inside me seemed to make the decision. I did not want to be made to stay in the background. I wanted to be in the front lines and I wanted to be one of those who made a difference, like Bill Kelly and Kenny Reecher and TC. The new job sounded as if it might take me there.

Soon I was packing my things into my parachute bag (the ATA had forgotten to reclaim it, or else they had looked the other way) and getting a plane ride to Algiers, where I would begin work in counterespionage—spy catching—that would take me from Algeria to Sicily to Italy and would finally land me in France on the tail of the Allied southern invasion.

PART TWO

Counterespionage

CHAPTER 15

On the Ground With the X-2

AFTER I RESIGNED FROM the ATA in late April 1943, where I was
flying planes for the RAF, and joined the OSS early the next month, where
our job was to capture enemy spies and turn them into double agents (D/
As), the most difficult thing for me to get accustomed to was not being in
the air most of my working day.

While I was in the ATA, no matter how gray and foreboding the
morning dawned, I knew that at some point in the day I probably would
take off in an airplane, charged with finding my way alone across the skies
to deliver that plane to some distant, camouflaged destination. I would
look down between the clouds on a grim and struggling England, feel my
utter freedom up there in the plane, and know I was part of the vast and
determined effort to free our world of Hitler and his Nazis.

For me, all of that changed abruptly the day I entered service with OSS.
Instead of looking down on England from an altitude of one thousand feet
on a daily basis, I was looking up at the planes passing overhead and both
my feet were planted firmly on the ground (see Map 15.1).

In the ATA I had settled into a grueling but satisfying routine of daily
piloting. I was looking forward to two big—for me—future events. First,
I had been slated to report for conversion instruction as soon as a slot
opened up for me in the class-conversion to Spitfires. And how I longed to
fly a "Spit." The other event would occur after the impending invasion of
the continent had taken place and ATA pilots would be assigned aircraft
deliveries or pilot and plane pick-ups on the continent. Peter, Scotty, and
I had our first visit to Paris planned out to the smallest detail. We could
hardly wait.

None of that was to be, at least not for the women pilots of ATA.
Suddenly it was announced that we women pilots were to be left in England

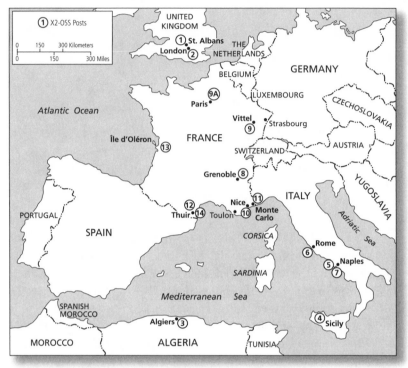

MAP 15.1 *X-2 OSS Posts*

and only the men pilots would see continental duty. As Scotty and Peter already had declared, "It was no big deal."

Maybe to them it was no big deal, but it was to me. I had not come all this way from the farm in Maryland to be left flying around foggy Great Britain. No, not me: I was going to the continent with the rest of the warriors.

William Stephenson happened to be in London at that moment. I took up my complaint with him and he facilitated my rapid transfer into a service that definitely was going to the continent. It was the counterintelligence branch of the OSS (X-2) that I joined. Until World War II we Americans did not have a national or international intelligence service. We viewed "spying" as a very impolite activity. When the creation of a spy service was suggested during President Herbert Hoover's term in office, his secretary of state is alleged to have remarked, "Gentlemen do not read other people's mail." In the newly created OSS, gentlemen and gentlewomen were going to learn to read other people's mail in a hurry.

William J. Donovan is the acknowledged founder of the OSS. When war first threatened the United States, setting up an intelligence-gathering force had not been his original goal. Donovan was a World War I veteran. He had been a battalion commander in the 165th U.S. Infantry regiment and rendered outstanding service in France with the American Expeditionary Force (AEF). After the war, he opened a highly successful law firm in New York City. In 1940, as Britain found itself drawn into what would become World War II, Donovan went to Washington with the express intention of getting back into active Army service. He knew that the United States Army would someday be involved in the war and he wanted a front seat to the action.

Because of his age, he was discouraged on all sides from seeking military service. While his plans were still in a state of flux, he had conversations with President Franklin Roosevelt and realized how misinformed Roosevelt was about what was going on in Europe. To add to the confusion, Charles Lindbergh, the famous pilot, had come back from a fact-finding visit to Germany pushing the policy of making a deal with Hitler and of staying out of the European conflict.

In this confusing situation, Donovan, with his sharp intuition, sensed a new way to render service to his country. To the president, he proposed going to Europe; he was going anyway at the behest of administration members for the purpose of assessing war damage. To Roosevelt, he proposed expanding his mission to visit both England and Germany and report back with the firsthand knowledge he would gain about the current state of affairs.

On that fact-finding trip, while conferring with Prime Minister Winston Churchill in England, Donovan met up briefly with William Stephenson, whom he had first encountered at the end of World War I. Stephenson pointed out the lack of intelligence-gathering means in the hands of the Americans. At the time of this encounter, Stephenson was setting up his BSC office in New York City. Stephenson never told me how much of BSC activities he divulged to Donovan at this time, but surely Donovan realized his friend was not just issuing passports to British citizens. Anyone who cared to look would know that Stephenson was setting up a British intelligence headquarters in the United States. Donovan and Stephenson agreed to keep in close touch with each other.

At the same time, Stephenson was using all his considerable influence to persuade Churchill to offer help in training an American intelligence force. Toward this ultimate goal, he pushed Roosevelt and Churchill together on various occasions.

About the time these two agreed to collaborate on an American intelligence service, Donovan returned from his first-fact finding trip to Europe and presented his findings to our president. His conclusions were entirely the opposite of Lindbergh's and were alarming. He, too, urged Roosevelt to consider forming a central intelligence organization. Roosevelt had already decided on that path of action and Donovan, standing conveniently idle, seemed the natural choice to head up the new service. Out of these casual and coincidental encounters, after passing through one or two preliminary forms—the Coordinator of Information being one such form—the OSS came into being and Donovan was formally designated to head the new service. It was not the military service he had sought, but he could foresee plenty of activity in this new field.

George Bowden and James Murphy immediately set up a counterintelligence branch. Murphy was another well-established lawyer who had worked with Donovan. Quite soon, Bowden went on to other duties; Murphy became the titular head of the service and is thought to have given it the "X-2" designation.

It was Murphy himself who interviewed me briefly in Stephenson's Claridge Hotel office on a Friday morning. He was a small, unassuming man with twinkling eyes and an easy, informal manner. He talked very little about the work to be done, only told me I would "start Monday" at a St. Albans address. My luck was holding: a St. Albans work location would put me within easy reach of Peter, Scotty, and Kenny for playtime.

I had become adept at billet hunting, and over the weekend I talked my way into a house within bicycling distance of my new work site at St. Albans. The owner was an attractive young woman named Maisie whose husband was on service in Burma. All my GI visitors would be very interested in Maisie.

Monday after my meeting with Murphy, his chauffeur drove me out to St. Albans. The chauffeur was Gwen de Haviland, and she was much more than a driver. (Stephenson had introduced me to Gwen, of the famous aviation family, and we had become friends.) In St. Albans she dropped me off at what was referred to quaintly as "the hut," a drab adjacent building within the MI6 quarters. MI6 was British counterintelligence; it was under MI6's tutelage that we Americans were going to learn the spy-catching business and start our own counterpart, X-2. The other American trainees were already at the hut, having arrived from the United States some days before. They were Dana Durand, John McDonough, and Norman Pearson; Robert Blum would arrive later. Upon my arrival they looked to me expectantly for secretarial help. Immediately and emphatically I informed these strangers that I did not type, I did not make tea, and the only pencils I sharpened were my own. "I am here, like you are, to learn the spy-catching business and then to get to the continent where the war is."

My compatriots showed great disappointment. They set about learning to brew their own tea and sent off to the States for private secretaries.

That first day on the job, I learned the most flabbergasting fact of the war: the British had broken the German radio code and, on a daily basis, were able to read the German field traffic with their Berlin headquarters. It was amazing. It was even more amazing that this information was such a closely guarded secret and remained so for the duration of the war. The code cracking had been made possible partly through Stephenson. On one of his trips to Poland, long before hostilities started, he had come across a curious machine, the purpose of which was to encode radio messages. Stephenson, realizing its potential value to MI6, acquired one of the machines, had it disassembled, smuggled the pieces into England one by one, and had the machine reassembled by British intelligence. This was the Enigma machine (an enigma is a riddle) and it is credited with playing a major part in winning the war for the Allies. Now, after much negotiating between Roosevelt and Churchill, the British were going to teach us Americans how to analyze the intercepted, encrypted messages and make use of the information for our own combat deception purposes.

To guard the secret of the source, the British insisted that only a limited number of Americans be briefed. To guard the secret even further, Frederick Winterbotham, head of the Secret Intelligence Service's Air Department, devised a plan whereby "Ultra" as the British called it and "Ice" as the Americans dubbed it, using nicknames for the data that was produced by the intercepted messages, was passed to various U.S. Army headquarters only through special liaison units (SLU), who had to be British subjects. On a daily basis, the SLU agent received the decoded messages from British intelligence and, working with the U.S. military special intelligence officer, disguised the original source of the material. The resulting intelligence reports proved to be so useful in planning military field operations that the SLU agents were highly sought after by the U.S. COs.

As our British instructor was telling us about this awesome secret and explaining how it worked, a light flashed on in my head and suddenly I knew with complete clarity where I could fit into service on the continent. I would become one of those SLU agents. Although I now worked for an American agency, the OSS, I still carried the British passport that had taken me to England. Being twenty-one and exuberant, I announced my intention to my compatriots right away. They shook their heads and sighed. If I was not going to type their memos and make their tea, they would just as soon I worked out in the field where I would not set a bad example for their secretaries.

When I told Murphy my idea, he thought it was a good idea for X-2. He had always favored maintaining close ties with the British service and voiced his opinion that my association through the SLUs would help to serve this purpose. Thereafter I thought of myself as an SLU agent, even though I worked in Algiers, Sicily, and Italy without a title and was finally working in France before I was given the title of the SLU counterintelligence liaison with the American Seventh Army.

The next weeks were ones of intense pressure as I set about getting acquainted with the extensive database the British had developed, the names of hundreds of strategic locations, what was manufactured there, such as ball bearings, aircraft, tanks, and bombs; what activity occurred, such as training wireless operators and pilots; and hidden aerodromes and locations that could become targets. I was introduced to files with the names and whereabouts of hundreds of high-ranking German military officers, what their commands were, and where they fit into Hitler's ruthless war plans. At the same time, I was reading the daily intake of decryptions and learning which materials would benefit the American commanders in the field and in what form it could be presented to them in order not to compromise the real source.

Besides pressing on us masses of intelligence materials, the British were intent on teaching us proper antisocial behaviors: to become aware at all times whether we were being followed, to avoid getting drawn into conversations with strangers on trains, on buses, in pubs, or in shops—conversations we just naturally fell into as civilians or service personnel. If we noticed the same "stranger" lurking around several times, we were instructed to report the incident so the British could investigate. The British were good at following up with those investigations.

On the social side I could still visit Kenny, first at the hospital and, when he was back on duty, at nearby Thurleigh air base. I was also able to keep seeing Peter and Scotty because they were assigned to a nearby ferry pool. We three spent a lot of time with my new billeteer, Maisie. She was easy going and good looking. As I had predicted, my GI callers loved her. Besides, she had chickens and chickens laid eggs.

The most difficult part of it all was keeping "the Secret": the fact that the radio codes used by the Nazis to communicate with each other had been broken. I did not dare take part in anybody's conversation for real fear of saying something that was not an opinion of my own, but a reflection of "the hut." My compatriots said that after a few months they could not remember whether their knowledge came from a newspaper article or from our secret intercepts. We all agreed that the safest solution was to stay away from all political topics. All their letters became amusing ramblings about the sheep in the pasture behind our hut, the meals they were cooking, and the important job of mowing the grass. I tried following their lead in a long letter to my family, writing pages about nothing in particular.

I still had to compose a letter to beloved TC, explaining my change of service. I kept putting it off, expecting the telephone to ring any day and to hear the familiar, happy voice announcing his arrival in England with his fighter squadron. A year had gone by since we spent TC's leave together in Baltimore. Since then, we had both passed through trying experiences apart from each other. Yet our bond had remained strong and I knew when TC appeared in England we would still feel the same, comfortable and familiar with each other. Of course my new service, taking me to the continent while he remained in England, was not going to be easy to sell. In fact, it was going to be hard to get across to him, but I tried to put it out of my mind for the moment.

We X-2 apprentices to the British spent our time between our designated hut in St. Albans and the new offices in the Ryder Street quarters of British intelligence; some days we were in one place, some days the other. I was in Ryder Street one ordinary day, reading background files on a dangerous spy still at large. Sometimes a most trivial observation about a spy could be the key clue to running him down. Did he spend his leisure in the pubs or the cinemas? Was he superstitious about anything? What kind of food did he prefer—were we likely to find him in a fish and chips joint or in the steakhouse of an inn? As I passed through the hall, my arms full of files, a staff member approached me and said that Stephenson wished to see me urgently in the office he kept in the building. I returned the files to the guardian clerk and made my way to Stephenson's office. There was nothing alarming about his message. If he knew I was around, he always sent for me and it would turn out to be lunch together or tickets for a play that night—he was a good friend of the playwright Noël Coward. And every encounter was urgent to Stephenson. So, tickets or lunch, which would it be? I knocked on the door of his office and pushed it open. Stephenson was sitting behind a big, old-fashioned desk. He asked me to sit down and indicated a chair. I said, "No thanks. I have work to do. What did you want to see me about?"

"I have this cablegram from your mother." He picked it up, "She says that your friend, TC, has been killed in an automobile accident."

A searing pain passed through my body from head to toe, as painful as if I had been struck by a bolt of lightning. I could not breathe for a moment, trying to understand the message. Stephenson did not get up from his chair behind the desk. In World War I he must have had this heartbreaking experience many times when he reported the loss of a squadron pilot to the parents. He held out that poisonous piece of paper to me. I backed away, out the door, without being able to utter a word. Across the hall was a large room, stacked from floor to ceiling with shelves full of intelligence files. I went deep into the shelves and leaned my forehead against some files. I must have stayed that way for half an hour, trying to come back to life. The pain was so intense I kept waiting to pass out. Nobody came to look for me. After awhile I could breathe again. I found my way back to the office niche where I had been working, excused myself, and blundered out into the city to deal with our tragedy. I had often imagined this moment, as I know TC had, but nothing I ever conjured up could match the reality. It would be many years before I got used to not having TC around.

I requested to be sent as soon as possible to my assigned post, Algiers, and mercifully my plea was granted. I loaded onto a cargo plane, bucket seats, with my parachute bag, and was flown through the dangerous corridor from southern England, skirting Portugal, and landing at Algiers airport. Recently, British actor Leslie Howard had been killed on this same route, shot down by enemy fire. The Luftwaffe was ever aprowl for unarmed aircraft.

Algeria was my first experience with a truly foreign country. Britain was foreign, of course, but sharing a language and our Anglo-Saxon heritage lessened the impact. Algeria was another world. The landscape was semitropical, with palm trees poking up their heads on the city streets. The population was a clashing mixture of French and Arabic. From the airport I reported to the X-2 office and my commanding office, Major Frank Holcomb. He was a Marine specializing in counterintelligence and he would prepare the X-2 unit for its participation in the invasion of southern France. We were housed in a fine dwelling, the Villa Magnole, requisitioned from the French. My billet had been selected for me already; no need for me to go knocking on doors as I did in England. The billet was in an apartment on nearby rue Michalet, presided over by a kindly, elderly French widow.

Algiers was teeming with British, French, and American forces, all preparing in one way or another for the looming invasion of Europe. General Eisenhower had his headquarters here and could be seen in the street every day on his way to and from his office. Soon he was to be designated CO of the Normandy invasion forces and he would transfer his headquarters to London. Meanwhile, among the Allies chaos ruled without much clear vision of how any of us would be contributing to the invasion.

The members of Secret Intelligence, OSS were the exception. They had dozens of sabotage agents wreaking havoc in the south of France, controlled mostly by radio from Algiers. Until the American troops had landed in France and the Germans had begun to retreat up the valley, leaving their spies behind them, there was little our X-2 unit could do. I did make my call on the British every day to examine the Ultra/Ice harvest, select what the Seventh Army could use, and deliver it to them in a disguised form. We were told later that the material had been very useful in selecting targets in France for sabotage and destruction.

In August Murphy passed through Algiers on an inspection trip and changed the designation of our unit from the 88th Special Counter-Intelligence (SCI) to the 69th SCI. He said this was to honor the World War I outfit of our chief, General Donovan, but the connection was hard to explain to our French and British counterparts and even to our own Seventh Army. "Who are you, anyway?" they asked.

Another confusing action of Murphy's was to order our competent and compatible leader, Maj. Frank Holcomb, back to London to prepare the participation of an X-2 unit in the Normandy invasion. Major Holcomb, who had been our commanding officer since our formation in London, was now leaving us. A new CO would be leading us into the southern France invasion, Murphy had chosen for us an officer who had no previous training or experience in counterintelligence and who soon antagonized our Seventh Army counterparts with his authoritarian behavior while attempting to act as the X-2 liaison with them.

The X-2 team reported its distress to London. Immediately a genuine Army officer was sent as a replacement. This officer was to be not only the X-2 commanding officer, but also the SCI liaison officer to the Seventh Army. This was an important position at that time—August of 1943—because the Seventh Army would participate to the fullest in the coming invasion of southern France. By more bad luck, the new leader's communication skills were as poor as that first CO. Within weeks both of these failures had drifted away, leaving us with an urgent need for competent leadership.

In this chaotic atmosphere, I liked to think of myself as an oasis of rational calm. I saw exactly where I could fit in and contribute to ending this war. In my capacity as an SLU agent, I reported every morning to the British intelligence office. This office moved along on a regular basis, as X-2 accompanied the Allied troops from Algiers to Sicily to Italy and finally into southern France. During the daily meetings, between whichever British intelligence officer was in charge of receiving Ultra/Ice from London and myself as the SLU liason, the daily crop of Ultra/Ice intercepts were examined. Together we tried to figure out where the German troops were being sent and at what points on their route they would be most vulnerable to Allied sabotage. We searched for mention of strategic war matériel plants along the route. If troops were not mentioned as being on the move, we tried to reason why they were stationary. Were they resting? Were they resupplying other units? Were they out of fuel? Could they be awaiting attack orders? With the help of the British staff members who had been cleared to handle Ultra/Ice, I reworked the intercepts so that they appeared to originate from other sources: Allied spies on the ground, for example. In achieving our goal—to impart valuable intelligence information to our troops—we were greatly aided by the Nazi's total ignorance of the Ultra/Ice—the broken code. Because they firmly believed that their codes were protected from detection, they "spoke" freely in their messages and gave us much useful information. Sometimes we were forced to withhold potentially good material because we were unable to pull off a believable disguise and the chance of blowing the Secret was too great. I took these doctored reports over to the Seventh Army HQ for their use in planning sabotage missions and other actions. The British were always willing to supply the Americans in this way as long as they kept control and we did our best to protect the secret of their precious Ultra/Ice.

Not much has been written about the subject, but as late as April or May 1944 there was still a serious alternative plan to invade Europe through Spain. Although Franco, the Spanish dictator, was pro-Hitler, the rationale for such an invasion was that, seeing the end of the war approaching with an Allied victory, Franco would not oppose Allied troops pouring through Spain en route to occupied France. It was probably wishful thinking, but in preparation for such an invasion X-2 had been ordered to install a network of clandestine radio operators along the Mediterranean coast of Spain. This project, Operation Banana, was entrusted to Donald Downes of X-2. Since Downes did not speak Spanish and was not familiar with the Spanish coastal area, carrying out this task fell on the shoulders of Richard Sickler, the "nom de guerre" for Ricardo Sicré. He was a former volunteer in the Spanish Republican Army who had found his way to the Coordinator of Information, the precursor of the OSS. Sickler recruited his radio agents from the abject holding camp the French had set up in Algeria and into which they dumped any Spaniards who crossed over their border as exiles from Franco's brutal dictatorship. If any sponsor wished to take over a detainee, the French were only too willing to get rid of that person: one fewer mouth to feed.

Thus, Sickler would interview and recruit his agents, have them hastily but properly trained to operate their radios, and personally install them along the Spanish Mediterranean coast. This was exceedingly dangerous work since it required rowing ashore with the operators, guiding them to their contacts, and rowing back to the motorized mother ship, a trawler under British command, hovering at the legally allowed distance from the shore. This was all done in the pitch black of a moonless night and under the possible observation of the Spanish Guardia Civil (Civil Guard) patrolling the beaches. Each time Sickler made one of these hazardous trips, he was required to write out a formal report for the X-2 files. Since English was not one of the three or four languages Sickler spoke well, I was asked to render his torturous reports into X-2 English. Most of his sentences were about a page long, so I spent a lot of the time I had free from my Ultra work with Sickler discussing the meaning of what he had written. The resulting reports were fascinating James Bond stuff on the Spanish coast and our unit members lined up to read them before they were sent off to X-2 London. Operation Banana ended badly. Worse than that, it ended in tragic disaster. From one day to the next the mission was cancelled by London HQ–X-2 with absolutely no provision designed to retrieve the eighteen brave Spaniards who, with their radio sets, had already been rowed ashore by Sickler. He protested vehemently, all the way to Seventh Army HQ, but to no avail. Seventh Army judged it to be an X-2 folly and would not rescue the operators. The Spaniards, after waiting for six futile, dangerous days and nights on the beach for the promised rescue, were captured one by one, tortured for what they might have known about future Allied invasion plans, and executed as spies. Robin W. Wink, in his very reasoned *Cloak and Gown: Scholars in the Secret War, 1939-1961,* concludes that all those men should have been decorated for their bravery. Instead, after their violent and torturous deaths, their names were never recalled.

With the demise of his assigned project, it was decided to add Sickler to our modest SCI unit, along with two of his Spanish recruits, code-named Mike and Frank, who had had the good luck not to have been dropped on the Spanish coast.

The Allied invasion of Normandy went forward in June 1944 as planned. We watched from afar in Algiers, watched our friends die on the beaches, my "cousin" Bill Kelly among them, and felt left out and useless. However, we were assured again by Murphy that ours would be a full participation in the southern France invasion.

From our chaotic beginning, little by little we were establishing order, selecting compatible, qualified members, and defining their future tasks. Most of the Seventh Army units had moved on to Sicily or Naples in preparation for a southern France coastal invasion; our X-2 unit was soon to follow.

One of our last nights in Algiers we were sitting around in our splendid requisitioned Villa Magnole living room, half-heartedly attempting to bond. Sickler announced that he was going into the casbah for coffee and would any of us accompany him? The casbah was the Arab quarter of the city. He knew that we knew how dangerous the Algiers casbah was for foreigners and that we had all been ordered not to set a foot in there. Silence followed Sickler's invitation. He put on his smug face, as if to say, "You Americans have no guts."

To save our American honor I spoke up, offering to go with him. Off we went to the casbah, walking deep into the dark, twisted alleys, sometimes so narrow that the walls touched above our heads. We came to what appeared to be a café of sorts. We entered, sat down at a rickety little table in the corner, and asked in French for some tea. Neither of us spoke Arabic. Tea was brought by a man in a *djellaba* (a loose outer robe worn by Moroccan men), but near the door several other Algerians were gathering. I could read body language well enough to realize that the group was planning to do us damage. "I think we better get out of here," I observed.

We gulped down our tea and left some local money on the table. Sickler pulled out his .45 and held it in full view as we made our way to the door. The menacing group fell to one side—nobody wanted to get shot—and we departed unchallenged. My heart was banging in my chest. Never again did I venture into such a one-sided situation without my own .45. In fact, my gun was not really my own, since I had not been issued a weapon of any sort. My .45 was a gift from a would-be suitor trying to impress me. He must have borrowed it from supplies. He taught me how to strip it and reassemble it in the dark. I never had occasion to use this gun and probably would not have pulled the trigger even if I were in danger.

Our subsequent trip to Sicily and our short days there are a blur in my mind. The X-2 Unit traveled by boat this time and on arrival we requisitioned our usual commanding villa. Since all our target materials were at OSS HQ in Caserta, a town just north of Naples, Italy, we could do little counterintelligence preparation and instead spent our time having discussions and working out a counterintelligence methodology for after the invasion. We kept in mind that there was no precedent for what we were about to do, that many eyes would be on us, and that we had better be good at it.

At this point Murphy made another inspection tour. He told us that we were the official X-2 unit attached to the Seventh Army and were cleared all the way to Washington, DC, to make the southern France invasion with them. He said that further personnel for our invasion unit would be meeting us in Naples. Then he was gone again, leaving us to close out our presence in Sicily and get ourselves to Naples.

Once in Italy the X-2 unit did indeed have additional personnel for the invasion, but it was scattered to the winds. Our personnel, both new and seasoned, came from the following sources: From Algiers there was Sickler and his two Spanish recruits, Mike and Frank, Hagler, Dodge, Rijos, and me. From Washington, DC, came Lenington, Marquand (the son of the author J. P. Marquand), Parker, Androvich, Zimmer, and Merrick. From London came Goiran and Fawcus. Rome supplied us with our required French liaison, Bellin. On paper this invasion X-2 unit looked like a fine working machine, covering all the bases in several languages. In reality it was a messy nightmare. All our members who were not officers in the Army had been snatched off the boat and assigned to Pozzuoli in southern Italy, where they did daily physical exercises all day and reported for roll calls and bed checks. The two civilians coming from OSS Washington arrived with matching luggage, beautiful wardrobes of sports, business, and dress suits, and vague orders to attach themselves to American consulates. U.S. consulates in wartime Italy? The impending invasion was a big surprise to these two. One of them immediately went off to the Isle of Capri for a self-awarded vacation. Any other leftover X-2 personnel were pressed into guard duty at the OSS HQ in Caserta. I was left untouched because of my SLU status and my daily duties examining and distributing Ultra/Ice.

The general staging area for the southern invasion was a small seaside Naples suburb, Pozzuoli. The area was crawling with U.S. Army vehicles, personnel, and matériel, as well as an impressive number of agile Italian pickpockets. To my great relief the personnel arrivals from London included our new CO, Capt. Roger Goiran. He was serious and well trained. With the authority of his captain's bars, we were able to round up all our scattered X-2 members from OSS HQ Caserta, from the Pozzuoli general staging area, and from the vacation island of Capri. X-2 had them officially relieved of the unrelated duties that had been imposed on them as they stepped off the boat from Sicily. X-2 commandeered a separate villa in Pozzuoli and got down to assigning administrative duties such as outfitting our unit with Army equipment and transportation, reserving shipping space for ourselves in the invasion fleet that was gathering in the bay of Naples, and getting our unit attached to the Seventh Army.

Parallel to these administrative tasks, we went forward with the counterintelligence training of our new unit members, training in enemy agent identification, capture, and interrogation. While in London our new CO, Goiran, had been indoctrinated in the existence and use of Ultra/Ice so he and I set up a small office under the wing of the British SCI Italian HQ in Naples; there we prepared extensive target materials for the use of our units following the invasion. We drew our targets from the Supreme Headquarters Allied Expeditionary Force (SHAEF) southern France suspect card set, a French blacklist (the list drawn from French citizens who were known to have collaborated willingly with the Nazis), the German Federal Intelligence Service (Bundesnachrichtendienst, or BND) organization handbook, and the most recent set of OSS regional studies. All this material, especially that from French sources, had to be utilized with skepticism and would have to be double-checked carefully once X-2 was in France because of the great possibility it could be tainted by personal vengeance. X-2 expected less of that from our American sources, such as the OSS regional studies, since X-2 were not so emotionally involved.

The date of the southern invasion approached and I was insistent that I had to be included in the "first lift" to leave from Naples harbor for France. After all, I was the original member of this unit and the only one besides Goiran authorized to handle Ultra/Ice. Goiran agreed that my SLU status merited me a place on the ship. "I will work it out with the Seventh," Goiran promised. "You be ready at 6:00 in the morning on loading day and we will pick you up in our weapons carrier on the way to the harbor." Once again I packed my old parachute bag—what do you take to an invasion?—and sat down on the edge of the bed to await my 6:00 pick up. I had my hair stuffed out of sight in a cap so I did not resemble a woman too much. By 8:00, still sitting optimistically on my bed and clutching my parachute bag, it became clear to me that I had been abandoned. So much for my SLU status. Goiran had decided it was too risky and too illegal to smuggle me on the invasion. I expect he was thinking also of the damage to his own career if we were discovered by higher authorities. Nevertheless, I was irate. But it turned out to be a wise decision of Goiran's because the invasion fleet sat for five long, unexpected days in the harbor, unable to get moving. The toilet arrangements alone would have been awkward and embarrassing.

After I recovered from the shock of being left behind, I decided I was not going to sit around Naples waiting for what someone else deemed female appropriate transportation. Instead I hitched a ride in a passing jeep and treated myself to a drive north up the coast to Rome. The departing Germans, who had been in charge in Italy, and the advancing American pursuers had decided independently to spare the great classic city from bomb damage.

Bits of our drive north passed over the ancient Appia Antica (Appian Way) and I was awed at the feeling of treading on stones that Roman soldiers had trod long before me. Because of the unwritten pact to protect Rome from the war, all the historical sites were unharmed: the coliseum where the gladiators fought their last battles, the Sistine Chapel, and the Vatican, with a pope still in residence. If only I could have found a postcard to send to my teachers at home. They would have been overwhelmed. And if only TC had lived to share this with me.

⚜ ⚜

I did get to meet the pope, Pope Pius XII. The Italian X-2 unit had added the services of a Women's Army Corps, Sergeant Verga. Besides being the most efficient administrator in three languages that I have ever met, she must have had impressive connections with the Catholic Church because one day she announced to me that she was going to meet the pope that afternoon, was nervous about going alone, and would I accompany her?

"You know I am not a Catholic," I told her.

"The pope doesn't care," answered Verga.

Off we went in a borrowed jeep to the Vatican. I envisioned being in a group of dozens of faithful followers, but, no, it was just the three of us: Verga, Pope Pius XII, and me. He was very tall and thin. He asked me where I came from and when I said, "Baltimore," he commented that he remembered that city well. He and Verga had some serious conversation in Italian that I did not follow, and then our visit was over.

To ease my guilty conscience at taking a holiday in Rome in the middle of a war, I reported to the X-2 villa there and the British Ultra/Ice hideout and spent several days bringing X-2 up to date on the German radio traffic that they could use. There was no other SLU agent available to serve them until my appearance, and I made it known that I was needed at Seventh Army HQ in France and would not be staying with their X-2 unit in Rome. Soon after, I returned to the X-2 villa in Pozzuoli and set about figuring out a way to rejoin the X-2 unit that had abandoned me.

During one evening foray into a U.S. military club, I overheard an officer who was wearing U.S. Air Force wings explaining to his companion that his mission was to fly one of the generals around in the general's exclusive plane. By the end of the evening, I had persuaded that pilot that I was a valuable radio technician, urgently needed at the front in France. I even tossed around Colonel Bruskin's name. (Colonel Bruskin was one of the officers in charge at Seventh Army HQ in southern France. When he and I had met in Algiers, he had shown interest in receiving Ultra/Ice when a SLU agent was available to retrieve it from the British.)

The pilot and I made a rendezvous date for several days hence at the Naples airport and I hustled down to Naples from Rome ahead of my new friend. I had to pick up my tired parachute bag and find a friendly general who would cut me some travel orders. True to his word, unlike Goiran, the pilot appeared, loaded me on board, and skirted the Mediterranean

Sea to France. I showed great interest in his single-engine Fairchild and never let on that I had piloted this model many a time.

⁂

The Seventh Army had come ashore in mid-August without me, and, meeting no resistance from the demoralized German troops, had sped up the Rhone Valley. "It was like invading Palm Springs," Marquand later described the landing to me. I had the pilot drop me at the Grenoble airport and from there made my way by jeep to the Seventh Army HQ in the small town of Vittel. Vittel is southwest of Strasbourg and north of Dijon, France's mustard town. The Allied troops were pausing there to regroup and resupply. I reported to Bruskin, who remembered me from Algiers and was delighted to resume our contact. I located the British controllers of Ultra/Ice; within the day I had become the SLU liaison for the Seventh Army. Bruskin supplied me with a room of my own in a temporary barracks. A room of your very own was a luxury up there on the battlefront. Soon I was making my daily visit to the British intelligence office and returning to Bruskin's HQ with valuable intelligence. The German forces were now in hectic disarray, retreating north up the valley and getting careless about security in their radio traffic. Eavesdropping on Ultra/Ice we were able to supply estimates of German troop strengths as they retreated, how great their recent losses had been, where they had decided to stand fast, and where they were continuing to give ground. To supply all this intelligence, Bruskin assumed the British had an entire platoon of spies out there in enemy territory and somehow getting it back to us. He was content with his new reports.

I was content myself. After my long tussle to be of genuine help in the war, here I was, on the front with the guns booming day and night, performing a valuable service as the SLU agent. My preference would have been to finish out the war in this Seventh Army job, under the wing of kindly Bruskin, but it was not to be. My messy 88th X-2 SCI, which had been renamed the 69th, was scattered all over the French Riviera. They needed organizing. Emissaries were sent up to Vittel to lure me back south. As a bribe I was offered an enticing visit to newly liberated Paris, which I accepted: soon I had the humble feeling of riding up the Champs Élysées where just a few short weeks before the German troops had ruled, passing the Ritz Hotel where we had heard Ernest Hemingway was hanging out, seeing the breathtaking Notre Dame cathedral on the Seine, and receiving the outpouring of gratitude from the French people who showered favors on anyone appearing to be an Ally. It was overpowering, but it was not my real world. The real world was a sheaf of formal orders sending me back to my unit in the south. I returned to Vittel, zipped up my parachute bag once again, and informed Colonel Bruskin that I had to rejoin my X-2 unit. He was disappointed to lose my SLU services and we both hoped to meet again.

Merrick, the Washington, DC, recruit dispatched to X-2 with the matching set of luggage, had been sent to retrieve me. We drove south from Vittel back down the Rhone Valley from which Merrick had come in a requisitioned car. We hardly spoke to each other: me annoyed because Merrick was taking me away from the Seventh Army HQ, he annoyed because he had been sent on such a trivial errand.

Having arrived in France by plane, so not able to see much of the land, the car ride was fascinating to me. The roads were narrow by American standards and closely lined with the graceful but dangerous plane trees—dangerous because they were so close to the two-lane road, and allowed no margin for error when cars passed each other. Jeeps and weapon carriers full of GIs sped by us endlessly with no concern for safety, and some of them ended up crashed against the plane trees. Because there was no fuel to be had on our route, we carried some "jerry cans" containing a supply of gasoline that we had begged from the Seventh Army. When we stopped for food, café owners heaped their best dishes on us and refused payment. "Welcome to France," they said and, *"Merci milles fois."*

Merrick and I passed through Monte Carlo on our way to the Riviera. Allied troops—French, British, and American—were swarming all over the tiny, jewel-like principality of Monaco. The young Prince Rainier, serving as an officer in the French army, was permitted to lead the troops back into his country. What a feeling of accomplishment it must have been for the prince, barely out of his teens. Sickler later told me that American troops burst through the front entrance of the world-famous Monte Carlo casino, fingers on their triggers and ready to rescue whatever personnel were trapped in the gambling rooms, as the Germans retreated out the back doors and headed toward Italy. But there were no hostages in distress in the casino. The croupiers and the players, long-time residents of Monaco, merely looked up a moment, curious about all the ruckus, noticed the change of uniforms, and went back to gambling. The casino was under new management, so to speak, but Nazis or GIs were not of much concern to them.

When Merrick and I rolled into the Riviera, dusty and tired from our long drive from Vittel, we found a chaos even greater than Naples. It was only a few short weeks since the Allied troops had come ashore in Marseilles, Toulon, and Cavalaire and the Nazis had begun retreating up the

Rhone Valley in disarray. French, British, American, and Canadian troops were swarming all over as they carried out the basic tasks of liberation and occupation. They secured the means of transportation, such as bus and railway lines, and they took over communications and administration, such as radio stations, telephone centers, police stations, and town halls, and turned them over to the French civilians. The French were delirious with their recent liberation and zoomed around on their bicycles getting in touch with relatives and attempting to ascertain the fate of missing family members. The general atmosphere was one of supreme joy. Some French people were taking advantage of the roiled-up situation to assassinate known collaborators The newly placed French administrators were not able to do much to stop those actions.

In the midst of the pandemonium, our CO, Goiran, was having a hard time getting control of our X-2 personnel scattered along the Riviera and establishing some kind of order. Goiran finally sent Parker, one of the unit, out to requisition the Villa Isabella in Cannes and we set up our unit headquarters there. We turned two or three back rooms on the second floor into our offices and quickly installed our precious target materials there. We chose the second floor for maximum security; the Army assigned us a detail of five young military police for guarding our materials and any suspect "spies" we might be interrogating. We had the sensation of security, but in reality nothing was totally secure. It seemed that every second person on the street was a potential spy.

Our target materials continued to be those described before, but now they were more specific to the south of France: the SHAEF name cards, the French blacklist, the updated OSS regional studies, the BND organization handbook, and such extracts from Ultra/Ice as we were allowed to reveal. X-2 was very skeptical in the use of the French blacklist because we discovered so many of their personal and political grudges were being played out there. In addition to Villa Isabella in Cannes, we took over a nearby hotel, the Château de la Tour, to serve as our mess, motor pool, and billets. We also used Château de la Tour as a holding area for suspects under interrogation

Once we had these two properties functioning, we set up a tight schedule of meeting every morning, briefly reviewing our cases in progress, closing out interrogations that had proven unproductive and returning the "bodies" to the French, then assigning new target leads to our agents. We always kept in our minds that what we were doing—tracking down possible left-behind Nazi spies, detaining them for interrogation, and either turning them over to the French for trial and disposition or forcing them to become our D/As—was a first-time activity for American civilian intelligence personnel. We were pioneers in untried waters, constantly designing, redesigning, and adjusting our methodology. Out of this came several innovative practices. We formed two or three mobile units, each of which had two compatible X-2 agents having language capabilities and armed with a radio, a jeep, and a specific target list. Each morning, after our work conference, they would zoom off to track down those latest leads or to make the arrests of the day. We also hit up the Seventh Army for the use of a direction finding (D/F) unit. A D/F was a vehicle with equipment capable of pinpointing radio transmissions within a certain area. With the D/F van on call, we had more chance of pouncing on a Nazi spy during his radio transmission to his controller in Berlin. The disadvantage of the D/F system was that it immobilized too many personnel—six persons were needed for blanket coverage—on mere speculation. Although our unit was never able to take full advantage of the relatively new D/F system, the assigned Army personnel directed us in setting up a smoothly functioning radio station in the tower of our Villa Isabella. The radio station was code-named Goodyear. From there we had twenty-four hour contact with Seventh Army HQ, with X-2 and OSS HQs in Paris, and with our mobile teams.

The Allied troops had progressed up the Rhone Valley beyond Grenoble, all the way to Strasbourg, with the Germans retreating before them. Since they were in retreat, we could assume that the German commanders would not be sending new spies back over the front. Therefore, those spies left behind in place were the ones we needed to go after. Our short-range mission then was to clear out all the left-behinds from the Lyon–Marseilles–Riviera area. To accomplish this aim we distributed our unit as follows:

1.   Parker became our valued administrator, getting requisitions, property, and cars legalized with the French, supervising the kitchen staff, acquiring rations and supplies, and doing a large share of the French language interrogations.
2.   Rijos, Androvich, and Marquand worked on the interrogations of suspects being detained at our hotel–prison and helped with the overflow of reports we had to produce.
3.   Test and White, the surviving Banana Boys, assisted in making arrests, some of which turned violent, and did service tasks.
4.   Hagler took up service tasks.

5. Fawcus and Lenington covered the suspect cases in the Marseilles area.

6. Zimmer also was assigned to Marseilles where he examined the documents captured by the Allies at Gestapo HQ there. His German was flawless.

7. I continued as the SLU liaison agent, receiving Ultra/Ice from the British and passing along extractions to our X-2 Unit and G-2 (Army intelligence) of the Seventh Army HQ.

8. Merrick became our first full-time case officer.

9. Bellin, our French liaison, and Dodge were reassigned: the former to OSS Italy, the latter to X-2 London.

10. Goiran, still our CO, carried out an effective roving supervision from Marseilles to the Riviera to Lyon, our three areas of responsibility.

We functioned in this fashion from September to October 1944, when Holcomb, now CO of all X-2 in France, made his inspection tour and reorganized our areas of operation. Until that moment we had been working as we saw fit, with no formal direction from X-2 headquarters. Yet during that disorganized period, with no specific directive, our unit processed 930 target persons in ninety-two far-flung villages and cities. This, with our roster never more than fifteen or sixteen agents. To be given an actual directive with written assignments was reassuring.

Who were these spies we were looking for and hoping to put out of business? To find our enemy, we started by eliminating those who could not be spies. At the top of the list of the "nots" was any citizen of the occupied country. The thought of the harm they would be doing to their own relatives and fellow citizens would prevent them from even considering such a job, regardless of the amount of money offered. We could also eliminate men and women who had lived ten or twenty years or more in one community. The concept of embedded spies is a romantic notion that plays well on television or in the movies, but no country has a spy budget that allows it to support a "sleeper" spy and his family for ten years. Three youngsters in college? Automobiles for everyone? Forget it. I never came across such a spy nor did anyone I know.

Who, then, were these spies we were seeking? First, we limited our search to a manageable area. Next, we evaluated the damage done to us by the intelligence emanating from the area we were working. Had there been attacks on our troops? On their equipment? In our harbors? How recent was the intelligence in the enemy's hands? This we could deduce by what the Germans were saying on Ultra/Ice, which helped us decide if the source was an operating radio set, had come from recent intelligence collection, or from a courier passing a pouch. From the police and post office we could get a list of those who had moved into the neighborhood in the past two or three years. After we had eliminated the nationals, we looked more closely at the remaining few outsiders: What did they do all day? Who were their friends? We also consulted the SHAEF card file and the French blacklist for known suspects. If any of the names on these lists were still around (most of them fled when an Allied army approached), we brought them in for interrogation. Insurance information proved helpful in the field for selecting targets. Before the war started there were some two thousand British insurance companies; many of them had insured German war materiel plants and factories. Detailed plans and maps of these sites were still in the hands of the insurance companies and supplied valuable information for interrogations. For those of our members who passed through London, method information was gained in lectures given by British agents who had been captured and interrogated by the Gestapo, later to be exchanged or to have escaped.

In September 1944 alone we uncovered twenty-seven enemy spies with radio sets. Some suspects surrendered immediately and insisted that such had been their intention when they signed up with the BND. Others had to be tracked down and intimidated into giving up their radio sets.

Our most likely spy profile turned out to be a male of North African origin, usually Algerian. The Algerians had a burning hatred for the French because of France's occupation of their country. They admired the aggressiveness of the Germans. Algerian immigrants were generally short of money, too. The retreating German Army bought handfuls of these prospective spies, taught the intelligent ones to operate a simple wireless set, and tossed them to the wolves. They reasoned that out of ten maybe two would be productive. As I say, at the first opportunity many of them turned themselves over to us with their radio sets and the codes. Others pocketed what money they had been paid, buried their radios, and went off to find less hazardous work; the docks in Marseilles were full of retired spies. It was a good place to hide.

We never uncovered an effective enemy woman spy in the south of France. The few possibles that we came across were always in relationships with male spies. They were untrained in collecting intelligence so they generally operated as couriers or supply lines for their lovers. We did interrogate two or three of these women after we spotted them acting as couriers. Most of them were of French background and had spent long stretches of time in Algeria where they had become romantically involved with Algerians.

The few serious spies we apprehended had working patterns similar to the British. They were taught radio transmission and Morse code, given a transmitting schedule, usually once a week, steered into a "safe house," and hooked up with a supply chain and a secure pay system. Sometimes they lived at their safe house. Sometimes they only transmitted from the safe house and lived elsewhere. The pay system was important because if a spy missed two or three paydays he was tempted to consider changing sides. Last, but most important, a spy with a radio set had an alarm code, a word that if transmitted would alert his case officer that he has been captured. To spy catchers it was of utmost urgency to force a captured spy to reveal his alarm code immediately.

The British boasted that by using Ultra/Ice and their tried-and-true methodology they effectively identified and eliminated or doubled all the Nazi spies sent to their island during the course of the war.

In Italy an estimated one hundred spies were left behind by the Nazis. Of these, only 50 percent were operationally successful. The fact that they were willing to leave behind this many indicates poor recruiting criteria.

What material were these spies who had been left behind asked to collect? If we knew what they were after, we would know more specifically where they would be working. Sometimes it depended on how much mobility they had in their "straight" life. It also depended on what the two opposing armies were doing; a retreating army desperately needs information about what reinforcements the pursuing army is receiving. An advancing army needs to know what is going on at the front. Early on we were fortunate in getting our hands on a detailed list of information the Germans were seeking as they backed up the Rhone Valley. The list came to us from "MAC," a spy who called himself our D/A, but who was really for sale to the highest bidder. His list was written in German and is the only such list I saw during the war (see Figure 15.1).

Having stated above emphatically that nationals never spy against their mother country in wartime, I now admit that our most successful case on the Riviera was just such a person. For two weeks high-class intelligence

SECRET

(Translation - 9 February 1945)

1) Details on the new gasoline product called "TRIPTAN", quantities, process, what raw materials are used?

2) Information on all types of technical publications, illustrations, newspapers of technical interest etc. of American source, is of interest.

3) Results of the use of the weapon V1 and V2 in Belgium and France.

4) Information both military and political on Belgium and France.

5) Details on production in the "CAUDRON" Factory in Paris (Le Moleneux?). What is being produced? If German style airplanes, what type? What quantity? Other details.

6) What is being produced in MEAUX? In the factory formerly called POTZ which formerly worked for the Germans in the manufacture of airplanes?

7) Toulouse: what is being manufactured in the factory called BREQUET formerly DEVOUITINE? Exact details, types, class, quantities, etc?

8) Toulouse: the airplane pilot called "DORET", head of a squadron - what type of aircraft does he have in his squadron? What armament? Number of planes? What is his function in the squadron?

9) Paris: concerning the factory formerly called Konzern "Brandt" in Paris, a munitions factory (also manufactured cannon) -- what is its production now? What type of cannon? Munitions? If new models are being produced, what kind, maximum details?

10) Marseille: details with an indication of number of troops arriving by sea. Where are they divided to be sent to different fronts? Can you watch these troop camps continually? All sorts of details are of interest. Can the arrival of troops into Marseille and Toulon be constantly watched? Let us know the results.

11) French Mediterranean Ports - Watch and communicate to us arrival of troops from overseas and Africa in all ports (Marseille - Toulon). It is necessary to indicate exact quantities belonging to each group of soldiers. (Translator's note: probably means exact number of soldiers in each group). Indicate number of divisions, regiments, battalions; their strength, insignia, uniforms, equipment, type of vehicles.

FIGURE 15.1 *Secret: Sample Information Requested by the Germans*

had been leaving the area of Toulon by wireless transmission and no one in our unit could identify the source. The radio operator always seemed to know the exact location and composition of Allied troops in the valley, as well as what ships were coming in and out of Marseilles harbor. We could document this from our readings of the Ultra/Ice traffic. Sickler assigned himself to solve the mystery. We did not yet have access to the Seventh Army D/F equipment to help us. Sickler reexamined all the records that had been cleared previously: postal information, police lists, and resident registrations. Everyone looked clean, or at least not of radio operator caliber. However, Sickler noticed one resident who seemed out of place. This was a highly decorated Armée de l'Air (French air force) officer who, according to postal records, had taken up residence recently on a farm near the town of Draguignan with his wife and child. Sickler asked himself some questions: Why had this officer retired so young? Had he been wounded? Even if he was disabled, why had he chosen a remote farm, far from the school his son must need to attend? Was he a supporter of the Vichy government and thus being allowed to live where he chose? Sickler decided to give him a closer look. He picked up a CounterIntelligence Corps, U.S. Army for authority to make arrests (fairly soon after this, X-2 was accorded arrest permission by the Seventh Army), and drove in a jeep to the farm address that he had obtained from the post office. He arrived there over a dirt road of deep cart ruts. The house was L-shaped. One wing seemed to shelter the animals and farm equipment, and the other held the family living quarters and was painted an attractive yellow with green shutters. Right away Sickler deduced that no farmer in wartime could afford to buy so much expensive paint. Something was slightly off here. In the courtyard in front of the house a spring bubbled up into a little pond. It was in this bucolic setting that Sickler began to have doubts. He jumped out of the jeep, drew his gun, and knocked on the door. The French pilot himself answered. Before the man could say anything, Sickler demanded, "Where is your radio set?"

The Frenchman was caught completely off guard, noted the .45, and turned pale. He pointed toward the part of the L-wing where the animals were kept. "Show me," ordered Sickler.

In the stable, concealed under a bale of hay, the Frenchman uncovered a battered suitcase. Inside the suitcase was the radio that had been emitting so much damaging intelligence against the Allied troops. This decorated Armée de l'Air officer, disgruntled with France and very anti-Semitic, was throwing in his lot with the Nazis. He approved of their ghoulish philosophy.

The first moments of capturing an active enemy spy are extremely delicate. After locating the actual radio set and establishing the connection between it and the spy, the spy must be isolated immediately from family and friends. This isolation erodes his self-confidence, prevents him from giving instructions to them, and sets him to wondering what has happened to them and what information they might be divulging. The next step is to extract from him his danger signal. The danger signal, remember, is the word he has been trained to transmit along with his message to his handler in Berlin so they will know he has been captured. It is in these first moments of capture that the spy is most vulnerable to giving up his danger signal. After we obtained that signal, a third step was to maintain the setting exactly as it was. This was to prevent outside observers from noticing any change and reporting it to the Germans from another radio set. We maintained the setting as it was so we could use the spy as a D/A, if we decided to do so. That decision was made after hours of interrogation and depended on how stable and reliable we ascertained the spy would be in our service and how much the Nazis seemed to rely on the intelligence he sent them. If we decided to double a spy, we always looked for some solid psychological hold over him. In the case of this French spy, we gave him the code name of "Forest." We used his young son and his wife who were living with him on the farm. At the moment of capture, we removed them discreetly and refused to tell Forest where they were. His self-confidence was thus further shaken. We told him that he would never see them again if he refused to cooperate. Forest became a textbook perfect D/A. Merrick was assigned as his case officer and moved into the farmhouse. To curious acquaintances of Forest, Merrick was explained as a relative visiting from Paris. Merrick's French was good enough for that ruse. The wife and son were returned to their fake farm life with dire warnings of what would happen to the household head if they sought German help. The radio was given into Merrick's custody and the Berlin-assigned transmission schedule was resumed, but only under Merrick's supervision. Every spy has a distinct sending style, his "fist," and no other operator can substitute for him. The captured spy must do it himself or the operation would be at risk of being detected in Berlin. Replacing some spy's fist would be like trying to hand write a message in someone else's handwriting. Forest had to send his own Morse code message and Merrick had to supervise.

A further element and, really, the most important, is the information the D/A would now pass to his handler. It was important that X-2 supply enough authentic intelligence through Forest's radio transmissions so the Germans would not lose confidence in him and recruit additional agents in the area who would be unknown to us. The Berlin handler had to continue to be convinced that he was receiving authentic intelligence. Sometimes they were able to check the facts through another spy in the area that we had not uncovered. Again, we did not want the handler to lose faith in our D/A and recruit other agents in the area.

Before his capture, Forest had been sending accurate intelligence to Berlin concerning shipping activities and troop movements in the Marseilles and Riviera areas. He had been supplying precise coordinates for artillery attacks. After we took over his transmissions, we still sent coordinates, but we altered them slightly, shorter or longer, so that the shots dispatched would fall short or long of the ships or troops or equipment involved. The daily intercepts of Ultra/Ice were useful in getting an accurate reading of Berlin's reaction to our controlled messages.

Of the several D/As we ran on the Riviera, Forest was by far the most successful: the Germans trusted him entirely and therefore would accept our "misinformation" messages without too much scrutiny. Because he had made the fatal mistake of keeping his wife and child with him—in harm's way, so to speak—we were able to use them as a threat to keep him under our control.

By October 1944 we felt we had the spy situation in the south of France pretty much under control. We had swept back and forth, east and west, between Marseilles and Monte Carlo; had interrogated dozens, if not hundreds, of possible suspects; and had selected and were running several quality D/As. We had either released other suspects for lack of sufficiently incriminating evidence or turned the "possibles" over to the French for their swift and cruel justice. We were feeling comfortable with the methodology we had developed.

Our CO, Holcomb, made another inspection tour. Accompanied by Sickler, he visited Monte Carlo, Nice, Cannes, Toulon, Marseilles—the entire south of France. He also visited Toulouse, Tarbes, and Pau in the Pyrenees and Biarritz on the Atlantic Coast. After surveying the widespread territory we were covering, Holcomb agreed that changes had to be made. He departed for Paris and Parker and I joined him there to review our past and current work patterns and come up with a plan for the future. We came up with the following new division of territory:

1. The newly named 11th SCI Unit would cover territory west of the Italian border, east of the Rhone Valley, and south of Lyon. HQ would be in Marseilles. Goiran would be CO.
2. The old 69th/88th SCI Unit would cover the area west of the Rhone Valley south of the Loire River, and all the French–Spanish border territory over to the Atlantic Ocean. HQ would be in Perpignan, on the Mediterranean coast just north of the border. The CO would be Sickler.
3. The 55th SCI Unit would work in the territory north of Lyon and now under Seventh Army occupation. HQ would be in Vittel; Quirk, an unknown to us, would be the CO.

When Parker and I returned to Nice with the new operational chart, there were mild complaints before everyone settled down to make it work. Within a week we had finished up the suspect interrogations and relinquished the bodies to the French. We returned the hotel and villa to the French in good condition. Most of the requisitioned cars were returned to their owners. The underused D/F unit went back to Seventh Army HQ. The military police unit that had been guarding our suspects under interrogation was transferred. Our wireless communications were reduced to one operator. Our office files, D/A case records, SHAEF cards, and remaining supplies were all packed and moved over to Marseilles. There, British SCI were finding the requisitioned Petit Nice Hotel too large for their needs so they gladly gave it over to Goiran, soon to be CO of that area. Working with him would be Lenington, Androvich, and Schowel.

We divided personnel up as much as was practical along compatibility lines. Merrick stayed with the Riviera unit so he could continue watching over the ever-productive D/A Forest. Marquand stayed as our liaison with the French services. Hagler was assigned to service duties, but was soon recalled to the short-handed Seventh Army.

The newly invented 55th SCI Unit would consist of Fawcus from the 88th Unit and some newcomers from X-2 Paris, with Quirk as CO.

We who retained the original X-2 unit designation, the 88th/69th Unit, moved ourselves to the Perpignan area. We chose Perpignan because it was a hot spot for spies crossing the border between France and Spain. Franco's Spain was still 100 percent in the Nazi camp. The town was a strategic location, but for day-to-day operations it was much too public, so we requisitioned a well-hidden property, Villa Violet, near the village of Thuir, about ten miles outside Perpignan. Violet was the wealthy maker of a popular "aperitif" and was known to have collaborated closely with both the Vichy government of France and the German Nazis. Now he was eager to do what he could for the Allies who were going to win the war.

Violet's property was ideal for our spy-catching purposes—large, sprawling, and enclosed by a tall iron picketed fence. The mansion, too, was oversized. We fitted all our personnel into its lower quarters and still had ample room to set up our files and offices on the second floor. Without much fuss, we moved into Villa Violet taking our share of the SHAEF cards, the OSS regional study, the French blacklist, the BND organizational handbook, and our current, ongoing intelligence reports. Our unit personnel consisted of Parker, Rijos, White, Test, me, and Sickler, who was our CO. We soon had to double this number after one extraordinary interrogation, which I describe below. To those we had contact with we identified ourselves as a Psychological Warfare Mission from the OSS and attached to the U.S. Army.

It was October 1944 when we set up this new office; by December we were so active that we were pleading for more bodies. An American friend of Sickler's, Johnson, was transferred to us. Like Marquand, he was the son of a well-known author. Johnson had parachuted into France the year before and had spent a year with the Maquis (guerilla resistance fighters) in the Jura mountains. He was rail thin from that ordeal. He ate a lot and became invaluable as an interrogator. To my delight, my sister Nita was able to join us after leaving the RCAF where she was spotting submarines off the coast of Vancouver and passing through London to be indoctrinated in the use of Ultra/Ice out at St. Albans. She was valuable in retrieving the Ultra/Ice material from the British, but Goiran, short-handed in Marseilles, soon wangled her away from us. We were able to replace her with Army Sergeant Verga, with whom I had visited Pope Pius XII in the Vatican.

The extraordinary interrogation I mentioned happened like this: The French counterintelligence picked up a German national in civilian clothes who told a murky story. He claimed he was a noncommissioned officer from the German army. If true, it would remove him from spy status and save him from a quick death. The French interrogated him in their usual ungentle manner. In spite of the beatings, he stuck to his story and yielded no immediate intelligence. The French were in a hurry so they turned him over to the British. Technically the Allies were supposed to share enemy agents, each service conducting its own questioning, but if you received such an offer, you could be sure the subject had nothing of importance left to cough up or his services would not be offered to you. A day later we got a call from our British counterparts. Were we interested in interrogating the German suspect further? Why not? For some unfathomable reason, the British had taken the suspect all the way to Gibraltar before they had lost interest in him. Sickler hopped on a British military plane, flew down to Gibraltar, and claimed the German, code-named "Max," returning with him to the villa. He was a short, round little man, very sweaty, nervous, and frightened still from the treatment the French had given him and the confusing plane rides to Gibraltar and back.

Sickler conducted his interrogation in the basement of Villa Violet in French, which Max spoke well. Sickler's method of questioning was on the gentle side. He figured that since Max had not responded to the stick maybe he would respond to the carrot. He offered Max a cigarette and a cup of coffee. He mentioned that he was Spanish and how close Spain and Germany were. He observed that the war was winding down and it looked like the Allies were going to win and, by the way, what did he, Max, plan to do after the war? Max, grateful to have someone friendly to talk to, grateful to imagine he had a future, explained that he yearned to go to Hollywood and become a comedian. He would model himself after Charlie Chaplin, his idol, he said. After another cigarette and another cup of coffee, Sickler allowed as how we might be able to help him get to Hollywood when the war ended. Max's face lit up.

Sickler continued, "But you need something substantial to trade for your trip to Hollywood. You look like a very serious man to me. Surely you had an important job with the Germans, didn't you?"

Max hesitated for a long, long moment. He had come to the inevitable crossroad in the game of spying. He could either adhere obstinately to his cover story, knowing he would be tortured some more and finally die as a patriot, shot in the back of the head by the French. Or he could put himself in the hands of this sympathetic Spaniard who admired the Germans and maybe get to Hollywood and become a star after the war.

"I do have something important to trade," Max announced.

His something-to-trade was unbelievable. He was the current paymaster for a network of thirty-five spies who operated for the Nazis from Marseilles all the way from the French–Spanish border to Bordeaux on the Atlantic Coast. He lived modestly in Barcelona where the cooperative Franco bureaucrats helped him with his bank account. Once a month he was supposed to slip into France and quietly pay his agents with cash arranged for him in Barcelona, to avoid contact with the banks, and return immediately to the safety of Spain. Last payday, contrary to his orders, he had loitered on in France, enjoying the good food and wine. An alert gendarme had picked him out of the crowd. Pure bad luck for Max. More bad luck was the fact that he had never memorized his pay list and destroyed the paper record, as any professional spy would have done. No, Max had written all thirty-five names and addresses on one piece of paper which, when retrieved from a locker in the Perpignan railroad station, he handed over to Sickler, sure that he was paying his way to Hollywood and indifferent to betraying his collaborators.

With such an accurate list, we were able to arrest all thirty-five agents. Banking heavily on what we had learned already about running D/As, we turned eight of them into productive D/As. When the war ended, most of them suffered the common fate of spies: after summary military trials by the French, they were shot, the comedian paymaster included, still showing no remorse for having given up his network.

From October when we arrived on the French–Spanish border until December we swept our assigned territory clean of suspected spies. Those remaining at liberty for lack of incriminating evidence were mostly freelancers with no serious allegiance to the German Abwehr (German military intelligence). They were prowling around on the outskirts of the spy world, picking up irrelevant tidbits to sell for cash to whatever buyer came forward. We had settled into running Max's eight D/As, retaining Max as a controlled paymaster. I was shuttling back and forth between the British office in nearby Perpignan and Villa Violet in Thuir with Ultra/Ice material that was appropriate for our D/As.

As the German Army retreated north through the Rhone Valley, we Allies started to need specific intelligence. For instance, our military needed to know where the left-behind mine fields had been set, where roadblocks had been established, and what radio stations and gun placements were active in the valley. Train schedules and troop movements were fairly easy to come by because they were planned in advance. Prize intelligence was the location of their antiparachutist pickets, steel spikes driven into the ground where the Germans expected invasion from the air, a terrible reception for Allied parachutists. With adroit questions, sometimes we could worm some of this information out of the handlers of our D/As.

Many French, British, and Americans involved in counterintelligence came to visit us at Thuir because we had gained the reputation of being a model worth emulating. The British especially were impressed because they remembered vividly when we were a mere half-dozen bewildered students, taking lessons from them in counterintelligence at St. Albans.

Among the visitors was Frederick Winterbotham, head of the British Secret Intelligence Service. He and I recalled each other from the early days in St. Albans. He went off to have a private talk with our CO, Sickler, during which he began to talk freely about Ultra/Ice. To his utter astonishment, he discovered that Sickler had never been briefed on Ultra/Ice and did not know what Winterbotham was talking about. Winterbotham had assumed I had briefed Sickler, however contrary that would have been to my orders. They had told me in St. Albans not to tell anyone their secret and I had complied. Sickler believed that the British had some hot spies on the ground in Berlin, feeding them intelligence. Winterbotham was doubly embarrassed and chagrined because he was the one who had developed the complicated security system (the SLUs) to protect Ultra/Ice. Sickler did not speak to me for days, so angry was he at being left out all those months.

⁓⊚ ⊚⁓

Off the coast of Rochefort, to the north of Bordeaux on the Atlantic Ocean, is a small but strategic island called Île d'Oléron. It was strategic because it helped guard the French coastline from unfriendly attackers. The Germans loved the Île d'Oléron because it gave them a sweeping view of the ocean. For that purpose, during the war they always kept a strong military presence there, with radio communications to Berlin. As the Germans retreated north, naturally all their military placements joined in the retreat—that is, all except the troops still stationed on the Île d'Oléron. For some unexplained reason, they decided to hunker down on that island and hold out. And for another unexplained reason, instead of leaving the German soldiers on the island until they got hungry, the French decided to go in after them. If I had been in command (which I was not), I would not have made that decision. The French had endured years of humiliating occupation by the Nazis, though: maybe they didn't want to suffer it even one more week. Maybe they saw the recapture of the Île d'Oléron as a swift victory that would take away some of their pain.

The French announced an invasion date and, again for some unexplained reason, they requested that the 88th/69th SCI of X-2 mount one of our mobile units to accompany them and sweep up the pesky spies. We were happy to do this. We figured it was more like coastal tourism than real war. We hastily assembled what little operational intelligence information we had in our files and drove ourselves to the coast in a weapons carrier and a couple of jeeps; we were going to war. The mobile unit was made up of Marquand; Parker; my sister, Nita, borrowed from the Marseilles unit; me; and maybe two others, all under the command of Sickler.

The taking back of the Île d'Oléron turned out to be more like war than we had anticipated. Before our arrival, B-26 bombers from the 320th Bomb Group flew eight dawn-to-dusk missions against that tiny island and the 99th Group bombarded the island with heavy artillery for ten days. You would think the Germans would get the message and come out of hiding, but they did not. Impatient invading French forces stormed ashore, accompanied by our eager X-2 mobile unit. We were ferried from the Rochefort area to the island by a unit of American soldiers. They ferried us across the water in some neat amphibious carriers that, once returned to land, could be used as weapons carriers.

Once ashore we double-checked with each other and confirmed the village where we would rendezvous shortly with the French to take up the mutual spy hunt. Nita and Marquand were sent ahead to tell the French we were coming. The rendezvous village was on the main road that cut straight through the island, impossible to miss. But these two rambunctious twenty-year-olds, unaccustomed to what a French village looked like, barreled right through the tiny village in their jeep, and soon were in the middle of the island, which was still in German hands.

Before long they made out a lone figure standing in the middle of the road, waving a white shirt. On getting closer, they realized it was an unarmed German soldier. They stopped. Neither Marquand nor Nita spoke German, but the soldier pointed to his white shirt and motioned he wanted to surrender. Marquand and Nita understood that and indicated he should get into the back seat of the jeep. The soldier shook he head and pointed to a house off the road. "He wants to go get his gun and surrender it," said Marquand, nodding his permission.

The soldier hustled over to the house he had pointed out and made a signal with his hands. To Nita's and Marquand's astonishment, a line of fifteen soldiers emerged from the cellar of the house; arms held high, clutching their rifles. X-2 was being asked to take the surrender of sixteen German soldiers. After they recovered from the shock, Nita indicated for the soldiers to deposit their rifles in the back of the jeep and to march up the road in front of the jeep. The lead soldier shook his head and pointed back down the road Marquand and Nita had just traveled. "They want to surrender to Americans," said Nita and so it was that those fifteen German soldiers, holding their hands over their heads, returned to the Americans in the dock area, followed by a jeep loaded with their guns and driven by Nita, while Marquand sat behind the machine gun that was mounted on the jeep. Later, both admitted that neither of them knew how to arm and fire their weapon. If any of those soldiers are alive, they must still tell their grandchildren how the Americans sent two schoolchildren to take their surrender in the waning days of the war.

The rest of the Île d'Oléron mission went smoothly. We all found the village holding the French HQ. We identified enough suspect enemy spies to satisfy the French. All the Germans finally came out of the cellars and surrendered. The French held an impressive ceremony in a soccer field and presented medals to some of the military participants; Nita and Marquand missed out on a medal because they were civilians.

It was April 1945. As we drove our vehicles back across France, we visited some of the vineyards in the famous wine country. We sampled the vintages and bought some bottles to take back to our HQ. It was during that drive that I heard the first details of the Nazi death camps. I was stunned. We had heard disturbing rumors over the past several months, rumors so gruesome that we had refused to believe them. No human being could behave like that. We concluded that the rumors had to be exaggerated. Now we were being told details, related by our own soldiers, and we were coming to know the true nature of Hitler's inhuman plan for the world. Even today it is hard to believe that human beings could treat other human beings in such a manner. The realization of the true horror made me satisfied to have come over to help stop it.

We had no sooner returned to the relative quiet of the Villa Violet than our D/A radio traffic began to heat up with what appeared to be a frantic request to be put in touch with what the messages referred to as "American intelligence." (This was further proof they did not know they were already in touch with "American intelligence.") The name of Rear Adm. Wilhelm Canaris was being evoked.

Rear Admiral Canaris, although he was a naval officer, had spent the better part of his career as head of the Abwehr, German intelligence. In that capacity he had persuaded Hitler to support Franco during Franco's rebellion and cold-bloodedly approved the bombing of civilians by the Luftwaffe (German air force), with the 1937 bombing of Guernica being a notable example. Germany's support was one of the main factors in the defeat of the Republic's army. Early in World War II, Canaris became disillusioned with Hitler's plan for Europe's future. He tried to steer Hitler away from his violent actions. When he found himself unable to influence Hitler to take a more moderate direction, he surreptitiously joined the opposition, while maintaining his rank in the military. As early as 1938 and as late as 1943, he involved himself in failed coups aimed at assassinating Hitler. In February 1944 Hitler finally removed Canaris from his Abwehr post and placed him under house arrest. As far as we knew officially, he was still under house arrest. Now our D/A was bringing us messages in his name.

"Maybe he has escaped," we conjectured. "Maybe he has a plan to escape in the future and is hoping to arrange a coming over to us." Whatever the case we went right along with it. After three or four more message exchanges through our D/A, we had a firm rendezvous with a German U-boat on a beach near Bordeaux for a certain date in April 1945.

We were excited. At that point we made a tactical mistake that ensured the failure of our mission. Our Parker was set up operationally in Bordeaux and the practical plan of action would have been to radio him to quietly take a mobile unit down to the beach and meet whoever appeared. Instead, we enthusiastically informed X-2 Paris of our forthcoming meeting. We were asked to supply Paris with all the detailed information and to back off from the rendezvous; X-2 Paris would take over and make the meeting. We had put so much tedious and careful work into arranging this rendezvous and we felt we knew these agents and their methods better than anyone and now we were being ordered not to be there in the triumphant moment of a possible surrender. We of the 69th/88th were crestfallen, but we complied.

The rest of the story came to me from one of the motor pool noncommissioned officers who attended the spectacle as a jeep driver. We were friends from past assignments together and I have no reason to doubt his version of this event. Imagine this picture. It was dawn and a surprising number of Paris X-2 officers had congregated in the dunes above a stretch of beach near Bordeaux. It was here our messages pinpointed the appearance of the U-boat. The X-2 officers spread themselves out in both directions along the beach and hid themselves behind the dunes. They were armed and they all carried binoculars. My informant said he hid among the officers, but he was not armed. Everyone peeked out to sea—mercifully, a calm sea. In the distance, a speck appeared. As it got near, it turned into a dinghy with a man rowing (perhaps it was two men). The dinghy got closer and closer. Suddenly there was a sharp crack among the dunes: a gun had been discharged accidentally. The rower looked over his shoulder, startled and afraid. A gunshot was not what he had been told to expect. He swung his dinghy around quickly and started rowing back to his submarine in a panic. The hidden observers also panicked. They rose from their hiding places as one man and started shooting wildly at the retreating dinghy. Later, when the dinghy was retrieved and the body examined, my observer insists there were more than forty bullet holes in the body.

History tells us that Admiral Canaris probably was deprived of his life a month or two before this botched rendezvous, either by being hung in a laundry room or by being given a pistol and asked to shoot himself. I like to think that somehow he faked his death and was sitting out there in that U-boat, waiting to come ashore and surrender to X-2. We will never know the truth.

Epilogue

Suddenly, from one minute to another, the war in Europe was over. Hitler had killed himself and the German military had surrendered unconditionally. Three long years of war were over for me. It seemed entirely fitting that my sister Nita and I, who had begun this experience as teenage students at the University of Maryland, vowing to serve in battle, should finish up marking the end of the war together in a liberated France. In the next few months, the OSS was disbanded and we were all released to go home and begin to live our normal lives.

Corp. Bill Kelly was killed in June 1943 in France, defending the right of the rest of us to be free.

Scebeli was sunk by a Nazi torpedo in the northern Atlantic in April 1943; I don't know if Ole was still with the ship, but at least he was not listed as being one of the two killed.

TC was killed in his blue Nash on the eve of his departure for England with his fighter pilot squadron.

Scotty, Peter, Tony, Kenny, and I survived the war and went on to live our separate lives around the world.

Abbreviations and Acronyms

ATA	Air Transport Auxiliary
BND	German Federal Intelligence Service (Bundesnachrichtendienst)
BSC	British Security Coordination, USA
CO	commanding officer
CPT	Civilian Pilot Training
D/A	double agent
D/F	direction finding
MI6	British CounterIntelligence, foreign
OSS	Office of Strategic Services
RAF	Royal Air Force
RCAF	Royal Canadian Air Force
SCI	Special CounterIntelligence
SHAEF	Supreme Headquarters Allied Expeditionary Force
SLU	special liaison unit
U/S	unserviceable (aircraft)
X-2	counterintelligence branch of the OSS

Some of the ATA Cross-Country Routes

Barton–Thame–Bicester–Chipping Warden–Barton

Barton–Little Rissington–Harwell–Barton

Barton–Honington–Caxton–Barton

Barton–Marlow–White Waltham–Halton–Bicester–Barton

Barton–Luton–Radlett–Barton

Barton–Bourbourne–Sawbridgeworth–Debiden–Great Sampford–
   Castle Camps-Steeple Morden–Barton

Luton–Morton-in-the-Marsh–Wellesbourne–Luton

Luton–Cranfield–Halton–Luton

Luton–Cranfield–Wittering–Duxford–Luton

Luton–Brizi Norton–Colerne–Andover–Luton

References

Chant, Christopher, Brigadier Shelford Bidwell OBE, Anthony Preston, and Jenny Shaw. *World War II: Land, Sea and Air Battles, 1939– 1945*. London: Octopus Press/Treasure Press, 1986.

OSS X-2 files. National Archives, London.

Pre–World War II British Road Map, n.d. (np).

Index

About the Author

BETTY LUSSIER was born on the desolate plains of Alberta, Canada, to a Miss West Canada and a DFC-decorated fighter pilot who had survived World War I. She was only four years old when her family moved to the United States and bought a dairy farm on the Eastern Shore of Maryland.

It was there that she learned to fly. By the time she enrolled in the University of Maryland she was accepted for the Civilian Pilot Training program (CPT). Women would-be pilots were discouraged from applying, but there happened to be an empty slot in Maryland's program, so she slipped into it. After the Japanese attacked Pearl Harbor she dropped out of Maryland and took "defense" jobs. The British nation, desperate for war workers, offered to transport to England any citizen who could do a war job. Having been born in Canada, Betty qualified as a British subject, and this earned her passage on a Norwegian cargo ship to England. Once there she joined the Air Transport Auxiliary (ATA) and soon was delivering new planes to the RAF's operational aerodromes and flying damaged planes back to repair stations.

After the Normandy invasion, when women pilots were barred from delivering planes to the combat zones on the continent, she joined the counterintelligence branch of the recently founded Office of Strategic Services (OSS) and served for the remainder of the war as an OSS field agent in France, receiving, analyzing, and delivering to American forces secret intercepted Nazi messages known as "Ultra." She now is retired and lives in Pacific Palisades, CA.

THE NAVAL INSTITUTE PRESS is the book-publishing arm of the U.S. Naval Institute, a private, nonprofit, membership society for sea service professionals and others who share an interest in naval and maritime affairs. Established in 1873 at the U.S. Naval Academy in Annapolis, Maryland, where its offices remain today, the Naval Institute has members worldwide.

Members of the Naval Institute support the education programs of the society and receive the influential monthly magazine *Proceedings* or the colorful bimonthly magazine *Naval History* and discounts on fine nautical prints and on ship and aircraft photos. They also have access to the transcripts of the Institute's Oral History Program and get discounted admission to any of the Institute-sponsored seminars offered around the country.

The Naval Institute's book-publishing program, begun in 1898 with basic guides to naval practices, has broadened its scope to include books of more general interest. Now the Naval Institute Press publishes about seventy titles each year, ranging from how-to books on boating and navigation to battle histories, biographies, ship and aircraft guides, and novels. Institute members receive significant discounts on the Press's more than eight hundred books in print.

Full-time students are eligible for special half-price membership rates. Life memberships are also available.

For a free catalog describing Naval Institute Press books currently available, and for further information about joining the U.S. Naval Institute, please write to:

Member Services
U.S. NAVAL INSTITUTE
291 Wood Road
Annapolis, MD 21402-5034
Telephone: 800.233.8764
Fax: 410.571.1703
Web address: www.usni.org